From Latin to Romance in Sound Charts

Peter Boyd-Bowman

Georgetown University Press, Washington, D.C. 20057

Library of Congress Cataloging in Publication Data

Boyd-Bowman, Peter.
    From Latin to Romance in sound charts.

        1. Romance languages--Phonology, Historical.
I. Title.
PC76.B6   441'.5   80-11645
ISBN 0-87840-077-X

International Standard Book Number: 0-87840-077-X

CONTENTS

RULE

RULE

Map. The Roman Empire on the eve of the barbarian invasions (c. A.D. 395).

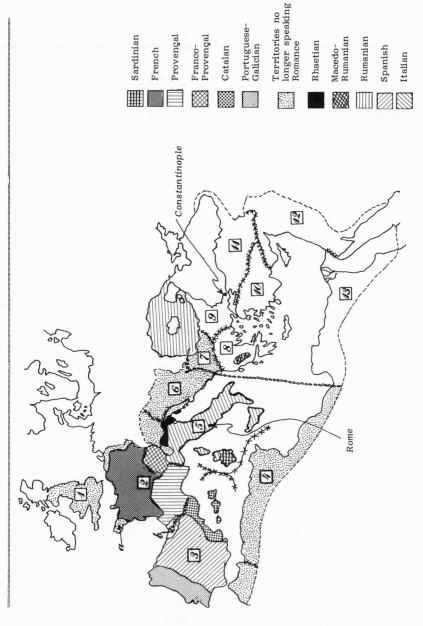

KEY: ---Boundary of the Roman Empire; ∘∘∘∘Division between East and West; ⩽⩾ Boundaries of Roman Dioceses
Roman Dioceses: 1 = Britannia; 2 = Gallia; 3 = Hispania; 4 = Africa; 5 = Italia; 6 = Illyricum; 7 = Dacia;
8 = Macedonia; 9 = Thracia; 10 = Asia; 11 = Pontus; 12 = Orientis; 13 = Aegyptus [1-7, Latin-speaking;
8-13, Greek-speaking]
a = Breton; b = Basque

Sardinian

French

Provençal

Franco-
Provençal

Catalan

Portuguese-
Galician

Territories no
longer speaking
Romance

Rhaetian

Macedo-
Rumanian

Rumanian

Spanish

Italian

INTRODUCTION

This handbook has two purposes: (1) to help college students to recognize related words in the Romance languages and to associate them with their English cognates; and (2) to provide students and scholars of Romance philology with a synopsis of the regular changes that Latin words underwent in the course of their evolution into the modern Romance languages.

Though English belongs to the group of Germanic languages, which includes such languages as Dutch, German, and the Scandinavian languages, some 60 percent of our English vocabulary is taken from Latin or Romance sources. This significant fact is one of the reasons why the study of Latin is essential to the mastery of our own language. Conversely, it can also be of great help to English speakers studying modern forms of Latin such as French, Spanish, Portuguese, and Italian.[1] These languages still are Latin, in the same way that English, though changed beyond recognition since the days of King Alfred, has never ceased to be English.

Students of Romance philology will find this volume useful as a ready reference and as a source of abundant examples of Latin sound changes. The arrangement of the sound charts makes it possible to trace the development of a sound in various phonological environments or in one or more of the Romance languages.

Classical and Vulgar Latin. The Latin taught in our schools, generally known as Classical Latin, was a highly refined literary medium cultivated during the period of transition between the Roman Republic and the Empire (roughly, 100 B.C. to A.D. 100). But it was not Classical Latin that was carried by Roman soldiers, merchants, and slaves into the conquered provinces of the Empire and which in time became the common tongue of the many races that peopled the Mediterranean. This everyday, colloquial 'vulgar' (or popular) Latin of the Roman Empire, with its modified pronunciation and its relatively uncomplicated, analytical structure, already bore some

striking resemblances to modern Italian. With the decentrali-
zation that characterized the later Empire, regional differences
(peculiarities of pronunciation and vocabulary, preferences for
certain expressions) began to assert themselves in the use of
Vulgar Latin. These regional variations, negligible at first,
assumed much larger proportions when the territories of the
Empire were broken up and isolated from each other by the
barbarian invaders. Held together by the spiritual power of
the Church and by the manifest superiority of Roman culture
over that of Western Europe's new barbarian masters, the con-
cept of a united Roman Empire lingered on in men's minds long
after the political Empire had ceased· to exist. Gradually the
image faded, however. Romans and Barbarians merged to produce new ethnic groups and a new social structure (feudalism).
Linguistically, the practice of speaking ROMANĬCE ('in the
Roman fashion', i.e. Romance) triumphed almost everywhere
over the languages of the invaders,[2] but by then the forms of
Romance spoken in the different regions of the former Western
Empire had drifted so far apart that they were no longer
mutually intelligible. Thus out of a group of dialects, all of
them claiming to be Latin or at any rate modified forms of it,
new languages came into existence.

Organization. The synopsis is presented in the form of
separate charts for each major sound change. For easier
reference by students not trained in phonetics I have arranged
the charts in alphabetical order, departing from this order
only when the parallel or identical treatment of certain sounds
might otherwise escape notice. In such cases, however, the
table of cross references at the end of the volume will direct
the student to the other sounds.

The charts are almost self-explanatory. A careful compari-
son of the words in each column will lead most students to
guess in advance the simple formula which appears below each
chart. The rule is stated as simply as possible; it does not
generally explain the evolution, but only the end results. For
those anxious only to improve their vocabulary, this is quite
enough. But for the student of Romance linguistics desiring
further information, there are notes after almost every rule,
outlining exceptions to or modifications of that rule, and often
sketching successive stages in the development that the sound
underwent. Several minor or sporadic sound changes are also
treated in note form.

Each chart is supplemented by a short list of additional
words illustrating that sound change. I hope that students
who use this handbook will take pleasure in writing down
further obvious examples as they encounter them in their
readings. They may also enjoy testing themselves on the
exercises, the answers to which will be found at the back of
the book. Those wishing to read more specialized treatments
of the subject are referred to the short bibliography.

Whether a student is familiar with several languages or is studying only one, I think that he will derive from these charts a fascinating glimpse into the family relationship existing among the Romance languages of today.

NOTES

1. These languages, together with Rumanian and Catalan, are known collectively as the Romance languages. Provençal, a Romance language which flourished in Southern France during the Middle Ages (ca. A.D. 1000-1300) and which was the literary medium of the troubadours, has since been relegated to the status of a patois by the southward expansion of French.

2. Exceptions: Britain, the frontier provinces along the Rhine and the Danube, the Austrian Alps together with most of Switzerland, Illyria (modern Jugoslavia), and North Africa. In North Africa Latin was obliterated by the Arabs, in Illyria it succumbed to Slavic infiltration, while in the other regions it succumbed to intensive settlement by speakers of Germanic (today represented in these areas by German, Dutch, Flemish, and English. (See map.)

ABBREVIATIONS
AND SOME BASIC TERMINOLOGY

Amer.-Sp. American-Spanish
Ar. Arabic
cp. compare
cons. consonant
CL Classical Latin
dial. dialectal
dimin. diminutive
Eng. English
esp. especially
fem. feminine
form. formerly
Fr. French
Gm. German
Gmc. Germanic
Gk. Greek
It. Italian
LL Low Latin
masc. masculine
met. metathesis (the transposition of sounds within a word)
O. Old; used with the abbreviation for any language, it
   refers to that language as it was spoken during a certain
   period in its development, generally between A.D. 950 and
   1300
onomat. onomatapoetic
orig. originally
poet. poetic
pop. popular
Ptg. Portuguese
Rum. Rumanian
Sp: Spanish
sup. supplement
var. variant
VL Vulgar Latin
C(a) or C(o,u) represent the sound of Latin c before a
   following a or a following o or u respectively
Ć or C(e,i)⁻ represent the sound of Latin c before a following
   front vowel (e or i)
G(a) or G(o,u)⁻ represent the sound of Latin g before a
   following a or a following o or u respectively

Ǵ or G(e,i) represent the sound of Latin g̲ before a following
front vowel (e̲ or i̲)

I̯, U̯ represent respectively semi-consonantal i̲ like the y̲ in
y̲et, and semi-consonantal u̲ like the w̲ in we̲t. They occur
only in combination with other vowels

Ê, I̯, J-, -J-, Y are all to be pronounced [j] like the y̲ in
Eng. y̲et

(1.) means that the preceding word shows learned influence.
To this category belong the numerous late borrowings from
Latin which did not undergo popular development; e.g. Sp:
artículo, Fr: exact.

(s.l.) means that the preceding word is semi-learned, in
general a word whose popular development has been partly
obstructed through scholarly or ecclesiastical influence; e.g.
Sp: siglo, Fr: sìecle

A syllable is said to be 'open' if it ends in a vowel: FĬ-DE,
BŎ-VE, CA-NE. In the foregoing examples the Ĭ, Ŏ, and A
are said to be 'free'

A syllable is said to be 'closed' if it ends in a consonant (see
Glossary) PAS-CIT, MĔN-TE, FŎR-TE, MĬL-LE. In the
foregoing examples the A, Ĕ, Ŏ, and Ī are said to be
'checked'

SYMBOLS

˘ indicates a short vowel; e.g. NŎVEM
− indicates a long vowel, e.g. FĪLU
( ) indicate a sound that tended to be omitted in pronunciation; e.g. ŎC(Ŭ)LU
· indicates a vowel pronounced with the mouth relatively open;
e.g. fǫrte [fɔrte], pę̣de [pɛde]
. indicates a vowel pronounced with the mouth relatively shut;
e.g. rẹge [rege], flọre [flore]
< 'derives from'; e.g. Fr: fait < FACTU
> 'becomes, develops into'; e.g. FACTU > Fr: fait
− stands for a vowel. For example: -t- 't between vowels',
t- 'initial t', -t 'final t'
* indicates that the following word form is presumed to have
existed at some time or other even though it has never been
found in written form.
[] indicate that the letters and symbols enclosed between them
are phonetic symbols. The latter are explained in the sec-
tion 'Phonetic Symbols'.
(()) denotes a word that means the same as the others in a
series, but is not a cognate.
(+) means that the preceding word is archaic or obsolete;
e.g. Fr: choir (+) 'to fall'
(´)(`) Where necessary the acute accent (´) is used with cer-
tain Italian words to indicate the stressed vowel. Actually,
the grave accent (`) alone is found in Italian spelling, and
then only with final accented vowels (più, fò).

THE PHONETIC ALPHABET

Phonetic symbols and transcriptions in the text are shown enclosed in square brackets; e.g. Fr: chanter [šã:te]. The following are the symbols of the phonetic alphabet used in this book, together with their approximate equivalents in modern Romance languages.

[a]	a as in Fr: pâte
[a]	a as in It, Ptg: passo, Sp: paso, Fr: pas
[ã]	an as in Fr: chanter
[ɐ]	close a, as in Ptg: vida, Eng: ago
[b]	b as in It, Sp, Ptg: banco, Fr: banc, Eng: bank (voiced bilabial stop)
[ƀ] or [β]	b as in Sp, Ptg: cabo (voiced bilabial fricative)
[d]	d as in Eng: do, Fr: deux, Sp, Ptg: dos, It: due (a voiced alveolar stop in English; a voiced dental stop in Romance)
[ẟ]	th as in Eng: they, z as in Castilian Sp: juzgar (voiced interdental fricative)
[đ]	d as in Sp, Ptg: nada (voiced dental fricative)
[ɛ]	ea as in Eng: pear, e as in It, Ptg: perdo, Sp: pierda, Fr: perds (open e)
[ɛ̃]	in as in Fr: vin
[e]	e as in It: secco, Sp: sé, Ptg: sêlo, Fr: ses (close e)
[ə]	e as in Eng: open, Ptg: pedir, Fr: venir
[f]	f as in Eng: (voiceless labiodental fricative)
[g]	g as in Eng: game (voiced velar stop), gh as in It: ghetto
[ǥ]	g as in Sp, Ptg: digo (voiced velar fricative)
[i]	i as in Eng: machine, Fr, Sp: venir, Ptg: vir, It: venire
[j]	(yod) y as in Eng: yes, Fr: yeux, Sp: yo, VL *fīlyo, i as in It: Pietro, Ptg: pior; J as in Latin JULIU, MAJOR: j as in Gmc: *warjan, Gm: ja; ll as in Mexican Sp: ella, caballo

[k]   c as in Eng: scare, Fr: cas, Sp, Ptg: cama, It:
            casa (voiceless velar stop); ch as in It: che,
            chiaro; qu as in Sp, Ptg, Fr: que
[l]   l as in Eng: lip (alveolar lateral)
[ʎ]   lli as in Eng, Fr: million; ll as in Castilian Sp:
            millón; lh as in Ptg: milhão; gli as in It:
            miglione (prepalatal lateral)
[m]   m as in Eng: mail (bilabial nasal)
[n]   n as in Eng: no (alveolar nasal)
[ŋ]   ng as in Eng: sing; n as in Eng: sink (velar
            nasal)
[ɲ]   ni as in Eng: onion; gn as in Fr: seigneur, It:
            signore; ñ as in Sp: señor; nh as in Ptg:
            senhor (prepalatal nasal)
[ɔ]   o as in It, Ptg: porta, Fr: porte, Sp: portero
            (open o)
[o]   o as in It: bocca, Ptg: bôca, Sp: bola, Fr: côté,
            Eng: hotel (close o)
[œ]   eu as in Fr: neuf, oeu as in Fr: boeuf, oeuf
            ([ɛ] pronounced with rounded lips)
[œ̃]   un as in Fr: lundi
[ø]   eu as in Fr: jeu ([e] pronounced with rounded
            lips)
[õ]   on as in Fr: mon
[p]   p as in Eng: spill, It, Ptg: passo, Sp: paso,
            Fr: pas (voiceless bilabial stop)
[r]   In It, Sp, and Ptg, a simple trill made by vibrat-
            ing the tip of the tongue against the alveolar or
            gum ridge; e.g. It, Sp, Ptg: caro. (The sound,
            also that of the well-known Scotch 'burr', is
            not unlike the t or tt of American Eng: meter,
            bitter pronounced very quickly.) In French,
            [r] represents a voiced uvular fricative, as in
            Fr: riche, grand.
[r̄]   In It, Sp, and Ptg a multiple trill produced in the
            same way as [r]; e.g. It, Sp, Ptg: carro, It:
            ricco, Sp, Ptg: rico
[ɹ]   r as in Sp, Ptg: cantar (voiced apico-alveolar
            fricative)
[s]   s as in Eng: see, It, Sp, Ptg, Fr: si; c
            in Amer.-Sp: ciento, Ptg: cento, Fr: cent;
            ç as in Ptg: braço, Fr: garçon; z as in Amer.-
            Sp: hizo, feliz (voiceless dorso-alveolar sibi-
            lant). In Castilian (but not in Spanish American)
            Sp: [s] is apico-alveolar, that is to say, a hiss
            produced between the tip of the tongue and the
            gum ridge. The tongue surface is concave.
            (Castilian [s] is sometimes mistaken by foreign-
            ers for the sound of sh in Eng: usher.)

[t]	t̲ as in Eng: stool, It, Sp, Ptg, Fr: tu (a voiceless alveolar stop in English; a voiceless dental stop in Romance)
[u]	oo̲ as in Eng: boot; u̲ as in It, Sp, Ptg: tu, Fr: tout
[v]	v̲ as in Eng: vast, It, Ptg: vasto, Fr: vaste (voiced labiodental fricative)
[w]	w̲ as in Eng: went; u̲ as in It: quattro, Sp: cuatro (labiovelar semiconsonant)
[x]	j̲ as in Sp: ojo: ch̲ as in Gm: ach, Scottish: loch. (The voiceless velar fricative produced in attempting to prolong a k̲)
[y]	u̲ as in Fr: une, Gm: über (i̲ pronounced with rounded lips)
[z]	s̲ as in Eng: visit, It: sdegnare, Sp: desde, Ptg: visita, Fr: visite (voiced alveolar sibilant)
[θ]	th̲ as in Eng: think; c̲, z̲ as in Castilian Sp: ciento, hacer, zona, esperanza (voiceless interdental fricative)
[š]	sh̲ as in Eng: shop, sc̲i as in It: uscire, ch̲, s̲, x̲, as in Ptg: chave, costa, extranho; ch̲ as in Fr: château (voiceless prepalatal sibilant)
[ž]	s̲ as in Eng: measure, Ptg: mesmo, j̲, ǵ as in Ptg: justo, gema, Fr: jour, âge (voiced pre-palatal sibilant)
[tš]	ch̲ as in Eng: child, Sp: chico, c̲ as in It: dieci, cento
[dž]	j̲ as in Eng: joy, g̲i as in It: giorno
[y̯]	u̲ as in Fr: lui, puis (semiconsonantal [y])

The symbol ~ (Sp: tilde, Ptg: til) is used in Spanish orthography as a sign of the palatal n̲ (Sp: niño), but in Portuguese orthography and in phonetic transcription it denotes a nasalized vowel (Ptg: rã [rẽ], licões [lisõjs̃], Fr: pain [pẽ]).

The accents [´] and [`] placed over vowels are occasionally used to indicate, respectively, the primary and secondary stress of a word; e.g. vèntilátion, SÀCRAMÉNTU.

SYNOPSIS OF VULGAR LATIN

The Romance languages of today evolved not out of the literary refinements of Roman statesmen, orators, and poets like Caesar, Cicero, or Ovid, but out of the colloquial, everyday speech of the common people of the Empire. Inasmuch as the vast body of Latin literature is written in the standardized literary language (Classical Latin), our knowledge of the spoken language of the Empire (i.e. Vulgar Latin, the Latin of the *vulgus* or common people) has had to be reconstructed from various fragmentary sources. These are: (1) literary lapses on the part of Roman authors; (2) the deliberate use of popular Latin by writers seeking comic effect, e.g. Plautus, Petronius; (3) the observations and censures of Roman grammarians, e.g. the *Appendix Probi*; (4) archaeological inscriptions found on walls, tombstones, tablets, and other objects; (5) the works of ignorant writers, e.g. the *Peregrinatio ad loca sancta*; (6) Latin words borrowed by the peoples with whom the Romans came in contact; (7) the evidence furnished by Latin's Romance descendants.

Vulgar Latin differed from Classical Latin in accentuation, pronunciation, grammar, and to some extent, in its choice of vocabulary. Here, in outline, are the principal characteristics of Vulgar Latin accent and pronunciation.

1. **Accentuation.** Classical Latin had a musical accent, that is to say, accented syllables were differentiated from unaccented ones not by greater loudness or length but by a higher pitch level. In Vulgar Latin this musical accent was replaced by a stress accent, under which all accented syllables became longer and louder while unaccented syllables were shortened and weakened correspondingly.

This Vulgar Latin habit of bearing heavily upon accented at the expense of unaccented vowels caused many of the latter to drop out entirely in certain positions, e.g. PÓPŬLŲU became PÓP'LO, PŎSÍTU became PÓS'TO, CÁLĬDU became CÁL'DO.[1] As for the place of the accent, this remained, with certain few

1

exceptions, the same in Vulgar as in Classical Latin. The Classical Latin rule for accentuation was extremely simple, to wit:

(a) Words of two syllables regularly stressed the penult (CÁSA, HÉRĪ).

(b) Words of three or more syllables stressed the penult if it contained a long vowel (AMĪCU), a diphthong (ACQUAERO), or ended in a consonant (HĬBĔRNU); otherwise they stressed the antepenult (PŌSĬTU, CŎLLŎCO, DĪCĔRE). In words like CŎLŎBRA, CATHĔDRA, ĬNTĔGRUM, both the stop consonant and a following L or R were considered part of the next syllable. Therefore CŎLŎBRA, CATHĔDRA, ĬNTĔGRU were stressed on the antepenult in Classical Latin.

(c) Compound words of three syllables that in Classical Latin stressed the prefix (RÉCĬPĬT, RÉFĬCĬT), in Vulgar Latin shifted the stress to the stem vowel, which was often restored to its original quality by analogy with the simple verb (RECĬPĬT, *REFÁCĬT).

2 (a) Accented vowels. Classical Latin had five pairs of accented vowels, to wit: Ī Ĭ, Ē Ĕ, Ă Ā, Ŏ Ō, Ŭ Ū. The opposing vowels in each pair were differentiated as to length or quantity, but qualitatively they were held to be the same.

These ten accented vowels were reduced in Vulgar Latin to seven long vowels, distinguished no longer by length but by clear-cut differences in quality. Figure 1 shows what happened.

Figure 1.

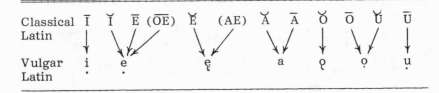

Two of the Classical Latin diphthongs, OE and AE, also disappeared in Vulgar Latin, falling together with ẹ and ę respectively. Thus Vulgar Latin ẹ represented Classical Latin Ĭ, Ē, and OE, while Vulgar Latin ę represented Classical Latin Ĕ and AE. Ă and Ā were no longer distinguished. AU, the remaining Classical Latin diphthong, was preserved for a time but eventually became ǫ, e.g. AŲRU(M) It, Sp: oro, Fr: or.

2 (b) Unaccented vowels. In the unstressed position, ǫ became ọ (but see Grandgent 1927:§228 and Williams 1938:§99, 5A) and ę became ẹ, thus reducing the number of vowels from seven to five, while in the final position a further change of -i > -e and -u > -ọ reduced all final vowels to just three (-a, -e, -ọ).

3. Consonants.

(a) In Vulgar Latin, h fell silent, also final -d (AD > a, QUĬD > que, ILLUD > ello), -m except in certain monosyllables (AMABAM > amába, ILLUM > ello, JAM > ja, SŬM > so, but CŬM > con, TAM > tan), -t (ĔT > e, AMAT > áma, AMANT > áman) [Exception: N. Gaul, where -t was preserved after a consonant.], and in Italy and Rumania, -s (TRĒS > tre, MĬNŬS > meno).

(b) The group NS > s; PS, RS both gave ss (MENSE > mése, ĬPSE > esse, PERSĬCA >péssega); NCT > nt except in Gaul (SANCTUM > sánto), PT > tt (SĔPTEM > sétte), X (+cons.) > s (+ cons.) (EXTRANĔU > estrányo).

(c) B between vowels or in the medial groups -BR-, -BL-, became the bilabial fricative [β] in some regions, the labio-dental fricative [v] in others. Consonantal Ụ [w], spelled v in Latin, became [β] or [v] also. Examples: HABĒRE > aβére or avére, FĔBRE > féβre or févre, NŎVUM > noβo or novo.

(d) Initial S (+ cons.) > es- (+ cons.) (usually spelled is (+ cons.)):SCHŎLA > escóla, iscóla.

(e) C > [tš] or [ts]: CĔNTU > tšénto, tsénto.

(f) CY > [tšj] or [tsj] : FACĬAM >[fatšja] or [fatsja].

(g) ŢY > [tsj] > [ts] : PRETĬU > [prétso].

(h) G, GY, DY > [j] : GENTE > yénte, FAGĔU > fáyo, RADĬU >ráyo.

(i) P, T, K, when intervocalic or in medial groups whose second element was L or R, tended to voice to b, d, g: DŬPLŬM > dóblo, MATRE > mádre, FŎCUM > fóco.

4. Gender, cases, and declensions.

Many students will remember that Classical Latin had a complex declensional system involving two numbers, three genders, and six cases. But in French, Spanish, Italian, and Portuguese there are just masculine and feminine,[2] singular and plural. How and when did such a striking change come about? Stated as concisely as possible the explanation is as follows:

(a) The blending of final vowels in Vulgar Latin, coupled with the widespread tendency to drop -m, -t, and in Italy -s, levelled most of the endings upon which the case system depended.

(b) A concomitant tendency in Vulgar Latin was to rely upon unambiguous prepositions such as de, ad, in, cum, together with a more rigid word order, to indicate grammatical relationships formerly expressed by the case endings alone. Case distinction, now superfluous, was abandoned in due course. Latin speakers came to use a single form of the word that was usually though not always based on the old accusative.[3] However, in Gaul (France), a two-case system (nominative-vocative and 'oblique') was retained right up until the thirteenth century, when the nominative-vocative was finally discarded. Only a few modern French nouns denoting persons (e.g. fils, soeur, prêtre, sire, Charles) go back to the Old French nominative-vocative form.

(c) As for the neuter gender, Vulgar Latin dispensed with it by treating neuter singulars, like VĔNTU(M), TĔMPU(S), as masculine singulars, and neuter plural collectives in -A, like FŎLĬA, as feminine singulars.

5. **Other grammatical changes.** (a) The number of declensions was reduced from five to three, with nouns of the fourth declension in -US, -U (FRŪCTUS, CŎRNU) and those of the fifth in -ĒS (RABĬĒS) going over to the second (masculine) in -ŬS and the first (feminine) in -A, respectively. Defective or irregular declensions were eliminated, and in the third declension new nominatives were formed to replace contracted ones like REX, NOX, LAC, PES, which became *RĒGIS, *NOCTIS, *LACTE, *PEDIS.

(b) The demonstrative ĬLLE 'that' acquired a new declension based on the endings of the relative pronoun QUĪ. Personal pronouns developed two forms, one stressed and the other unstressed, e.g. MĒ (stressed) It: me Sp: mí Ptg: mim Fr: moi, but ME (unstressed) It: mi Sp, Ptg, Fr: me.

(c) Comparative and superlative endings (FŎRTĬOR 'stronger', FŎRTISSĬMUS 'strongest') were gradually abandoned in favor of the simple adjective preceded by PLŪS or MAGĬS. Only a few irregular comparative forms were preserved (like MAJOR, MĬNOR, MĔLĬOR, PĔJOR). Beginning in adverbial phrases like SĪNCĒRĀMĔNTE 'with a sincere mind', the word -MENTE generalized its use to become in time a mere adverbial suffix, replacing the Classical Latin -ĬTĔR.

6. **Conjugations and tenses.** With the exception of the past participle, the entire passive voice was lost, its forms being replaced by the past participle conjugated with ESSE (or *ESSĔRE). In addition, the passive was frequently avoided by using indefinite pronouns like HŎMO or ŪNUS, or the reflexive construction with SĒ. Deponent verbs (verbs with passive form but active meaning, like SĔQUĪ, FABŬLĀRĪ) acquired an active conjugation (SĔQUĔRE, FABŬLĀRE). The future indicative was replaced by the infinitive conjugated with the present tense of auxiliaries like DĒBĒRE, VADĔRE, VĔLLE, and VĔNĪRE, but more especially with HABĒRE (CANTĀRE (H)ABĔT It: canterà Sp, Ptg: cantará Fr: chantera).

The infinitive used with the imperfect indicative of HABĒRE was used to express a new past future or conditional (CANTĀRE HABĒBAM). In addition, a whole series of tenses compounded of forms of HABĒRE plus the past participle came into being, some of them, like HABĒBAM CANTĀTUM, and HABŬISSEM CANTĀTUM, replacing the Classical Latin pluperfects indicative and subjunctive. CANTĀREM, the Classical Latin imperfect subjunctive, disappeared (except in the province of Lusitania, where it survives as the so-called 'personal infinitive' of Portuguese) and its function was assumed by the once pluperfect subjunctive in -ĬSSEM (CANTAVĬSSĒM or CANTASSĒM).

7. **Syntactical changes.** As stated earlier, word order became increasingly important in Vulgar Latin as the atrophy of case and verbal endings continued.[4] At the same time, the speaker, to make his meaning clear, would rely more and more upon prepositions, AD generally replacing the dative, DĒ the genitive or possessive, and CŬM the instrumental ablative.

ĬLLE and ŪNUS, their demonstrative and enumerative functions weakened through excessive use, acquired the respective functions of a definite and indefinite article, which Latin had hitherto lacked.

Lexical differences between Classical Latin and Vulgar Latin.

(1) A large number of Classical Latin words fell into varying degrees of disuse in Vulgar Latin and have left no trace in popular Romance. Among these, to mention only a few, were PŬER 'boy', PŬELLA 'girl', VIR 'man', UXOR 'wife'), ĔQUUS 'horse' (but ĔQUA 'mare' survives in Sp: yegua Ptg: egua) FĒLIS 'cat', SŪS 'swine', CRŪS 'leg', VŬLTUS 'face', TERGUM 'back', RŪS 'country', OPPĬDUM 'town', DŎMUS 'house, home', IGNIS 'fire', IMBER 'rain', PROCELLA 'storm', TELLUS 'sea', CLASSIS 'fleet', HIEMS 'winter', HŪMUS 'soil', BELLUM 'war', PROELĬUM 'battle', TELUM 'spear', GLADĬUS 'sword', ENSIS 'sword', CAEDES 'defeat', SCELUS 'crime', VIS 'force', SPĒS 'hope', NEX 'violent death', LAEVUS 'left', PULCHER 'pretty', FLAVUS 'yellow', INGENS 'huge', SAEVUS 'cruel, fierce', TŪTUS 'safe', CANĔRE 'to sing', JŪBĒRE 'to command', ĬNTERFĬCĔRE 'to kill', LOQUĪ 'to speak', FIERĪ 'to become', NOLLE 'to refuse to', MALLE 'to prefer', ULCISCĪ 'to avenge', UTER 'which of two', IS 'he', HIC 'this', QUISQUE 'whoever', NĒMO 'nobody', ĒTĬAM 'also', -QUE 'and', VEL 'or', SIVE 'or', VIX 'hardly', MOX 'soon', NUPER 'lately', TAMEN 'however', IGITUR 'therefore', CLAM 'secretly', CORAM 'in person', PROCUL 'far away', HAUD 'not', SIMUL 'together', AT 'but', ENIM 'for', QUOQUE 'also'.

(2) Like the popular speech of lower classes everywhere, Vulgar Latin was rich in colorful metaphors and charged with emotional content. Speakers made abundant use of prefixes, suffixes, diminutives, and augmentatives of every kind; reinforced prepositions by the process of accumulation (e.g. Sp: desde DE + EX + DE, Sp: adelante AD + DE + IN + ANTE, or Fr: jusqu'à DE + USQUE + AD); and coined new words from other parts of speech (CAPĔRE > CAPTUS > *captare, SĔDĒRE > SĔDĔNTE > *sedentare). Many adjectives came to be used as nouns, e.g. HĪBĔRNU replaced HĬEMS 'winter', VĬATĬCU 'pertaining to a road' replaced ĬTĔR 'journey', and in Italy and Gaul, the adjective DĬŬRNU supplanted DĬĒS 'day'.

(3) Vulgar Latin borrowed extensively from the languages of neighboring peoples such as Celts, Germans, and Greeks. Believed to be of Celtic origin are CAMĪSĮA 'shirt', CÉRÉVĪSĮA 'beer', CABALLU 'horse', BRACAE 'breeches', LEŲCA 'league', CAPANNA 'cabin', LANCĘA 'lance', and others.

Germanic supplied hundreds of words, of which *WERRA 'war', HÉLMU 'helmet', RĪCCU 'powerful, rich', *ORGŌLĮU 'pride', *WĪSA 'way, manner', HŌSA 'hose', BANDA 'band', BLANCU 'white', BRŪNU 'brown', STALLA 'stable', STACCA 'stake', *RAŲBĀRE 'to rob', are only a few. In general, the lexical influence of Germanic was greater in Italy and Gaul than in the Iberian Peninsula.

NOTES

1. The lengthening of the stressed vowel was later to give rise to the phenomenon of diphthongization in Italian, French, and Spanish. The stressed vowel would double its length, e.g. ǫ́ > óó, then its two elements would dissimilate: ǫǫ́ > oǫ́ > uǫ́ in Italian, or uǫ́ > uá > uę́ as in Spanish.

2. Vestiges of the neuter in Spanish are esto, eso, aquello, ello, and the neuter article lo (lo bueno, lo difícil).

3. Italian, which lost -s, could not use the accusative plural endings -A(S) to distinguish plural from singular. Instead, Italian kept the nominative plurals -AE and -I (modern Italian -e, -i). Nouns of the Latin third declension (e.g. It: padre, madre, latte) probably owe their plural in -i to analogy with the second (masculine) declension, though some scholars have claimed that -ES > -i in Italian was a regular phonetic change.

4. Whereas Classical Latin could say with equal facility FĪLĮA AMĪCAM VĪDÉT, FĪLĮA VĪDÉT AMĪCAM, AMĪCAM FĪLĮA VĪDÉT, AMĪCAM VĪDÉT FĪLĮA, VĪDÉT FĪLĮA AMĪCAM, or VĪDÉT AMĪCAM FĪLĮA, all meaning 'the daughter sees a friend', Vulgar Latin tended to standardize the subject--verb --object sequence: filya vęde(t) amica(m). Moreover, whereas the Classical Latin sentence is ambiguous (does AMICAM mean 'a friend' or 'the friend'?) Vulgar Latin would use ILLE to designate a particular friend: vęde(t) ęlla(m) amica(m).

A SYNOPSIS OF THE ORIGIN
AND DEVELOPMENT OF FRENCH SIBILANTS

A. Old French. Old French had the sibilants outlined in Figure 2.

Figure 2. The Old French Sibilants.

(1) [s] as in O.Fr:	sel, passer	
(2) [ts] as in O.Fr:	cent, place, laz	
(3) [tš] as in O.Fr:	chanter, vache	
(4) [z] as in O.Fr:	rose, asne	
(5) [dž] as in O.Fr:	jambe, mangier	

The sources of these sibilants are outlined in (1) through (5).
   1. O.Fr. [s] developed from Latin S or SS in all positions except those described in (2), also from C'T, CTY, SCY, SSY, STY, TY (when final), and X: SĔPTEM > set, FĔSTA > feste, FALSA > false, MŪRŌS > murs, MĒSE > mois, CANTA(VĬ)SSEM > chantasse, ESSĔRE > estre, PRAEPŎS(Ĭ)TU > prevost, PLACĬT > plaist, DIRECTIĀRE > dresser, *PĬSCĮŌNE > poisson, BASSĮĀRE > baissier, ANGŬSTIA > angoisse, PĂLATIU > palais, LAXĀRE > laissier.
   2. O.Fr. [z] was the pronunciation of Latin S between vowels or before a voiced consonant; it also came from intervocalic Ć, SY, and TY: RŌSA > rose, ASĬNU > asne, CO(N)S(UĔ)RE > cousdre, PLACĒRE > plaisir, BASIĀRE > baiser, RATIŌNE > raison.
   (3) O.Fr. [ts] came from Latin Ć (initial, protected, or final), from CY, and from TY preceded by a consonant other than S: CĔNTU > cent, DŬLCE > dolce, PŪL(I)CE > puce, *RAD(I)CĪNA > racine, VŌCE > voiz, *FACĮA > face, SEDANTĮA > seance, CAPTĮĀRE > chacier, MARTĮU > marz.
   4. O.Fr. [tš] developed from C[a] when initial, protected, or preceded by an unstressed vowel that dropped early, also from PY: CAPU > chief, CAMPU > champ, MERCĀTU > marchié, VACCA > vache, CŎLL(O)CĀRE > coulchier, MAN(Ĭ)CA > manche, SAPĮAM > sache.

7

(5) O.Fr. [dž] came from Latin G$^{(a)}$ when initial, protected, or preceded by an unstressed vowel that dropped early, from C$^{(a)}$ preceded by a vowel that dropped late, from the suffix -ATICU, from BY, MY, MNY, and VY, from initial Ǵ-, J-, DY-, or GY, and from R'G, RDY, NGY, and RGY: GAUD̦IA > joie, VȊRGA > verge, NAV(Ȋ)GĀRE > nagier, VȊNDȊCĀRE > vengier, CARRȊCĀRE > chargier, VĪSATȊCU > visage, RAB̦IA rage, SĪM̦IA > singe, SŎMN̦IU > songe, CAVEA > cage, GENTE > gent, JŎCĀRE > jo(u)er, D̦IU̇RNU > jorn, GȨORG̦IUS > Georges, ARGENTU > argent, HORDȨU > orge, VȊRD̦IAR̦IU > vergier, ȊNGȨN̦IU > engin.

B. **Modern French.** During the thirteenth century the French sibilants underwent simple changes that have survived to this day. First, [tš] became [š], [dž] became [ž], [ts] became [s]. Secondly, with few exceptions, [s] came to be silent before consonants and at the end of a word; some examples are listed in Figure 3.

Figure 3. Development of Old French Sibilants in Modern French.

O.Fr.	Fr.
chief [tšjɛf]	chef [šɛf]
champ [tšãmp]	champ [šã]
vache [vatšə]	vache [vaš]
juge [džydžə]	juge [žyž]
Georges [džɔrdžəs]	Georges [žɔrž]
chargier [tšardžɛr]	charger [šarže]
cent [tsẽnt]	cent [sã]
chacier [tšatsjɛr]	chasser [šase]
escu [esky]	écu [eky]
espede [espɛdə]	épée [epe]
nostre [nɔstrə]	notre [notr]
isles [izlɔs]	îles [il]
pris [pris]	pris [pri]
avez [avets]	avez [ave]
alz, aux [al(t)s, aus]	aux [o]
François [Frãntsojs]	François [Frãswa]

Liaison. Final -s survives as [z], i.e. is treated like intervocalic S, when linked in speech to a following word beginning with a vowel sound. For example, dix-huit [dizyit], les arbres [le zarbr], mes yeux ouverts [mezjǿzuvɛr].

Learned Words. A large number of learned words retain s before a consonant. Compare escalier, espèce, estomac, with échelle, épice, étroit, or vaste, funeste, schisme, poste, and juste with hâte, forêt, abîme, vôtre, dût. In a handful of

words final s̲ is pronounced [s]: fi̲ls̲, li̲s̲, ma̲rs̲, and in certain cases so is final x̲: si̲x̲, di̲x̲.

A SYNOPSIS OF THE ORIGIN
AND DEVELOPMENT OF SPANISH SIBILANTS

A. Old Spanish. Old Spanish had the sibilants shown in Figure 4.

Figure 4. The Old Spanish Sibilants.

Voiceless	Voiced
(1) [s] as in O.Sp: sal, passar	(2) [z] as in O.Sp: rosa, asno
(3) [ts] as in O.Sp: çiento, plaça	(4) [dz] as in O.Sp: fazer, tristeza
(5) [š] as in O.Sp: dixo, baxo	(6) [ž] as in O.Sp: ojo, muger
(7) [tš] as in O.Sp: lech(e), noch(e)	

Their sources were as follows:

1. O.Sp. [s] came from Latin S or SS in all positions except those described in (2): SĔPTE > siete, ĬSTU > esto, FALSU > falsso, MŪROS > muros, MĒSE > mes, CANTA(VI)SSEM > cantasse, PŎS(Ĭ)TU > puesto.

2. O.Sp. [z] was the pronunciation of Latin S between vowels or before a voiced consonant: RŌSA > rosa, AS(Ĭ)NU > asno, Ĭ(N)SŬLA > isla.

3. O.Sp. [ts] came from Latin Ć in an initial or strong position, also from (cons. +) CY, DY or TY, or from sporadic confusion with [s]: CĔNTU > çiento, VĬNCĔRE > vençer, LANCĔA > lança, *VĬRDĬA > berça, MARTĬU > março, SERĀRE > çerrar.

4. O.Sp. [dz] came from Latin Ć between vowels, from Ǵ preceded by N or R, and from CY, TY: FACERE > fazer, SĬNGĔLLU > senzillo, ARGĪLLA > arzilla, LAQ(U)ĔU > lazo, PŬTEU > pozo.

5. O.Sp. [š] came from Latin X, PSY, SSY, or from Ar: shin: AXE > exe, CAPSĔA > caxa, BASSĬU > baxo, Ar:

wa ša Allah > oxalá. There are a few cases of confusion between O.Sp. [s] and O.Sp. [š]; e.g. SAPŌNE > xabón,
SĒPĮA > xibia.
  6. O.Sp. [ž], formerly [dž], came from Latin C'L, G'L,
LY and from J (DY, GY) before o or u: ŎC(Ŭ)LU > ojo,
TĒG(Ŭ)LA > teja, MŬLIĒRE > muger, JŬVĔNE > joven.
  7. O.Sp. [tš] came from Latin CT, the groups FL, PL,
C'L when preceded by a consonant, or from sporadic confusion
with [ts]: NŎCTE > noche, INFLĀRE > (h)inchar, AMPLU >
ancho, CALCŬLU > cacho, MASCŬLU > macho, CĬCCU > chico.

  B. **Modern Spanish.** During the course of the sixteenth
century, Spain's great century of conquest and colonization,
the Old Spanish sibilants underwent a drastic change. The
voiced sibilants [dz], [z], and [ž] unvoiced to become identical, respectively, with [ts], [s], and [š].
  At about the same time [ts] advanced its point of contact to
between the teeth ([ts] > [tθ]>[θ]), while [š] retreated all the
way to back of the mouth to become the velar fricative [x].
The only sibilants not affected were [s] and [tš].
  The sibilant changes described above, embracing a span of
only 30 years, were by no means carried out uniformly. They
were completed in standard Castilian only after considerable
vacillation.

  Seseo. Some regions of Spain did not share with Castile its
peculiar concave [ś], pronounced with the tip of the tongue
against the gum ridge. Instead, they had the dorso-alveolar
[s], pronounced with the tip of the tongue against the lower
teeth, that is common to Portuguese, Italian, French, and English. The point of contact for this latter [s] lay in the path
of advancing [ts], whose [t] element had almost disappeared
by the time the positions of the two sounds came to coincide.
The hopeless confusion of the two almost identical sounds
could be solved only by equating them either as [s] or as [θ].
Result: whereas Castilian Spanish with its cacuminal [ś] distinguishes clearly between the sibilants in cinco and sí, señor,
part of Andalusia says θinco, θí, θeñor (ceceo), while another
part of Spain, together with the whole of Spanish America,
says sinco, sí, señor (seseo). In this respect the latter regions offer a close parallel with Portuguese and French, whose
[ts] has also become [s]: Ptg: cinco [sĩku] Fr: cinq [sɛ̃·k].
In Italian, where Latin Ć- had never advanced beyond the
[tš] stage, there was no possibility of confusion with [s],
hence It: cinque [tšiŋkwe] and si, signore.

A SURVEY OF THE PHONETIC
CHARACTERISTICS OF PENINSULAR PORTUGUESE

1. Unlike the other Romance tongues, Portuguese does not diphthongize Ĕ or Ŏ under any circumstances: PĔDE > pé, NŎVU > novo.

2. -LL- > -l-; -NN-, -MN- > -n̠-: CABALLU > cavalo, ANNU > ano, DAMNU > dano.

3. -L-, -N- disappear: FĪLU > fio, TENĒRE > ter.

4. The l of the definite article, treated as intervocalic in the stream of speech, drops: lo, la, los, las > o, a, os, as.

5. PL- > [pʎ] > [pj] > [ptš-] > [tš-] > [š], spelled ch-. CL- and FL developed in the same way: PLŌRĀRE > chorar, CLĀVE > chave, FLAMMA > chama. (An alternate development was pr-, cr-, fr-: PLANCTU > pranto, CLĀVU > cravo, FLACCU > fraco.)

6. ŬLT, CT > it: MŬLTU > muito, ŎCTO > oito.

7. C'L, LY > lh̠ [ʎ]: ŎCŬLU > olho, FĪLῘU > filho.

8. GN, NY > nh̠ [ɲ]: PŬGNU > punho, SENῘŌRE > senhor.

9. S (final before a pause) or S (+ voiceless cons.) > [š], S (+ voiced cons.) > [ž]. This also applies in liaison: [š] dois, gasto, espera, disco, esfera, boas tardes, muitas questões; [ž] desde, asno, cosmo, rasgo, deslial, desviar, as grandes nacões, as licões difíceis.

10. AU, together with au from AL (+ cons.), > ou (sometimes confused with oi): AURU > ouro (oiro), ALTĔRU > outro. Similarly, an ai of any origin > ei: LAICU > leigo, AMĀ(V)I > amei, MAJ(O)RĪNU > meirinho, PRĪMĀRῘU > primeiro.

11. Unstressed, a > [ɐ], e > [ə], o > [u]: APERTU > aberto [ɐbertu], VĒRITĀTE > verdade [vəɹdadə], VOCALE > vogal [vugal], LATU > lado [ladu].

12. Portuguese has several nasal vowels and diphthongs which arose from the influence upon a following or preceding vowel, of a nasal consonant, which itself sometimes fell and sometimes remained: LANA > lã [lɐ̃], VENDERE > vender [vẽdeɹ], FĪNE > fim [fĩ], CŬM - com [kõ], ŪNU > um [ũ],

TENET > tem [tẽi], MANU > mão [mɐ̃u], PŎNIT > põe [põi], MŬLTU > muito [mũitu].

13. -ĀNE, -ŌNE, and - ĀNU all give Portuguese -ão [-ẽu], though in the plural they are well differentiated: CĀNÉ > RATIŌNE > razão, MĀNU > mão, but plural cães [kɐ̃iš], razões [rʋzõiš], mãos [mɐ̃uš].

14. Metaphony or umlaut. In Portuguese nouns and adjectives, final -o often exerts a closing influence upon an accented e or o (that is to say, ę > e, e > i, ǫ > o, o > u), while final -a, -os and -as open ę >ę̣, o >ǫ. This phenomenon, by no means consistent, appears to have originated in a desire to distinguish more carefully between words differentiated only by their inflectional ending. Examples: TŌTU 'all' > tudo 'everything'; PŬTĘU > poço 'well', pǫça 'pond'; MĒTA 'goal' męda 'stack'; MĒTŬ 'fear' > medo; ŎVU > ôvo 'egg', plural ǫvos, ǫva 'fish roe', plural ǫvas; MŎRTU 'dead' > morto, but mǫrtos, mǫrta, mǫrtas; AŲRĒLLA > ouręla 'border, edge', ourelo 'trim, selvage (of cloth)'; PĒTRA > pędra 'stone', Pędro 'Peter'; ῨPSU > esso > isso 'that' but ῨPSA > essa > ęssa; *AVŎLU 'grandfather' > avô, but *AVŎLA 'grandmother' > avǫ́. In verbs, final -o tended to close the accented stem vowel, and final e to open it: devo but dęves, dęve; como but cǫmes, cǫme; verto but vęrtes, vęrte.

15. Contraction of vowels brought together (i.e. into hiatus) through the fall of an intervening consonant. Grouping Portuguese vowels into the following two series, (I) Front and (II) Back, as in Figure 5, we find as a rule:

(a) If the two vowels were identical in quality, they contracted: PALA 'shovel' > paa > pa; VIDĒRE 'to see' > veer > ver; PERĪCULU 'danger' > perigoo > perigo; PALATĮU 'palace' > paaço > paço; GĒNĒRALE 'general' > geral; CRĒDITŌRE 'creditor' > creedor > credor.

(b) If the unaccented vowel was one step more open (in the same series), it was assimilated and absorbed by the accented vowel: CALENTE 'hot' > caente > queente > quente; VENĪRE > vęir > viir > vir; CĪVĪLES 'civil' > civięs > civiis > civis; MŎLA 'mill-stone' > mǫa > mǫǫ > mó 'mill-stone, molar'; CRŪDU 'raw' > cruo > cru; MŪLU 'he-mule' muo > mú; ŬMBῨLĪCU 'navel' > embeígo > embigo.

(c) If the unaccented vowel was two steps more open, then mutual assimilation took place: SAGῨTTA 'arrow' > saęta > sęę̣ta > sęta; PALŬMBU 'dove' > paómbo > pǫǫ́mbo > pǫmbo; MAJŌRE 'greater' > *maór (by analogy with peor) > mǫǫ́r > mǫ́r 'chief, principal, major'; SŌLA 'alone' > soa > sǫǫ > sǫ́.

(d) If the unaccented vowel was three steps more open, then there was no change: SALĪRE 'to jump' > sair 'to come out'; LŪNA 'moon' > lua.

(e) If the unaccented vowel was closer (in the same series) than the accented vowel, it was repelled and if possible became closer still: MALU 'bad' > mao > mau; VADIT 'he goes' vae > vai; VOLĀRE 'to fly' > voar [vwar]; GELĀRE 'to freeze' >

gear [žjar], AFFĪLĀRE 'to sharpen' > afiar; GENERĀLĒS 'general (plur.)' > gerais.

(f) If the unaccented vowel was not in the same series, it also became closer: *MOLĒRE 'to grind' > moer_[mwer]; MOLĪNU moinho [mwiɲu], CAELU 'sky' > céu; SŌLĒS 'suns' > sóis; PĔDŌNE 'pedestrian' > peão [pjɐ̃u].

Figure 5.

	Open		Close	
I. Front	a	ę	ẹ	i
II. Back	a	ǫ	ọ	u

RULE 1

Á

Rule: Á generally remains in the Romance languages, but in French, if the syllable is open, it becomes e̲, and before a nasal, a̲i̲.

	Italian	Spanish	Portu-guese	French	English cognate
CAMPU 'field'	campo	campo	campo	champ	camp, champion
PASSU 'step'	passo	paso	passo	pas	pace
GRANDE 'big'	grande	grande	grande	grand	grand
PARTE 'part'	parte	parte	parte	part	part
AS(I)NU 'ass'	asino	asno	asno	âne	ass, asinine
FLAMMA 'flame'	fiamma	llama	chama	flamme	flame
MARE 'sea'	mare	mar	mar	mer	maritime
CARU 'dear'	caro	caro	caro	cher	cherish (i.e. 'to hold dear')
PRATU 'meadow'	prato	prado	prado	pré	prairie
FABA 'bean'	fava	haba	fava	fève	
PASSĀTU 'passed'	passato	pasado	passado	passé	past
PRĪVĀTU 'deprived'	privato	privado	privado	privé	private, privy

	Italian	Spanish	Portuguese	French	English cognate
PATRE 'father'	padre	padre	pai	père	paternal
MANU 'hand'	mano	mano	mão	main	maintain, manual
PANE 'bread'	pane	pan	pão	pain	companion (lit. 'one who shares bread')
SANU 'healthy'	sano	sano	são	sain	sane
AMAT 'loves'	ama	ama	ama	aime	amorous

Note 1. An A which for any reason came into contact with a following yod combined with it to give Ptg: ei, Sp: e: CANTĀ(V)I Ptg: cantei, Sp: canté; BASIARE Ptg: beijar, Sp: besar; OP(E)RĀRIU Ptg: obreiro, Sp: obrero; LACTE Ptg: leite, Sp: leche; ŜAPIA(M) Ptg: seiba, Sp: sepa.

Note 2. In French, an A, accented or not, usually combined phonetically with a following yod of no matter what origin: PACE 'peace' Fr: paix [pɛ], AREA 'threshing-floor' Fr: aire [ɛr], RADIU 'ray' Fr: rai [re], FÁC(E)RE Fr: faire [fɛr], MA(G)ÍS Fr: mais, CANTĀ(V)I 'I sang' Fr: je chantai [ŝa•te], LACTE Fr: lait, LAXĀRE Fr: laisser, BASSIARE 'to lower' Fr: baisser, SACRAMENTU 'oath' O.Fr: sairement, Fr: serment; ACRE 'sour, tart' Fr: aigre, MACRU 'thin, meager' Fr: maigre, AQUILA 'eagle' Fr: aigle, ACŪTU 'sharp, pointed' Fr: aigu [egy], ACŪC(Ū)LA 'needle, pin' Fr: aiguille, AQUAS 'waters' Fr: Aix, Aigues (Mortes) (place names), AQUA MARĪNA Fr: aigue-marine 'aquamarine'.

Note 3. In French, all final vowels weakened and tended to disappear at an early stage, with the exception of final -A which survived as [ə], the so-called 'mute' e: PARTE part, VENDÍT vend, VĪGINTĪ vingt, ŪNU un, MŪRŌS murs; but ŪNA une, *VIDŪTA vue. However, even the other final vowels generally remained as [ə] when needed to support (i.e. facilitate the pronunciation of) certain Latin or Romance consonant groups: MACRU maigre, V.L. QUATTRO quattre, PATRE père, DUPLU double, LĪBRU livre; ASINU âne (O.Fr: asne) METÍPSÍMU même (O.Fr: mesme); APIU ache, RŬBEU rouge; ARBŎRE arbre, LĔPŎRE lièvre, CARŎLUS Charles, CRĒDĔRE croire; ŬNDĔCĬM onze; VENDŬNT vendent. (It will be noted that in Modern French such support vowels survive even though the consonant group has in the meantime often disappeared.)

Additional Examples

SŬPERĀNU It: sovrano Sp: soberano Ptg: soberano
Fr: souverain (Eng: sovereign)
LANA 'wool' It, Sp: lana Ptg: lã Fr: laine
DĒ MANE 'in the morning' It: domani Fr: demain 'tomorrow'
EXAMEN 'swarm (esp. of bees)' It: sciame Sp: enjambre
Ptg: enxame Fr: essaim
FAME 'hunger' It: fame Sp: hambre (FAMĬNE) Ptg: fome
Fr: faim (Eng: famine)
CLAMO 'I call' O.Fr, Eng: claim
AXE 'axis' It: asse Sp: eje Ptg: eixo Fr: essieu (AXELLU)
LAĬCU 'lay' Sp: lego Fr: lai (Eng: lay)
ANTĔNĀTU 'born earlier' Sp: alnado 'step-child' Fr: aîné
'elder (son)'

Exercise

Opposite each of the words in Group A write down the number of its nearest cognate in Group B.
Group A
1. Sp: leche..... 2. Fr: laine..... 3. Ptg: sao.....
4. It: asino..... 5. Fr: fève..... 6. Sp: eje.....
7. Ptg: cantei... 8. Eng: meager... 9. Fr: faim....
10. It: sciame....

Group B
1. Sp: así 2. Eng: lane 3. Eng: sane 4. Sp: haba
5. Fr: âne 6. Fr: lait 7. Eng: fever 8. Ptg: lã
9. Eng: sing 10. Sp: humo 11. Fr: je chantai
12. Ptg: olho 13. Fr: maigre 14. Fr: essaim
15. Eng: exit 16. It: asse 17. Sp: mugre 18. It: fame
19. Eng: shame 20. Fr: lit

RULE 2

-ĀRĮU (cf. RY, p. 115)

Rule: The common Latin suffix -ĀRĮU(S) became -áio (sometimes -aro) in Italian, developed (via -airo) to Ptg: -eiro and Sp: -ero, while in Fr the result was -ier (fem. -ière).

	Italian	Spanish	Portu-guese	French	English cognate
ŎP(Ĕ)RĀRĮU 'worker'	operaio	obrero	ǫbreiro	ouvrier	
JAN(Ŭ)ARĮU 'January'	gennaio	enero	janeiro	janvier	January
FEBR(Ŭ)ĀRĮU 'February'	febbraio	febrero	febreiro	février	February
CAL(Ĭ)DĀRĮA 'cauldron'	caldaia	caldera	caldeira	chaudière	cauldron, chowder (Fr: chaudière)
ŪSŪRĀRĮU 'usurer'	usuraio	usurero	usureiro	usurier	usurer
DENĀRĮU 'penny'*	denaro (danaro) 'money'	dinero 'money'	dineiro 'money'	denier 'a former coin'	denier
PRĪMĀRĮU 'first'	((primo))	primero	primeiro	premier	primer, premier
SCŪTĀRĮU 'shield-bearer'	scudiero**	escudero	escudeiro	écuyer	squire, esquire
MAR(Ĭ)NĀRĮU 'sailor'	marinaio (marinaro)	marinero	marinheiro	O.Fr: marnier	mariner, (Silas) Marner
RĪP(Ŭ)ĀRĮA 'shore (adj.)'	riviera**	ribera 'beach, strand'	ribeira	rivière	river
FŬRNĀRĮU 'baker'	fornaio	hornero	forneiro	fournier ((boulanger))	furnace

18

	Italian	Spanish	Portu- guese	French	English cognate
CŎQUĪNĀRĮA 'cook'	cucinaia	cocinera	cozinheira	cuisinière	

*The British monetary symbols £--s--d stand for Latin libra (pound), sestertius (shilling), and denarius (penny), respectively.
**Scudiero, sentiero, and a few other words in -iero are adaptations from French.

Note: Sp: -ario (vario, diario, agrario, etc.), Fr: -aire (libraire, ovaire, commissaire) are learned or semi-learned forms.

Additional Examples

SŌL(Ĭ)TĀRĮU 'alone' Sp: soltero 'unmarried' Ptg: solteiro
 Eng: solitary
FERRĀRĮU It: ferraio Sp: herrero Ptg: ferreiro 'blacksmith'
ACĮĀRĮU 'steel' It: acciaio Sp: acero Fr: acier
SĒM(Ĭ)TĀRĮU (from SEMĬTA 'path') It: sentiero Sp: sendero
 Ptg: senda (SEMĬTA) Fr: sentier
*ALBĀRĮU (ALBU 'white') Sp: overo Fr: aubère '(of horses)
 dapple-grey'
*CARRĀRĮA 'carriage-road' (< CARRU 'cart, carriage') It:
 carraia Sp: carrera Ptg: carreira Fr: carrière (> Eng:
 career It: carriera)
OVĀRĮA,-U Sp: overa Ptg: oveiro 'ovary (of fowls)'
PANĀRĮU 'bread (adj.)' It: panaio 'mealy (of apples)' Fr:
 panier 'basket' Sp: panero 'bread basket'
LĪBRĀRĮU It: libraio Sp: librero 'bookseller' Ptg: livreiro
FOCĀRĮU,-ĀRĮA Sp: hoguera 'bonfire' Ptg: fogueira Fr:
 foyer 'hearth' (It: (pietra) focaia 'flint')
*FRONTĀRĮA Sp: frontera Ptg: fronteira Fr: frontière
 (Eng: frontier)
GLACĮĀRĮU 'of ice' It: ghiacciaio 'glacier' Fr: glacier (Eng:
 glacier)
*ŪSTĮĀRĮU 'janitor' (for OSTĮĀRĮU < OSTĮU 'gate') Fr:
 huissier Eng: usher
CABALLĀRĮU 'horseman' It: cavallaio, cavallero 'horse-trader'
 Sp: caballero 'knight, gentleman' Ptg: cavaleiro 'knight'
 Fr: chevalier (> It: cavaliere) 'knight' (Eng: cavalier)
MAN(Ŭ)ARĮA (MANU 'hand') Sp: manera Ptg: maneira Fr:
 manière (It: maniera) Eng: manner
*MŎLĪNĀRĮU 'miller' It: molinaio Sp: molinero Ptg: moleiro
 Fr: meunier
*PANATARĮU 'baker' Sp: panadero Ptg: padeiro
*FACĮĀRĮA (< FACĮES 'face') O.Sp: façera (h)açera Sp: acera
 'sidewalk'

DĮĀRĮA 'a day's ploughing' Ptg: geira 'acre'
AEST(Ŭ)ĀRĮU 'estuary, tideland' Sp: estero Ptg: esteiro
 Fr: étier
AQUĀRĮA, -U(< AQUA 'water') It: acquaio 'sink' Sp: agüera
 'irrigation trench' Ptg: agüero 'gutter, drain' Fr: évier
 'sink' (see Rule 33)

Exercise

Opposite each of the words in Group A write down the number
of its nearest cognate in Group B.

Group A
1. Sp: hoguera.... 2. Fr: chevalier.... 3. Eng: manner....
4. It: ghiacciaio..... 5. Ptg: escudeiro....
6. Eng: career... 7. It: acquaio.... 8. Eng: ovary....
9. Fr: acier... 10. It: caldaia.... 11. Sp: dinero...
12. Fr: panier... 13. Eng: usher.... 14. Ptg: padeiro...
15. Sp: soltero... 16. Ptg. janeiro... 17. Sp: sendero....
18. Sp: obrero.... 19. Ptg. livreiro... 20. Sp: herrero....

Group B
1. Sp: cabellera 2. Fr: ouvrier 3. Ptg: forneiro
4. Fr: chaudière 5. Sp: overa 6. Eng: liberator
7. Fr: foyer 8. Eng: scout 9. Ptg: ferreiro 10. Sp: maña
11. Sp: panero 12. Fr: meunier 13. Eng: acquire
14. Eng: glacier 15. Fr: usine 16. It: libraio 17. Sp:
pandera 18. Ptg: carreira 19. Eng: janitor 20. Fr: évier
21. It: acciaio 22. Ptg: primeiro 23. Eng: farrier
24. Eng: colder 25. It: gennaio 26. Eng: soldier
27. Sp: caballero 28. Fr: dîner 29. Sp: panadero
30. Eng: solitary 31. Fr: manière 32. Fr: j'acquiers
33. Eng: courier 34. Fr: sentier 35. It: denaro
36. Fr: ouvrir 37. Eng: squire 38. Sp: cartero
39. Fr: huissier 40. Eng: ovation

RULE 3

-ĀTĬCU

Rule: The suffix -ĀTĬCU, originally adjectival, became a fertile collective noun suffix in Provençal and Old French, whence it was borrowed by the other Romance tongues. Corresponding to French -age [-aːž] we find Italian -aggio [-adžo], Spanish -aje [-axe], and Portuguese -agem [-ažẽu].

	Italian	Spanish	Portu-guese	French	English cognate
VĬĀTĬCU (< VĬA 'way')	viaggio	viaje	viagem	voyage	voyage
*LĬNGUĀTĬCU (< LĬNGUA 'tongue')	linguaggio	lenguaje	linguagem	langage 'style of expression'	language
*SĬLVĀTĬCU (SALVĀTĬCU) (< SĬLVA 'forest')	selvaggio	salvaje	selvagem	sauvage	savage
*CŎRĀTĬCUM (< CŎR 'heart')	coraggio	coraje 'anger'	coragem	courage	courage
*PA(G)ENSĀTĬCU (< PAGENSE 'district')	paesaggio	paisaje	paisagem	paysage 'landscape'	
*LĪNĀTĬCU (< LĪNU 'line')	linaggio	linaje	linagem	--	lineage
*HŎMĬNĀTĬCU (< HŎMĬNE 'man')	omaggio	homenaje	(h)omenagem	hommage	homage
(LL) ABANTE 'forward' plus -ĀTĬCU	vantaggio	ventaja	vantagem	avantage	(ad)van-tage

Note 1. The French development went like this: -ÁTICU [-ád(i)jə] > [-ádjə] > [-áddžə] > [-á:ž]. But in words where the [j] came into contact with a voiceless consonant it palatalized to [tš] instead: PŎRTĬCU > [pórt(i)jə] > [pórtjə] > [pórttšə] > [pɔrš]--porche (Eng: porch). Showing a development like that of -ĀTĬCU are words like PĔDĬCA piège 'snare' and VĬNDĬCAT venge 'avenges'.

Note 2. The normal Spanish development of -ĀTĬCU was to -ad'go > -azgo, as found in mayorazgo, hallazgo, portazgo, alguacilazgo, and others. (TRĬTĬCU trigo represents an alternative development.) D'C developed in a similar fashion JŪDĬCĀRE Sp: juzgar Fr: juger (Eng: to judge), FŎRU JŪDĬCU Sp: Fuero Juzgo.

Additional Examples

*SALINĀTĬCU (< SAL 'salt') O.Fr: salinage Fr: saunage 'salt trade'

*MANSĮONĀTĬCU 'pertaining to the household' O.Fr: mesnage Fr: ménage 'household'

*BIBERĀTĬCU Sp: brebaje Fr: breuvage (Eng: beverage)

*NŪBATĬCU Fr: nuage 'cloud'

STĀTĬCU Fr: étage (Eng: stage)

(CASĘU) FŎRMĀTĬCU 'moulded cheese' It: formaggio Fr: fromage

*AETĀTĬCU (< AETĀTE 'age') O.Fr: e(d)age, aage Fr: âge (Eng: age)

*CALMĀTĬCU (< CALMARE 'to calm, cease') Fr: chômage 'work stoppage, unemployment'

VĪLLĀTĬCU (< VĪLLA 'estate') It: villaggio Fr: village Eng: village

OPERĀT(Ĭ)CU Fr: ouvrage 'work'

MĬSSĀTĬCU Sp: mensaje Eng: message

PASSĀTĬCU It: passaggio Sp: pasaje Fr, Eng: passage

*ŬLTRĀTĬCU (from ŬLTRA 'beyond, in excess') It: ultraggio Sp: ultraje Fr, Eng: outrage

Exercise

Opposite each of the words in Group A write down the number of its nearest cognate in Group B.

Group A
1. Eng: beverage.... 2. Ptg: selvagem.... 3. It: paesaggio.... 4. Sp: ventaja.... 5. Eng: outrage.....
6. Sp: homenaje... 7. Sp: portazgo.... 8. It: formaggio....
9. Ptg: viagem.... 10. Sp: lenguaje....

Group B
1. It: linaggio 2. Fr: fromage 3. Eng: sausage 4. It: vantaggio 5. Ptg: linguagem 6. Fr: page 7. Eng: sewage
8. Sp: brebaje 9. Eng: passage 10. Fr: sauvage
11. Eng: cottage 12. Fr: village 13. Eng: homage
14. Eng: forage 15. Eng: portage 16. Fr: voyage
17. Eng: strategem 18. Fr: paysage 19. Eng: vintage
20. Sp: ultraje

RULE 4

AṶ

Rule: In general, the diphthong AṶ monophthongized to o̱ in all four languages, with o̱u̱ and au͡ being common spellings in Portuguese and French, respectively. In French, however, the o̱ sound sometimes combined with a following vowel to form a new diphthong, e.g. *AṶCA oie (pron. [wa]); PAṶCU > póu > peu (pron. [pø]).

	Italian	Spanish	Portu-guese	French	English cognate
AṶRU 'gold'	oro	oro	ouro	or	
*AUSARE 'to dare'	osar	osar	ousar	oser	
PAṶSARE 'to rest'	posare	posar 'set down, rest'	pousar	poser 'to set'	pose, pause
THESAṶRU 'treasure'	tesoro	tesoro	tesouro	trésor	treasure, thesaurus
CAṶSA 'cause'	cosa 'thing'*	cosa 'thing'*	cousa 'thing'*	chose 'thing'*	
TAṶRU 'bull'	toro	toro	touro	taureau (TAURELLU)	taurus
AṶTŬMNU 'autumn'	autunno (s.l.)	otoño˙	outono	automne (s.l.)	autumn
AṶRĬC(Ŭ)LA 'ear-lobe'	orecchio 'ear'	oreja 'ear'	orelha 'ear'	oreille 'ear'	auricle
*AṶ(Ĭ)CA, *AṶCA (< AVE 'bird')	oca 'goose'	oca ((ganso)) 'goose'	((ganso))	oie 'goose'	

	Italian	Spanish	Portu-guese	French	English cognate
AU̯T 'or'	o (od before vowels)	o	ou	ou	
AU̯DĪRE 'to hear'	udire**	oír	ouvir***	ouir ((entendre))	(arch.) oyez!
LAU̯DĀRE 'to praise'	lodare	loar	louvar***	louer	laud, laudatory
PAU̯CU 'little (of quantity)'	poco	poco	pouco	peu (O.Fr: póu)	paucity
FAU̯CE 'throat; defile'	foce	hoz 'river mouth'	'defile, ravine'	foz	--

*It, Sp, Ptg: causa, Fr: cause 'cause' are later borrowings from CL.
**When initial, AU̯- occasionally gives u- in Italian.
***In Portuguese, a v̯ was developed to separate the diphthong ou from a following vowel: AU̯DĪRE ouvir, LAU̯DĀRE louvar, CAU̯LE couve 'cabbage' (via coue, see Rule 20). V̯ is found with a similar function in Italian and French, e.g. It: védova VĪDU̯A, Pádova PADUA, Fr: pouvoir PŎTĒRE.

Note 1. A few words with initial AU̯- followed by another U in the next syllable (e.g. A(U̯)GŪSTU, A(U̯)GŪRIU, AU̯SCŬLTĀRE) had lost their first U in VL times. Hence It, Sp: agosto Ptg: agôsto Fr: août; Sp: agüero 'augury, omen' Ptg: agouro O.Fr: eür (*AU̯GŪRIU) Fr: bonheur malheur; It: autore Sp: autor Ptg: autor Fr: auteur (AU̯(C)TŌRE) 'author'; Sp, Ptg: aula; Sp, Ptg: aumentar (AUGMENTĀRE); It, Sp, Ptg: austero Fr: austère It, Sp, Ptg: áureo; Sp, Ptg: auxilio, etc. are learned words. Beside Sp: cauto (CAU̯TU) 'cautious', there is also the popular development coto 'boundary, limit; fine or penalty', Ptg: couto 'shelter, enclosure'.

Note 2. In Old Portuguese, the group OCT developed in some regions to oit, in others to out. Gradually, forms like noite and noute became interchangeable. Later, in the sixteenth century, the confusion between the two diphthongs began to spread to words containing oi or ou from other sources, e.g. couro (= coiro < CORIU), coisa (= cousa < CAU̯SA). As a result, the diphthongs oi [oi] and ou (now [o]) are today generally interchangeable: ouro oiro 'gold', ouço oiço 'I hear' and so on. But in certain cases the ou [o] is obligatory: ou 'or', the preterit ending -ou (< VL -AU̯T for C.L. -AVĪT) as in comprou 'he bought', and the preterit stem of certain irregular verbs: coube (from caber 'to be contained') soube (from saber 'to know') trouxe (from trazer 'to bring').

Additional Examples

GAU̯DĮA 'joys' Fr: joie, whence It: gioia 'joy; jewel' Sp:
 joya 'jewel' Ptg: joia Eng: joy (Eng: jewel is from an O.Fr
 diminutive form of joie)
PARAB(Ŏ)LA (*PARAU̯LA) It: parola Fr, Eng: parole
 Gmc: kausjan 'to choose' Fr: choisir (Eng: choice) (But
 Eng: choose comes from Anglo-Saxon ceosan.)
NAU̯SĘA O.Fr: > Eng: noise
MAU̯RŬ Sp: moro 'moor'
AV(Ĭ)CĔLLU It: uccello** O.Fr: oisel Fr: oiseau
AU̯RA 'breeze' It: ora
A(V)U̯NC(Ŭ)LU 'uncle' Fr: oncle Eng: uncle
AU̯RĬDĮARE (< AURA 'breeze') Sp: orear 'to air'
AU̯RĬFABER 'goldsmith' Fr: orfèvre
*AD plus FAU̯CARE 'to go for the throat' Sp: ahogar 'to
 choke; drown'
CAU̯LE FLŌRE 'cabbage flower' Fr: chou-fleur Eng: cauli-
 flower
GAU̯DĮU Sp: gozo 'joy'
AU̯(C)TOR(Ĭ)CĀRE Sp: otorgar Ptg: outorgar 'to grant,
 authorize' Fr: octroyer (the c̲ is learned)
CLAU̯SU (past participle of CLAU̯DERE 'to close') Fr: clos
 Eng: close (adj.)
CLAU̯SA 'enclosures' Sp: llosa 'enclosed field'
CANTAV̎T, CANTAU̯T 'he sang' It: cantò Ptg: cantou
 (Fr: il chanta is from a different contracted form of -AVIT)
CAU̯DA 'tail' It: coda Sp: cola (Fr: queue 'tail' is from a
 VL *CŌDA; CAU̯DA would have become *choue. Cp. CAU̯SA
 chose.)
LAU̯SĮA 'flagstone' Sp: losa Ptg: lousa
CLAU̯STRU 'enclosed place' (influenced by O.Fr: cloison
 *CLAU̯SIŌNE 'partition') Fr: cloître Eng: cloister
INCAU̯STU 'ink' (associated in the early Middle Ages with
 monasteries, hence also INCLAU̯STRU) It: inchiostro Fr:
 encre Eng: ink

Exercise

Opposite each of the words in Group A write down the number of its nearest cognate in Group B.

Group A
1. Fr: automne... 2. Sp: loar.... 3. It: orecchio....
4. Ptg: cousa... 5. Eng: treasure..... 6. Fr: oiseau...
7. Sp: losa.... 8. Ptg: pouco.... 9. It: agosto....
10. Sp: otorgar.... 11. Sp: agüero.... 12. Ptg: foz....
13. It: coda.... 14. Fr: encre.... 15. Sp: oca....
16. Eng: cauliflower.... 17. Fr: or.... 18. It: gioia....
19. Ptg: ouvir... 20. Sp: faltó.....

Group B
1. Eng: augury   2. Eng: or   3. Fr: fou   4. Sp: otoño
5. Eng: lore   6. Ptg: faltou   7. It: uccello   8. Eng: fault
9. Eng: pause   10. Fr: peu   11. Sp: pozo   12. Fr: chose
13. Eng: anchor   14. Fr: ouvrir   15. It: lodare
16. Ptg: ouro   17. Eng: oracle   18. Sp: cola   19. Fr: août
20. It: o   21. Eng: case   22. Ptg: lousa   23. Fr: oie
24. Sp: tesoro   25. Fr: chou-fleur   26. Eng: loss   27. Sp:
orear   28. It: udire   29. It: inchiostro   30. Sp: gusto
31. Fr: jour   32. Ptg: orelha   33. Fr: avoir   34. Sp: hoz
35. Eng: oak   36. It: voce   37. Sp: joya   38. Fr: octroyer
39. Eng: anchor   40. Eng: poor .

RULE 5

C^a, G^a

Rule: In French, when initial or after a consonant, C^a became ch(i)e or cha, and G^a became g(i)e or ja, depending on whether the syllable was open or closed.

Between vowels, C^a became G^a, which then either went to y or was lost. In some words, the early fall of the preceding vowel forestalled this development (e.g. MAN(Ĭ)CA manche) or else halted it part way (CÀRR(Ĭ)CĀRE > *carr(e)gar > *carr'gar > charger). Intervocalic G^a is kept in Italian, frequently falls in Spanish and Portuguese, while in French its disappearance is often marked by a yod (plaie, nie).

Intervocalic C^a regularly voices to ga in Spanish and Portuguese, but in Italian only sometimes. In other positions C^a remains unchanged.

	Italian	Spanish	Portu-guese	French	English cognate
CAPRA 'goat'	capra	cabra	cabra	chèvre (O.Fr: chievre)	capricorn
CAPU (for CĂPŬT) 'head'	capo 'head, end'	cabo 'end'	cabo	chef (O.Fr: chief)	chief, chef***
CASA 'hut'	casa 'house'	casa 'house'	casa 'house'	chez 'at the house of' (CASAE)	
CARU 'dear'	caro	caro	caro	cher (O.Fr: chier)	cherish, i.e. 'hold dear'
CANE 'dog'	cane	can ((perro))	cão	chien	canine, kennel
SCALA 'ladder'	scala	escala	escada	échelle	scala, echelon

	Italian	Spanish	Portu-guese	French	English cognate
PĪSCĀRE 'to fish'	pescare	pescar	pescar	pêcher (O.Fr: peschier)	piscatory
PECCĀRE 'to sin'	peccare	pecar	pecar	pécher (O.Fr: pechier)	impeccable
MERCĀTU	mercato	mercado	mercado	marché	merchant
CABALLU 'nag'	cavallo	caballo	cavalo	cheval	cavalry,* chivalry
CAMĪNU 'furnace; (fig. highway)'	camino 'road'	camino 'road'	caminho 'road'	chemin 'road'	chimney_ (CAMĪNĀTA)
CAMĪS(I̯)A 'shirt'	camicia	camisa	camisa	chemise	
CAPĬLLU 'hair'	capello	cabello	cabelo	cheveu (O.Fr: chevel)	capillary, dishevelled
VACCA 'cow'	vacca	vaca	vaca	vache	vaccine
MŬSCA 'fly'	mosca	mosca	môsca	mouche	mosquito
FŬRCA 'pitchfork'	forca	horca	forca	fourche 'pitchfork'	fork*
CASTĔLLU 'castle'	castello	castillo	castelo	château (O.Fr: chastel)	castle*
CASTĪGĀRE 'to punish'	castigare	castigar	castigar	châtier (O.Fr: chastier)	chasten, chastise, castigate
CAPTĬARE 'to catch'	cacciare 'hunt, chase'	cazar 'hunt'	caçar	chasser (Norm. Picard: cachier)	chase, catch*
CAP(Ĭ)TĀLE 'capital'	capitale	caudal 'wealth' (O.Sp: cabdal)	caudal	O.Fr: chatel (Norm. Picard: catel)	chattel, cattle*
CAMBĬĀRE 'to change'	cambiare	cambiar	cambiar	changer	change
CANTĀRE 'to sing'	cantare	cantar	cantar	chanter	chant
CAŲSA 'cause'	cosa	cosa	cousa	chose**	cause
FRĬCĀRE 'rub'	fregare	fregar	esfregar	frayer	fray

	Italian	Spanish	Portuguese	French	English cognate
PACĀRE 'appease'	pagare	pagar	pagar	payer	pay
CARR(Ī)CARE 'load'	caricare	cargar	carregar	charger (O.Fr: chargier)	charge, carry*
AMĪCA 'friend (fem.)'	amica	amiga	amiga	amie	amicable
ŬRTĪCA 'nettle'	ortica	ortiga	ortiga	ortie 'nettle'	
MĪCA 'crumb'	mica	miga 'crumb'	miga	mie 'crumb; not at all'	
		'not at all'			
ADVOCĀTU 'lawyer'	avvocato	abogado	avogado	avoué (l. avocat)	advocate
MAN(Ī)CA 'sleeve'	mánica	manga	manga	manche 'sleeve'	
CŎLL(Ŏ)CAT 'places'	cólloca	cuelga	colga	couche (O.Fr: colche)	couch, cushion
GAUDĒRE 'to rejoice'; GAUDIU,-A 'joy(s)'	godere	gozo	gôzo (< Sp)	joie	joy
PLĀGA 'wound'	piaga	llaga	praga	plaie	plague
RŪGA 'furrow, rut'	ruga	ruga 'rut'	rua 'street'	rue 'street'	corrugate
NĔGAT 'denies'	nega	niega	nega	nie (via nie̯e)	negate, deny

*Eng castle, fork, carry, catch, cattle, cavalry are taken from the Norman Picard dialect, which did not palatalize C(a) > ch.

**CAUSA > chose, GAUDIA > joie give us an interesting clue to the sequence of sound changes in French. Figure it out: Which change must have occurred earlier: Cᵃ,Gᵃ > ch, j; or AU > o? (Note that the U is not really a vowel but the semiconsonant [w], therefore the syllable is closed.)

***In Old French, ch was pronounced [tš], but in Modern French it is [š]. English chief and chef are one and the same word, only borrowed at different stages in the evolution of French. A parallel change took place with the voiced palatal affricate [dž]. English judge [dž∧dž] reflects the Old French pronunciation of Modern French juge [žyž]. In both ch and j (ǧ) the affricate element (t or d) has been lost in French.

Additional Examples

CANTIŌNE It: canzone Fr: chanson
CHANŪTU 'grey-haired' It: canuto Sp: cano Ptg: cão (CANU) Fr: chenu
CĪRCĀRE 'to hunt around' O.Fr: cerchier (Eng: search) Fr: chercher (by influence of the second ch), but It: cercare
CANĪC(Ŭ)LA 'a little dog' Fr: chenille 'grub, caterpillar' Eng: chenille originally 'silky fabric'

DEL(Ĭ)CĀTU Sp, Ptg: delgado 'thin'
VOCĀLE 'vowel' It: vocale Ptg: vogal Fr: voyelle Eng: vowel
(Sp: vocal is learned)
CALMĀRE 'to calm, cease' Fr: chômer 'to cease work, be idle
or unemployed'
Gmc: kausjan 'to choose' Fr: choisir (Eng: choose is from
O.Eng: ceosan)
GAMBA It: gamba Fr: jambe
Gmc: GALB- 'yellow' O.Fr: jalne Fr: jaune
CAULE 'cabbage' Fr: chou
*AVICA, *AUCA (for AVIS) 'bird' It, Sp: oca Fr: oie 'goose'
NAV(Ĭ)GARE O.Fr: nagier Fr: nager 'to swim'
Gmc: GARD- 'garden' (plus -ĪNU) Fr: jardin
DECĀNU O.Fr: deien (Eng: dean) Fr: doyen Eng: deacon
LĒGĀLE 'legal' Sp: leal Ptg: lial Fr, Eng: loyal (It: leale is
apparently borrowed from O.Fr)
*MAGALĬĀTA (for MAGALIA) 'shepherd's hut' Sp: majada
Ptg: malhada 'sheepfold'
LĪTIGĀRE 'to dispute, fight' Sp: lidiar Ptg: lidar Eng: litigate
LĪGĀRE 'to find' It: ligare Sp: liar, ligar (1.) Ptg: ligar (1.)
Fr: lier Eng: ligament, lien
FŪMĬGĀRE 'to smoke' Sp: humear Ptg: fumear, fumegar Eng:
fumigate
GALLĪNA 'hen' (O.Fr: geline)
LĪGATĬŌNE 'binding' Fr: liaison
GALLŬ 'cock' (O.Fr: gel)

Exercise

Opposite each of the words in Group A write down the number of its nearest cognate in Group B.

Group A
1. It: calore.... 2. Ptg: manga.... 3. Fr: chanson.... 4. Fr:
jardin.... 5. Eng: chattel.... 6. Fr: chameau.... 7. Eng:
cancer.... 8. Sp: abogado.... 9. Eng: deacon.... 10. It:
canuto.... 11. Fr: cheveu.... 12. Eng: fumigate.... 13. It:
cacciare.... 14. Sp: mosca.... 15. Sp: lidiar.... 16. Fr:
cheval.... 17. Eng: delicate.... 18. It: legare.... 19. Sp:
caldera.... 20. It: gamba....

Group B
1. Sp: delgado 2. Eng: chimney 3. Sp: mancha 4. Sp: llegar
5. Eng: chapel 6. Fr: châlet 7. Eng: mosque 8. Sp: liar
9. Eng: abrogate 10. Fr: chaudière 11. It: canzone 12. Fr:
chancre 13. Fr: fumée 14. Eng: apocopate 15. Fr: chenu
16. Eng: garden 17. It: cavallo 18. Eng: leader 19. Sp:
deleite 20. Fr: jambe 21. Eng: litigate 22. Fr: doyen 23. It:
capello 24. Fr: mouche 25. Fr: chasser 26. Ptg: fumear
27. Fr: manquer 28. Fr: avoué 29. Sp: caudillo 30. Sp:
caudal 31. Eng: canton 32. Fr: manche 33. Sp: camelo
34. Eng: jargon 35. Fr: chaleur 36. Fr: fumée 37. It: duce
38. Ptg: formiga 39. Fr: délectable 40. Eng: gamble

RULE 6

Ć (=C^{e,i})

Rule: Initially or after consonants, c survives and is pronounced as [tš] in Italian, [θ] or [s] in Spanish, and as [s] in Portuguese and French. In the medial (intervocalic) position, Portuguese and French voice it to [z], spelling it z and s, respectively. In the final position, we find -z (pronounced [ž]) in Portuguese, but in French -is or -ix (both consonants silent).

	Italian	Spanish	Portu-guese	French	English cognate
CĔNTU 'hundred'	cento	ciento	cento	cent	cent
CĔRVU 'stag'	cervo	ciervo	cervo	cerf	
CAELU 'sky'	cielo	cielo	ceu	ciel	celestial, ceiling
CĪLĮU 'eyelid'	ciglio 'eyebrow'	ceja 'eyebrow'	celha	cil 'eyelash' (via *cieil)	supercilious
CĒRA 'wax'	cera	cera	cera	cire (via *cieire)	ceraceous 'waxy'
MERCĒDE 'reward'	mercede 'reward, grace, pity'	merced 'grace'	mercede	merci (via *merciei)	mercy
DŬLCE 'sweet'	dolce	dulce	doce	douce	dulcet
CĪV(Ĭ)TĀTE 'state'	città 'town'	ciudad 'town'	cidade	cité 'city'	city
RACĒMU 'bunch of grapes'	racemo	racimo	racimo (l.)	raisin 'grape(s)' (via *raisiein)	raisin

	Italian	Spanish	Portu-guese	French	English cognate
VĪCĪNU (*VĪCĪNU) 'neighbor'	vicino	vecino	vezinho	voisin	vicinity
PLACĒRE 'to please'	piacere 'pleasure'	placer 'pleasure'	prazer 'pleasure'	plaisir 'pleasure' (via *plaisieir)	pleasure
CǑCĪNA (for CǑQUĪNA) 'kitchen'	cucina	cocina	cozinha	cuisine	kitchen
PACE 'peace'	pace	paz	paz	paix	peace
VŌCE 'voice'	voce	voz	voz	voix	voice
PĬCE 'tar, pitch'	pece	pez	pez	poix	pitch
NŬCE 'nut'	noce	nuez (NǑCE)	noz	noix	
DĔCE(M) 'ten'	dieci	diez	dez	dix (via *die-is)	decimal, dime
VĬCE 'change, turn'	((volta))	vez	vez	fois	vice versa
CRŬCE 'cross'	croce	cruz (s.l.)	cruz (s.l.)	croix	cross
RADĪCE 'root'	radice	raíz	raiz	(racine (*RADĪCĪNA))	radish

Note 1. Latin C̲ was originally pronounced [k] in all positions. In the course of time, however, Latin speakers anticipated a following front vowel (e or i̲) by pronouncing the [k] with tongue contact further forward̲ than before other vowels. The result was that CĔNTU [kẹnto] came to sound like [kjẹnto] or [tjẹnto]; then, coming further forward still, like [tšẹnto], which is the Italian pronunciation of today. The other three languages carried the process further. In French and Portuguese, the pronunciation of C(e,i) went from [tš] to [ts] to [s] or [z]. Old Spanish shared [ts] with Old French and Old Portuguese, but in the sixteenth century shake-up of the Spanish sibilants, [ts] either went to [tθ] and then [θ] (the Castilian pronunciation), or in Spanish America and certain parts of Spain became [s], as in French.

Note 2. French has developed Latin C in three ways: C^a has become [š], C^{e,i} has become [s], while C^{o,u} remains as [k]. Italian, Spanish, and Portuguese distinguished two types only: C^{e,i} and C^{a,o,u}.

Note 3. In Old French, C^{e,i} had a curious tendency to generate a yod. Look at CĒRA cire and DĔCEM dix. According to Rules 13 and 12, we would expect *ceire and *dies. But this yod made it *ci̯eire and die̯s. As the triphthong i̯ei regularly contracted to i, we therefore find cire, dix. Between vowels, the Ĉ developed a yod on either side of it: RACĒMU, PLACĒRE passed through the stage *rai̯sei̯n, *plai̯sei̯r to give us raisin, plaisir. The yod also shows up in contact with a, o, and u (PACE paix, VŌCE voix, LŪCENT luisent) but before ī (ci̯ite), ie (ci̯iel) and e (ci̯erf) it was in time absorbed and lost. Lastly, ue̯ gave ūi: NŎCENT 'they harm' > *nue̯sent > nuisent.

Additional Examples

LĬCĒRE 'to be permitted'   O.Fr: leisir (Eng: leisure) Fr: loisir

PŪL(Ĭ)CE 'flea'   It: pulice   O.Fr: pulce   Fr: puce   (Sp, Ptg: pulga come from a form *PŪL(I)CA)

FAŬCE 'ravine'   It: foce   Sp: hoz   Ptg: foz

FALCE 'scythe'   It: falce   Sp: hoz   Ptg: fouce   Fr: faucille

LŪCE 'light'   It: luce Sp, Ptg: luz ((Fr: lumière))

CŎQ(U̯)ĔRE, *CŎQ(U̯)ĒRE   It: cuócere   Fr: cuire (via *cue̯re) but Sp: cocer

PERDĪCE 'partridge'   Sp, Ptg: perdiz   Fr: perdrix (Eng: partridge)

VĬNCERE 'to conquer'   It: víncere Sp, Ptg: vencer but Fr: vaincre (O.Fr: veintre < VĬNC(Ĕ)RE)

Exercise

Opposite each of the words in Group A write down the number of its nearest cognate in Group B.

Group A
1. Sp: ciudad....   2. It: luce....   3. Ptg: cozinha....
4. Fr: fois....   5. Fr: poix....   6. Sp: coger....
7. Eng: raisin....   8. Fr: ciel....   9. It: croce...
10. Fr: cimetière....   11. Ptg: foz....   12. Ptg: vezinho....
13. It: dieci....   14. Eng: please....   15. Fr: centime....
16. It: feci....   17. It: facciamo....   18. Sp: cera....
19. Fr: nous disons....   20. Eng: mercy....

Group B
1. Fr: nous faisons   2. Sp: lucha   3. Eng: cemetery
4. Eng: fez   5. Sp: centavo   6. Sp: raíz   7. Fr: je fus
8. It: foce   9. Ptg: mercede   10. Sp: decimos   11. Ptg:
vontade   12. Eng: peace   13. Sp: plaza   14. It: racemo
15. Eng: face   16. Ptg: prazer   17. Eng: crocus   18. Sp:
haz   19. Fr: dix   20. Ptg: céu   21. Fr: voisin   22. Eng:
civility   23. It: ciglio   24. Eng: poise   25. Eng: cement
26. It: città   27. Eng: lice   28. Fr: vous dites   29. It:
cuócere   30. Fr: je fis   31. Eng: cross   32. It: pece
33. Eng: faith   34. Fr: cire   35. Eng: crucial   36. Sp: vez
37. Fr: cuisine   38. Eng: decent   39. Sp: luz   40. Fr: je
fais

RULE 7

C'L

Rule: The group C'L, resulting from the fall of an unstressed vowel, has a very regular development in Romance. It becomes <u>cchi</u> [k:j] in Italian, <u>j</u> [x] in Spanish, <u>lh</u> [ʎ] in Portuguese, and <u>il(le)</u> [i:j] in French.

	Italian	Spanish	Portu-guese	French	English cognate
ŎC(Ŭ)LU 'eye'	occhio	ojo	olho	oeil*	oculist
AURĬC(Ŭ)LA 'ear'	orecchio (-ĬC(Ŭ)LU)	oreja	orelha	oreille	auricle
LENTĪC(Ŭ)LA 'lentil'	lenticchia	lenteja	lentilha	lentille	lentil
APĬC(Ŭ)LA 'bee'	pecchia	abeja	abelha	abeille	apiary
ACŪC(Ŭ)LA 'needle'	((ago (ACU)))	aguja	agulha	aiguille	acute
PARĬC(Ŭ)LU 'like, equal'	parecchio	parejo	parelho	pareil	pair, peer
VĔCLU (for VETŬLU) 'old'	vecchio	viejo	velho	vieil (vieux)	veteran
SPEC(Ŭ)LU 'mirror'	specchio	espejo	espelho	((miroir))	speculate
CŬNĪC(Ŭ)LU 'rabbit'	coniglio	conejo (-ĬC(Ŭ)LU)	coelho (-ĬC(Ŭ)LU)	((lapin)) (O.Fr: conil)	cony
VERMĬC(Ŭ)LU 'little worm'	vermiglio 'ruddy'	bermejo 'vermilion'	vermelho 'vermilion'	vermeil	vermilion
*FENŬC(Ŭ)LU (for -ĪC(Ŭ)LU) 'fennel'	finocchio	hinojo	funcho (see Note 2)	fenouil	fennel
TRABAC(Ŭ)LU (< TRABE 'heavy beam')	((lavoro))	trabajo	trabalho	travail	travail
GENŬC(Ŭ)LU 'knee'	ginocchio	hinojo ((rodilla))	joelho (via jeolho)	((genou <(GENU)))**	genuflection

	Italian	Spanish	Portu- guese	French	English cognate
PĔDŬ(Ŭ)LU 'little foot'	pidocchio 'louse'	piojo 'louse'	piolho 'louse'	((pou))	

*If you have ever wondered why the plural of oeil is yeux, here is the development: ŎC(Ŭ)L(O)S [ɥeʎs] (with palatal l̦) > [*ɥeu̯s] (l̦ regularly vocalizes before a consonant), then through dissimilation of the first of these u's we get [*ieus], spelled yeux.
**But note the verb agenouiller 'to kneel'.

Note 1. Spanish and Portuguese palatalize G'L also:
TĒG(Ŭ)LA 'tile' Sp: teja Ptg: telha (Fr: tuile): RĒG(Ŭ)LA 'bar' Sp: reja 'grill' Ptg: relha (O.Fr: reille > Eng: rail). COAG(Ŭ)LĀRE Sp: cuajar Ptg: coalhar 'to curdle' (Fr: cailler). The ecclesiastical words Sp: regla Fr: règle 'rule' and Sp: siglo Fr: siècle SAECŬLU 'generation, age' > 'century' show semi-learned development.
Note 2. After a consonant both Spanish and Portuguese usually developed C'L to ch. The preceding consonant was sometimes lost. Examples: TRŬNC(Ŭ)LARE 'to cut off, truncate' Sp, Ptg: tronchar 'cut off the stem, mutilate'; *MANC(Ŭ)LA (for MACŬLA) Sp, Ptg: mancha 'stain'; CONCHŬLA 'little shell' Sp, Ptg: concha 'shell' Eng: conch; MASC(Ŭ)LU Sp, Ptg: macho It: maschio Fr: mâle (O.Fr: masle) Eng: male, masculine; FENUCULU *fŭc'lu > *func'lu > Ptg: funcho '(bot.) fennel'; CALC(Ŭ)LU Sp: cacho Fr: caillou 'pebble' Eng: calculus; SARCULU 'a light hoe' Sp, Ptg: sacho.
Exception: MŪSC(Ŭ)LU Sp: muslo 'thigh'.
Note 3. NG'L gives Spanish ñ, Portuguese nh: ŬNG(Ŭ)LA 'fingernail' Sp: uña Ptg: unha, but It: unghia Fr: ongle (cp. A(V)ŬNC(U)LU Fr: oncle); SĬNG(Ŭ)LOS O.Sp: seños, modern sendos, O.Ptg: senhos, modern sendos 'one each'; CĬNG(Ŭ)LU Sp: ceño 'hoop, rim'; RĪVI ANG(Ŭ)LU 'bend in the stream' Sp: Riaño 'a town in León'.
Note 4. Here are some more Spanish developments of Romance groups ending in L: B'L may give ll as in SĪBĬLĀRE chillar 'to hiss, creak' Eng: sibilant; TRĪBULĀRE trillar 'to thrash' Eng: tribulation, but usually it remains: FABŬLĀRE hablar Ptg: falar; NĒBŬLA niebla 'fog, mist, haze' Eng: nebulous; NŪBĬLU nublo 'cloudy'; DIĀBŎLU diablo 'devil'; SĪBĬLĀRE silbar (met.) 'to whistle, hiss'. T'L popularly gave C'L: VĔTŬLU, VĔCLU viejo, MŬTĬLĀRE mochar 'to trim, lop off'; AD plus RŎTŬLĀRE arrojar 'to hurl, fling'. In semi-learned words both T'L and D'L metathesized to give ld: SPATŬLA espalda 'back'; TĪTŬLU tilde 'tilde, diacritical sign of the letter ñ'; CAPĪTŬLU cabildo '(eccles.) chapter' (Fr: chapitre (l.) Eng: chapter); MŌDŬLU molde 'pattern, mold' Eng: mode, mold).

Note 5. In many semi-learned Portuguese words the unstressed vowel survived through the tenth century, when -L-dropped out (Rule 20): TABŬLA taboa 'plank'; NĔBŬLA nevoa 'mist'; PERĪCŬLU > perígoo > perigo 'peril'; DIABŎLU > diáboo > diabo 'devil'; ORACŬLU > orágoo > orago 'oracle'; ANGĔLU > ángeo > anjo 'angel'; PŎPŬLU póboo > povo 'people'; ŬMBĪLĪCU > *embeígo > embigo 'navel'.

Note 6. In Spanish, C'LY gave unvoiced ch: COCHLEĀRE 'spoon' It: cucchiaio Sp: cuchara Ptg: colher Fr: cuiller.

Additional Examples

SŌLĪC(Ŭ)LU 'little sun' Fr: soleil
SŎMNĪC(Ŭ)LU 'sleep, nap' Fr: sommeil
MAC(Ŭ)LA 'spot, mesh' Fr: maille Eng: mail
OVĪC(Ŭ)LA 'little sheep' Sp: oveja Ptg: ovelha
CANC(Ĕ)RĪC(Ŭ)LU 'little crab' Sp: cangrejo 'crab' Eng: cancer

In Spanish, ARTĪC(Ŭ)LU gives both learned artículo 'article' and popular artejo 'knuckle' (Fr: orteil 'toe' < *ORTĪCŬLU for ARTĪCŬLU). Milagro (O.Sp: miraglo) 'miracle' and peligro (O.Sp: periglo) 'peril' are semi-learned.

Exercise

Opposite each of the words in Group A write down the number of its nearest cognate in Group B.

Group A
1. Fr: abeille.... 2. It: specchio.... 3. Fr: oeil....
4. Eng: vermilion.... 5. Ptg: nevoa.... 6. Fr: cailler....
7. Fr: caillou... 8. It: pidocchio... 9. Sp: cangrejo...
10. Eng: male.... 11. Eng: articulate... 12. Sp: peligro....
13. Ptg: coelho... 14. Fr: pareil... 15. Ptg: povo....
16. Sp: lenteja... 17. Fr: aiguille.... 18. Ptg: unha....
19. Sp: mochar... 20. Fr: oreille....

Group B
1. Eng: oil 2. Sp: cacho 3. Eng: parallel 4. Sp: artejo
5. Ptg: perigo 6. Sp: ajo 7. Fr: maille 8. Eng: cancer
9. Eng: speck 10. Sp: ojo 11. It: parecchio 12. Sp: abajo
13. Fr: neveu 14. Eng: coil 15. Eng: mock 16. Ptg: piolho
17. Eng: apiary 18. Eng: mutilate 19. Sp: aguja 20. Eng:
lens 21. Sp: coger 22. Fr: lenteur 23. Sp: bermejo
24. Fr: verrou 25. Eng: vehicle 26. Ptg: macho 27. Sp:
oreja 28. Ptg: espelho 29. Sp: conejo 30. It: lenticchia
31. Fr: ongle 32. Sp: niebla 33. Eng: pilgrim 34. Eng:
navel 35. Sp: cuajar 36. Eng: equal 37. Sp: pavo
38. Eng: populate 39. Sp: orilla 40. Fr: oncle.

RULE 8

$C^{o,u}$

Rule: $C^{o,u}$ usually remains in Italian; when preceded by a vowel the C voices to g in Spanish and Portuguese; in French, unless initial or protected, it disappears (k > g > y > —).

	Italian	Spanish	Portuguese	French	English cognate
CŪRA 'care'	cura	cura	cura	cure	cure
COLŌRE 'color'	colore (m.)	color (m.)	côr (f.)	couleur (f.)	color
CŎRPU(S) 'body'	corpo	cuerpo	corpo	corps 'body'	corpse
CO(H)ORTE 'retinue'	corte	corte	corte	cour	court
CŬRRĬT 'runs'	corre	corre	corre	court	course
CŬRTU 'short'	corto	corto	corto	court	curt
CŎ(N)STAT 'stands firm'	costa 'costs'	cuesta 'costs'	costa 'costs'	coûte 'costs'	costs
SCŪTU 'shield'	scudo	escudo	escudo	écu	
ACCŪSO 'I accuse'	accuso	acuso	acuso	j'accuse	accuse
SACCU 'sack'	sacco	saco	saco	sac	sack
PŎRCU 'pig'	porco	puerco	porco	porc	pork
SĒCŪRU 'safe'	sicuro	seguro	seguro	sûr (O.Fr: seür)	sure, secure
ACŪTU 'sharp'	acuto	agudo	agudo	aigü (s.l.)	acute

39

	Italian	Spanish	Portu-guese	French	English cognate
AMĪCU 'friend'	amico	amigo	amigo	ami	amicable
FŎCU 'hearth'	fuoco	fuego	fogo	feu	focus
PAŬCU 'little'	poco	poco	pouco	peu	paucity

Additional Examples

CAECU 'blind' It: cieco Sp: ciego Ptg: cego
GRAECU 'Greek' It: greco Sp: griego Ptg: grego
DĪCO 'I say' It: dico Sp, Ptg: digo Fr: dis [di]
CŪJU(S) Sp: cuyo Ptg: cujo 'whose'
AMAR(Ĭ)CU Sp, Ptg: amargo 'bitter'
ŬMB(Ĭ)LĪCU It: bellico Sp: ombligo Ptg: embigo 'navel'
(CANE) GALL(Ĭ)CU Sp: galgo 'greyhound'
*FACO (for FACĮO) 'I do' Sp: hago

Exercise

Opposite each of the words in Group A write down the number of its nearest cognate in Group B.

Group A
1. Sp: seguro..... 2. It: cieco..... 3. Fr: feu......
4. Ptg: embigo..... 5. Sp: griego.....

Group B
1. Sp: ambiguo 2. Sp: hago 3. Eng: sickle 4. Sp: ombligo 5. Fr: sûr 6. Sp: hogar 7. It: greco 8. Ptg: cego 9. Sp: seco 10. It: fuoco

RULE 9

CT

Rule: The Latin group CT develops to <u>tt</u> in Italian, to <u>ch</u> (ts) in Spanish, and in Portuguese and French to <u>it</u>.

	Italian	Spanish	Portu-guese	French	English cognate
NŎCTE 'night'	notte	noche	noite	nuit (via *nueit)	nocturnal
ŎCTŌ 'eight'	otto	ocho	oito	huit (via *ueit)	octave
BĪS plus CŎCTU 'cooked twice'	biscotto	bizcocho	biscoito	biscuit (via *biscueit)	biscuit
LACTE 'milk'	latte	leche	leite	lait	lactate
FACTU 'done'	fatto	hecho	feito	fait	fact, feat
LACTŪCA 'lettuce'	lattuga	lechuga	((alface))	laitue	lettuce
SATISFACTU 'satisfied'	soddisfatto	satisfecho	satisfeito (s.l.)	satisfait (s.l.)	satisfied
LĔCTU 'bed'	letto	lecho	leito	lit (via *lieit)	litter
PROFĔCTU 'advantage'	profitto	provecho	proveito	profit (via *profieit)	profit
DESPĔCTU 'contempt, anger'	dispetto	despecho	despeito	dépit (via *despieit)	despite
STRĬCTU 'narrow'	stretto	estrecho	estreito	étroit (O.Fr: estreit)	strait, strict

	Italian	Spanish	Portu-guese	French	English cognate
DĬCTU (*DĪCTU) 'said'	detto	dicho (O.Sp: decho)	dito (via *di-ito	dit (via *di-it)	dictation
TĔCTU 'roof'	tetto	techo	teto (s.l.)	toit	protect
DĪRĒCTU (*D(I)RĒCTU) 'right straight'	dritto, diritto	derecho	direito	droit	direct, adroit

Note 1. In Spanish, though not in French, the development CT > i̯t > [tš] prevented diphthongization of a preceding Ĕ or Ŏ. Hence ocho instead of *huecho, lecho instead of *liecho. ACT gives Ptg: eit, Sp: ech. ĪCT, as in FĪCTU 'fixed', FRĪCTU 'fried', gives Sp: it (hito, frito).

Note 2. In Spanish, words like delito 'crime', luto 'mourning', tratado 'treaty', fruto, distrito, respeto show semi-learned development, while acto, contacto, correcto, defecto, doctor, exacto, and many others are outright Latinisms.

Note 3. When preceded by a or o, CT could also give Ptg: ut; ACTU auto 'act'; DOCTU douto 'learned', DOCTŌRE doutor 'doctor'; OCTŪBRE outubro. When preceded by u, the result was t: FRUCTU fruto, TRŪCTA truta.

Additional Examples

SŬBSPECTĀRE It: sospettare Sp: sospechar Ptg: sospeitar
  Eng: suspect
OCTAGĬNTA It: ottanta Sp: ochenta Ptg: oitenta ((Fr:
  quatre-vingts))
TRUCTA It: trota Sp: trucha Ptg: truta Fr: truite
  Eng: trout
AQŬAEDŬCTO, AQŬADŬCTO It: acquedotto Sp: aguaducho
MAL(E)TRACTĀRE It: maltrattare Sp: maltrechar, maltratar
  (s.l.) Ptg: maltratar (s.l.) Fr: maltraiter Eng: maltreat
FRŪCTU 'fruit' It: frutto Sp: fruto (s.l.) Ptg: fruto
  Fr: fruit Eng: fruit
CONDŬCTA It: condotta Sp: conducta (1.) Ptg: conducta
  (1.) Fr: conduite Eng: conduct, conduit
VĬNDĬCTA 'revenge' It: vendetta
LŬCTA 'struggle' It: lotta Sp: lucha Ptg: luta Fr: lutte
PĔCTU(S) 'chest' It: petto Sp: pecho Ptg: peito O.Fr:
  piz (via *pieits)
VERVACTU 'fallow ground' Sp: barbecho
COLLECTA Sp: cosecha 'harvest' (via *cogecha)

TRACTU 'distance (in space or time)' It: tratto Sp: trecho
Ptg: treita (TRACTA) Fr: trait, traite (TRACTA) Eng:
trait
BĔNĔDĬCTU 'blessed' It: benedetto, Benedetto Sp: bendito
(l.) Benito (s.l.) Ptg: bemdito, Bento Fr: bénit, Bénoît
Eng: Benedict
ELĔCTA 'select, chosen' Fr, Eng: élite (via *eljĕte)

Exercise

Opposite each of the words in Group A write down the number of its nearest cognate in Group B.

Group A
1. Sp: ocho.... 2. Eng: lettuce.... 3. It: detto....
4. Ptg: doutor.... 5. Fr: lutte.... 6. Sp: pecho....
7. Eng: act.... 8. Sp: bizcocho.... 9. Fr: traité....
10. It: acquedotto.... 11. Fr: minuit... 12. It: frutto....
13. Ptg: estreito.... 14. Fr: droit.... 15. hecho....
16. It: tetto.... 17. Fr: truite.... 18. Eng: conduct....
19. It: vendetta.... 20. Sp: ochenta....

Group B
1. Sp: luto 2. It: mezzanotte 3. Fr: fait 4. Eng: auction
5. Sp: vendido 6. It: freddo 7. Fr: dette 8. Eng: fritter
9. Fr: douteur 10. Sp: lechuga 11. It: dottore 12. Eng:
aquatic 13. Eng: vindictive 14. Ptg: astuto 15. Fr: huit
16. Eng: extract 17. It: ottanta 18. Eng: friction 19. Ptg:
auto 20. Sp: tratado 21. Fr: dit 22. Eng: drought
23. Ptg: direito 24. Eng: strict 25. Sp: tacha 26. Eng:
lotto 27. It: condotto 28. Eng: fruit 29. Sp: contacto
30. Fr: hache 31. It: venduto 32. It: lotta 33. Sp: pito
34. Sp: trucha 35. Eng: tact 36. Fr: biscuit 37. Fr:
doigt 38. Ptg: peito 39. Sp: aguaducho 40. Fr: toit

RULE 10

Double Consonants

Rule: In Italian, double consonants regularly remain double both in spelling and pronunciation. Spanish palatalizes LL to ll and NN to ñ [ɲ], retains RR as a multiple trill (carro < CARRU, but caro < CARU), and simplifies all other double consonants to one without further change. Portuguese simplifies all double consonants except RR. In French, though double letters appear between vowels in spelling, all double consonants reduce to single sounds or disappear.

	Italian	Spanish	Portu-guese	French	English cognate
ABBĀTE 'abbot'	abate	abad	abade	abbé	abbot
SĬCCU 'dry'	secco****	seco	sêco	sec (fem. sèche SĬCCA)	desiccated
ADDŪCĔRE	addurre	aducir	aduzir		adduce
Gmc: KOFFJA	cuffia	cofia	cofiar (verb)	coiffe	coif
BELLA** 'beautiful' (fem.)	bella	bella	bela	belle***	belle
FLAMMA 'flame'	fiamma	llama	chama	flamme	flame
ANNU 'year'	anno	año	ano	an [ã]	annual
CŬPPA (for CŪPA 'cask')	coppa	copa*	copa	coupe*	cup
TĔRRA 'earth'	terra	tierra	terra	terre	terrestrial
PASSU 'step'	passo	paso	passo [paso]	pas [pa]	pace

44

	Italian	Spanish	Portu-guese	French	English cognate
GŬTTA 'drop'	gotta 'gout'	gota 'drop, gout'	gota 'drop, gout'	goutte 'drop, gout'	gout, gutter

*CŪPA 'cask' gave Sp: cuba and Fr: cuve.
**Latin -ĬLLU gave Spanish -ello, but -ĒLLU gave first -iello [-ję́ʌo] and then -illo.
***For O.Fr: -el > -eᵃu > -eau (pron. [o]), see Rule 21.
****In Italian, double consonants represent sustained consonant sounds such as those found, for example, in the English combinations bookcase, coattail, cart track, dip pen, thinness.

Additional Examples

SACCU 'sack' It: sacco Sp, Ptg: saco Fr: sac Eng: sack
VACCA 'cow' It: vacca Sp, Ptg: vaca Fr: vache Eng: vaccine
BŬCCA 'mouth' It: bocca Sp, Ptg: boca Fr: bouche Eng: buccal
*ĬN + ADDĔRE 'to add' O.Sp: enadir Sp: añadir 'add'
CABALLU 'nag' It: cavallo Sp: caballo Ptg: cavalo Fr: cheval Eng: cavalry, chivalry
AŬRĔLLA 'border' Sp: orilla Ptg: ourela
SĒLLA 'seat' It: sella Sp: silla** Ptg: sela Fr: selle 'saddle'
CĔRĔBĔLLU 'brain' It: cervello Fr: cerveau
ANĔLLU 'ring' It: anello Sp: anillo** Ptg: elo (via aelo, cf. Rule 24) Fr: anneau 'ring' (O.Fr: anel)
CASTĔLLU 'castle' It: castello Sp: castillo** Ptg: castelo Fr: château*** (O.Fr: chastel) Eng: castle
MARTĔLLU 'hammer' It: martello Sp: martillo** Ptg: martelo Fr: marteau*** (O.Fr: martel) 'hammer'
CAPĬLLU 'hair' It: capello Sp: cabello** Ptg: cabelo Fr: cheveu*** (O.Fr: chevel) 'hair' Eng: capillary, dishevelled
SĬGĬLLU 'seal' It: suggello Sp: sello** Ptg: sêlo Fr: sceau*** (O.Fr: sel) Eng: seal
*STĒLLA 'star' It: stella Sp: estrella** Ptg: estrêla Fr: étoile 'star' (STELA) Eng: stellar, stella
CĬPŬLLA 'onion' It: cipolla Sp: cebolla Ptg: cebola ((Fr: oignon)) (Gm: Zwiebel)
MEDŬLLA 'marrow (of bones)' Sp: meollo
RŎTĔLLA 'little wheel' Sp: rodilla 'knee-cap, hence knee'
VĬTĔLLU 'calf' It: vitello Ptg: vitela (s.l.) Fr: veau*** Eng: veal
AV(I)CĔLLU, *AŬCĔLLU 'bird' It: uccello*** Fr: oiseau*** (O.Fr: oisel)
PĔLLE 'skin, hide' It: pelle Sp: piel (final -ll > -l in O.Sp) Ptg: pele Fr: peau*** (O.Fr: pel)

CANNA 'reed' It: canna Sp: caña Ptg: cana Fr: canne
  Eng: cane
PINNA 'feather' It: penna Sp: peña 'pinnacle' Ptg: pena
  Eng: pen
GRUNNIRE 'to grunt' It: grugnire Sp: gruñir Ptg: grunhir
  Fr: grogner
GEMMA 'bud, gem, yolk' It: gemma Sp: yema Ptg: gema
  Fr: gemme Eng: gem
CIPPU It: ceppo 'stock' Sp: cepo 'branch' Ptg: cepo
  Fr: cep
MASSA 'lump' It: massa Sp: masa Ptg: massa [s] Fr:
  masse Eng: mass
GROSSU 'thick' It: grosso Sp: grueso Ptg: grosso [s]
  Fr: gros (fem. grosse) Eng: gross
CATTU 'cat' It: gatto Sp: gato Ptg: gato Fr: chat
  Eng: cat
MITTERE 'to send' It: méttere Sp, Ptg: meter Fr: mettre
  'to put'
MUTTU 'mutter, grunt' It: motto**** 'epigram' Fr: mot 'word'

Exercise

Opposite each of the words in Group A write down the number of its nearest cognate in Group B.

Group A
1. Sp: año.... 2. Eng: pace.... 3. Ptg: belo.....
4. Fr: château..... 5. Eng: abbot.... 6. It: gatto....
7. Sp: cebolla 8. Ptg: ourela.... 9. It: vitello....
10. Fr: anneau....

Group B
1. Eng: bellow 2. Sp: botella 3. Fr: âne 4. Ptg: elo
5. Eng: vital 6. Sp: peso 7. Fr: sèche 8. Eng: veal
9. Fr: gâteau 10. Fr: chat 11. Ptg: abade 12. Sp:
anillo 13. Sp: bello 14. Ptg: cebola 15. Fr: an
16. Eng: grotto 17. Sp: orilla 18. Fr: pièce 19. It:
passo 20. Sp: castillo

RULE 11

-DR, -GR-, -BR-

Rule: Medially before R, Latin D and G usually fell in Romance. B, however, was retained in Spanish, sometimes restored from a v in Portuguese, always went to v in French (like -PR-), while in Italian a reaction against its loss generally caused it to be doubled (an exception: libro 'book').

	Italian	Spanish	Portu-guese	French	English cognate
QUADRU 'square'	quadro	cuadro	quadro	carré (QUADRĀTU)	square
QUADRA(G)ĬNTA 'forty'	quaranta	cuarenta	quarenta	quarante	quarantine
CÁTHĔDRA (or CATHĔDRA) 'chair'	cáttedra (l.)	cadera***	cadeira***	chaire* 'professorial chair'	chair
HĔDĔRA 'ivy'	édera	hiedra	hera	lierre (l'hierre)	
PĬGRĬTĬA 'laziness'	pigrizia (l.)	pereza	preguiça (met.)	paresse (see Rule 40)	
NĬGRU 'black'	nero	negro	negro (< Sp.)	noir	negro
PELEGRĪNU (for PEREGRĪNU) 'foreign, strange'	pellegrino 'pilgrim'	pelerino 'pilgrim'	peregrino (l.)	pélérin 'pilgrim'	pilgrim
ĬNTĔGRU 'whole, complete'	intiero	entero***	enteiro	entier	entire

47

	Italian	Spanish	Portu- guese	French	English cognate
FĔBRE 'fever'	febbre	fiebre	febre (earlier, fevre)	fièvre	fever
FEBR(U̯)ĀRĮU 'February'	febbraio	febrero	fevereiro	février	February
LĪBRA 'pound'	libbra	libra	libra	livre	
FÁBRĬCA 'craft, work- shop'	fabbrica 'factory'	fragua (met.)** 'forge'	fragua (met.)** 'forge'	forge	forge, fabric
CǑLŎBRA, CŎLŬBRA 'snake'	colubro	culebra (via coluebra)	cobra (earlier coovra)	couleuvre	cobra (< Ptg.)

*Fr: chaise 'chair' is a survival from a seventeenth century Parisian fad for pronouncing -r- as -z- (mazi, Pazis). Ridiculed by many contemporary writers, the fad was short-lived.
**FÁBRĬCA > fábrega > frábega > frab'ga > frauga > fragua. Here is a test for you. Figure out how FÁBRĬCA yielded Fr: forge 'smithy' though AU̯RI FABRE 'goldsmith' gave Fr: orfèvre. (Hint: the group vr'g would be unpronounceable.) You can solve the problem by applying Rules 4 and 5.
***Sporadically D and G, in disappearing, generated a yod, the action of which can be observed in CATHĔDRA Ptg: cadeira Sp: cadera (instead of *cadiera) Fr: chaire; ĬNTĔGRU Ptg: enteiro Sp: entero; AGRU > eiro > Sp: ero; FLAGRĀRE (for FRAGRĀRE 'to smell') Ptg: cheirar; *FLAGRU Ptg: cheiro Fr, Eng: flair (lit.) 'keen sense of smell'.

Note 1. It: ottobre Sp: octubre Ptg: outubro Fr: octobre (< ŎCTŌBRE, ŎCTŪBRE) are learned or semi-learned.

Additional Examples

AGRU 'cultivated field' It: agro 'land around a city' but Sp: ero 'cultivated field' (The development was AGRU > *airo > eiro (dial.) > ero.)
FĬBRA 'fibre' Sp: hebra Ptg: fibra
LĪBRU It, Sp: libro Ptg: livro Fr: livre
ĒBRĮU 'drunk' It: ubbriaco (+ -ACU) Sp: ebrio Ptg: ebrio Fr: ivre Eng: inebriated
ĒBRĬTĮA 'drunkenness' It: ebrezza Sp: embriaguez (*INĒBRĮACU + -ĬTĮA) Fr: ivresse
PARÁB(Ŏ)LA 'word' It: parola Fr, Eng: parole and by meta-thesis Sp: palabra Ptg: palavra (Eng: palaver)
LABŎRĀRE 'to till' Sp: labrar Ptg: lavrar
QU̯ADRĬFŬRCU 'crossroads' (lit.) 'where four roads meet' Fr: carrefour

Exercise

Opposite each of the words in Group A write down the number of its nearest cognate in Group B.

Group A
1. Fr: chaire.... 2. Sp: negro.... 3. Eng: cobra....
4. It: édera.... 5. It: fábbrica... 6. Fr: paresse....
7. Ptg: fibra.... 8. Sp: labrar.... 9. Fr: carré....
10. It: febbraio....

Group B
1. It: febbre 2. Sp: pereza 3. Eng: cheer 4. Ptg: lavrar 5. Fr: fièvre 6. Sp: hebra 7. Fr: noir 8. Eng: liver 9. It: quaranta 10. Sp: culebra 11. Ptg: hera 12. Sp: cobre 13. Sp: parece 14. Eng: ether 15. Fr: forge 16. Sp: cuadrado 17. Fr: février 18. Eng: fever 19. Sp: cadera 20. cuivre

RULE 12

Ĕ, ÁE (VL ę̈)

Rule: In open syllables an accented ę̈ diphthongizes to ie [jέ] in Italian, Spanish, and French, but in Portuguese never. In closed syllables ę̈ diphthongizes only in Spanish.

	Italian	Spanish	Portu-guese	French	English cognate
PĔDE 'foot'	piede	pie	pe	pied	pedal, centipede
HĔRĪ 'yesterday'	ieri	ayer (AD plus HĔRĪ)	((ontem))	hier	
FĔL 'gall'	fiele	hiel	fel	fiel	
MĔL 'honey'	miele	miel	mel	miel	mellifluous
TĔNĔT 'holds'	tiene	tiene	tem	tient	maintain, tenure
DĔCĔM 'ten'	dieci	diez	dez	dix (via *dieis)	decimal
CAELU 'sky'	cielo	cielo	céu	ciel	celestial
PĔTRA 'stone'	pietra	piedra	pedra	pierre	petrified
LĔP(Ŏ)RE 'hare'	liepre	liebre	lebre	lièvre	
CAECU 'blind'	cieco	ciego	cego	((aveugle))	
CĔNTU 'hundred'	cento	ciento, cien	cem	cent	cent
VĔNTU 'wind'	vento	viento	vento	vent	vent
SĔPTE(M) 'seven'	sette	siete	sete	sept	septet, septennial
PĔRDĬT 'loses'	perde	pierde	perde	perd	perdition

50

	Italian	Spanish	Portu-guese	French	English cognate
FĔSTA 'feast'	festa	fiesta	festa	fête	feast
FĔRRU 'iron'	ferro	hierro	ferro	fer	ferrous

Note 1. Unstressed ę did not give a diphthong. Compare TĔNET It, Sp: tiene Fr: tient with TĔNĔTĬS It: tenete Sp: tenéis Fr: tenez or Sp: viento, siete, hierro with ventana 'window', setecientos 'seven hundred', herrero 'blacksmith'.

Note 2. Before a or o, ie reduces to i in Italian and Spanish: MĔU 'my' > *mieo > It: mio Sp: mío; JŪDAEU 'Jew' Sp: judío; DĔUS 'God' > dieo (CIL, VIII, 9181) > It: dio Sp: dios; Ĕ(G)O 'I' > *ieo > It: ío Sp: yo.

Note 3. In Spanish, but not in French, a yod of various origins would 'close' the ę to e before it could diphthongize. Thus LĔCTU 'bed' Sp: lecho, but Fr: *lieit > lit, SĔX (=SĔCS) > Sp: seis but Fr: *sieis > six, SPĔCŬLU > Sp: espejo (Sp: viejo VĔTŬLU is not of Castilian origin), MATĔRĬA > Sp: madera, GRĔ(G)E > Sp: grey, ĬNGĔNĬU > Sp: engeño but O.Fr: engin (Eng: engine). This is why tengo TĔNĘO failed to diphthongize while tienes, tiene (TĔNES, TĔNET) did. Only the yod from TY, CY had no effect: *PĔTTĬA > Sp: pieza. Occasionally, -DR- and -GR- generated a yod which prevented a diphthong: CATHĔDRA > Sp: cadera 'seat, buttock' but Fr: chair (with i < *iei), ĬNTĔGRA > It: intiera Fr: entière but Sp: entera.

Note 4. In Italian, diphthongization did not occur before G, LY, or NY: LĔGĬT > legge, MĔLĬU > meglio, TĔNĘO VĔNĮO Old It: tegno vegno, Mod.It: tengo vengo. Nor generally in words with a semi-learned flavor stressed on the antepenult, like décimo, pécora, ténero.

Note 5. After ģ-, ć-, and consonant plus r, the i of ie has disappeared in Standard Italian: gelo, breve, prego, and cielo, cieco in which the i is silent. This development is not unlike O.Fr: chief > Fr: chef, O.Fr: nagier > Fr: nager 'swim', O.Fr: brief > Fr: bref.

Note 6. The common suffix -ĔLLU gave O.Sp: -iello [-jeʎo]. The two palatals closed e to i, giving -illo (castillo, anillo vs. It: castello, anello).

Additional Examples

QUAERO Sp: quiero Ptg: quero
ADHAERO Sp: adhiero (s.l.) 'I adhere'
ĔRĬGĬT 'erects' Sp: hiergue
QUĔM 'whom' Sp: quien 'who' Ptg: quem

HÉDĔRA 'ivy' It: edera Sp: hiedra Ptg: hera Fr: lierre
(orig. l'hierre)
VĘNĔRĬS (DIES) It: venerdì Fr: vendredi, but Sp: viernes
MĔRCŬRI (DIES) It: mércoledì Fr: mercredi, but Sp:
miércoles
SĔXTA (HŌRA) Sp: siesta Ptg: sesta
NĔB(Ŭ)LA 'mist' Sp: niebla Ptg: nevoa
TĔMPTAT Sp: tienta Ptg: tenta Fr: tente 'tempts'
NĔP(Ŏ)TE Sp: nieto Ptg: neto 'grandson' (but NĔPŌTE
It: nipote Fr: neveu 'nephew')
GRAECU 'Greek' Sp: griego Ptg: grego
STĔPHĂNU O.Fr: Estienne Fr: Etienne Eng: Stephen
RĔM 'thing' Fr: rien 'nothing'
*CĔRĔSĮA 'cherry' It: ciliegia Fr: cérise (with i < iei), but
Sp: cereza (CĔRĀSĘA).
APĔRTU 'open' It: aperto Sp: abierto Ptg: aberto Eng:
aperture
SAEC(Ŭ)LU 'century' shows s.l. development due to ecclesi-
astical influence: It: sécolo Sp: siglo (O.Sp: sieglo)
Ptg: século Fr: siècle. For the normal development of C'L,
see Rule 7.
HĔRBA 'grass, herb' It: erba Sp: hierba (or yerba) Ptg:
erva Fr: herbe (Eng: herb)
ĔRĔMU 'deserted place' It: ermo 'solitary' Sp: yermo Ptg:
ermo 'deserted place' (Eng: hermit)
ĔQŲA 'mare' Sp: yegua Ptg: egua
LĔVAT 'raises' O.Sp: lieva Sp: lleva 'carries' (In Modern
Spanish this lle- (< lie-) has spread by analogy to forms of
the verb which did not have a diphthong originally, hence
llevar, llevó, llevamos. Similarly affected is the derivative
LĔVĪTĀRE 'to leaven', which in Modern Spanish is either
leudar or lleudar.)

Exercise

Opposite each of the words in Group A write down the number of its nearest cognate in Group B.

Group A
1. It: dieci.... 2. Ptg: cego.... 3. Sp: viernes....
4. Eng: certain.... 5. Sp: hiedra.... 6. It: sécolo....
7. Ptg: lebre.... 8. Fr: sent.... 9. Eng: centipede....
10. Ptg: neto.... 11. Sp: cielo.... 12. Eng: tempts....
13. Fr: pierre.... 14. Fr: couvert.... 15. Sp: hierro....
16. Ptg: erva.... 17. Sp: fiesta.... 18. Sp: piel....
19. Fr: pièce.... 20. Fr: hier....

Group B
1. Eng: net   2. Sp: cierto   3. Fr: fête   4. Eng: pier
5. It: pelle   6. Ptg: sesta   7. It: cicco   8. Eng: fist
9. Sp: nieto   10. Fr: douze   11. Fr: siècle   12. It: cieco
13. Fr: lèvre   14. Fr: ère   15. Sp: ciempiés   16. Fr:
vendredi   17. Fr: nid   18. Sp: cubierto   19. Fr: tempête
20. Eng: convent   21. Fr: poil   22. It: édera   23. Sp:
hierba   24. Eng: rigid   25. Fr: fer   26. Sp: tienta   27. Ptg:
dez   28. Fr: poule   29. Sp: ayer   30. Ptg: peça   31. Eng:
saccule   32. Sp: siente   33. It: pietra   34. Fr: lièvre
35. Sp: hervir   36. Fr: fier   37. Ptg: cem   38. Sp: viento
39. Eng: heir   40. Ptg: céu

RULE 13

Ē, Ỹ, Œ (VL ẹ)

Rule: In open syllables only, Latin accented Ē, Ỹ, and Œ (i.e. VL ẹ) diphthongized to Old French ei. Unless followed by n, this ei generally went on to become Modern French oi, now pronounced [wa].

	Italian	Spanish	Portu-guese	French	English cognate
MĒSE (for MENSE) 'mouth'	mese	mes	mês	mois	
TRĒS 'three'	tre	tres	três	trois (O.Fr: treis)	trey
PĒSU (for PENSU) 'weight'	peso	peso	pêso	poids (O.Fr: peis)	
CRĒDIT 'believes'	crede	cree	crê	croit	creed
PARĒTE (for PARĮETE) 'wall'	parete	pared	parede	paroi	parietal
FỸDE 'faith'	fede	fe	fé	foi (O.Fr: fei)	faith
PỸRA (for PỸRU) 'pear'	pera	pera	pera	poire	pear
PỸCE 'tar'	pece	pez	pez	poix	pitch*
MỸNUS 'less'	meno	menos	menos (earlier, meos)	moins	minus
VỸDET 'sees'	vede	ve	vê	voit	evident
POENA 'punishment'	pena	pena	pena (Sp: see 24) peine		pain, penalty

54

	Italian	Spanish	Portu-guese	French	English cognate
PLĒNU 'full'	pieno	lleno	cheio	plein	replenish
SĬNU 'fold, bosom'	seno	seno	seio	sein	sinus
VĒNA 'vein'	vena	vena	veia	veine	vein
VĬRDE (for VĬRĬDE) 'green'	verde	verde	verde	vert	verdant
SĬCCU 'dry'	secco	seco	sêco	sec	desiccated
MĬTTĬT 'sends'	mette 'puts'	mete 'puts'	mete 'puts'	met 'puts'	
DĒBĒRE 'to owe'	dovere	deber	dever	devoir	debit
MĒSŪRA (for MENSŪRA) 'to measure'	misura	mesura	mesura	mesure	measure
SĒCŪRU 'safe'	sicuro, securo	seguro	seguro	sûr (O.Fr: seür)	sure, secure
ĬNTRĀRE 'to enter'	entrare	entrar	entrar	entrer	enter
PĬSCĀRE 'to fish'	pescare	pescar	pescar	pêcher	piscine, piscatorial

*Eng: pitch is taken from the Norman-Picard dialect, in which č, cy > [tš].
Cp. Norm.-Pic: cacier [katšér] (Eng: catch) with Fr: chasser (Eng: chase).
The English botanical name vetch (VĬCIU) is also from this same dialect.

Note 1. The evolution was [éi] > [pái] > [ói] > [ɔέ] > [wέ] > [wá]. [wέ] was the elegant pronunciation of the seventeenth and eighteenth centuries but with the French Revolution was abandoned in favor of hitherto vulgar [wa]. An alternative development, [wε] > [ε], is also found, but spelling has been changed to ai. Cp. français [ε] with François [wa], anglais [ε] with suédois [wa], and avais, parlaient [ε] with older avois, parloient [wε].

Note 2. In contact with a preceding yod (e.g. CĒRA > *cĕire, PLACERE > *plaĭsĭéir), the result was iei, which then reduced to i (cire, plaisir). In contact with a following yod, the result was ei (STRĬCTU > *estreĭt > O.Fr: estreit (Eng: strait) Fr: étroĭt 'narrow'; FĒRĮA > *feĭre > O.Fr: feire (Eng: fair) > Fr: foire 'market').

Note 3. Before a vowel, é becomes i in Italian, Spanish, and Portuguese, e.g. VĬA 'way' It, Ptg: via Sp: vía, but Fr: voie; (H)ABĒ(B)AT It: avia Sp: había Ptg: havia, but Fr: avait (formerly avoit).

Note 4. In Italian, ę́ tends to become i before nc, ng: VĬNCĒRE 'to conquer' It: víncere (but Sp: vencer); CĬNGĒRE 'to gird' It: cíngere (but Sp: ceñir); LĬNGŲA 'tongue' It: lingua (but Sp: lengua). In Portuguese and Spanish, we sometimes find the same thing: DŎMĬNĬCU 'the Lord's (day)' Sp, Ptg: domingo, SYRĬNGA 'syringe' Sp: jeringa Ptg: seringa, LĬNGŲA Ptg: lingua. In all three languages, the development is sporadic and semi-learned.

Note 5. In Italian, Spanish, and Portuguese, we sometimes find i for e before [ʎ] or [ɲ]: CONSĬLĮU It: consiglio (but Sp: consejo); TĬNĘA 'book-worm' It: tigna Sp: tiña Ptg: tinha (but Fr: teigne), MĬRABĬLĮA It: meraviglia Sp: maravilla Ptg: maravilha (but Fr: merveille) 'marvel', ERVĬLĮA 'pea' Ptg: ervilha but Sp: arveja, MĬLĮU 'millet' It: miglio Ptg: milho Fr: mil but Sp: mejo.

Note 6. Unstressed initial ę gave Italian i and sometimes e, occasionally even o or u before labial consonants. Examples: DĒ POST dopo 'after', DĒ MANE dimani (or domani), DĒMANDAT dimanda (or domanda), DĒBĒRE dovere, *RĒVERSĮU rovescio 'reversed', *SĬMĬLĮARE somigliare 'to liken', ĒBRIACU ubbriaco 'drunk'.

Note 7. In the final position, Ē, Ĭ, Ĕ, and AE all blended to a VL ę. This e generally survives in Italian (PŪRĒ pure, CRĒDĬT crede, NŌMEN nome, FĬLĮAE figlie). Spanish drops final e after the single Latin consonants C, D, L, N, R, S, and T (VŌCE voz, MERCĒDE merced, SŌLE sol, BĔNE bien, MĀRE mar, MĒSE mes, ĪTE id), but keeps it after consonant groups (dulce, grande, doble, carne, padre, parte). This is frequently true even when the consonant group has since dissolved: PĔCT(Ĭ)NE peine, *DŌD' CE (for DUODĔCĬM) doce, SAL(Ĭ)CE sauce yet FALCE hoz). In French, all final vowels were lost except -A, which gave [-ə] in Old French and is now mostly silent. Examples: CLAVE clef, PĔRDĬT perd, HĔRĬ hier, ŎCTŌ huit, MŪRU mur, but RŌSA rose. Only if the preceding consonant group could not be pronounced alone were final vowels kept as [-ə], as in VĪV(Ĕ)RE vivre, *DŌD' CE (for DUODĔCĬM) douze, *QUATTRO (for QUATTUOR) quatre, MAGĬSTRU maître, DŬLCE douce, HŪM(Ĭ)LE humble.

Note 8. Portuguese dropped final e after the single Latin consonants C, L, R, S (VŌCE voz, SŌLE sol, MĀRE mar, MĒSE mes) but kept it after double consonants or consonant groups (PĔLLE pele, DĪXĬT disse, CARNE carne, DĔNTE dente). When the fall of a consonant brought -e into hiatus it became e or i depending on the quality of the preceding vowel and the nature of the fallen consonant (MERCĒDE > mercee > mercê, CRĒDIT > cree > crê, TĒNĒS > tẽes > tens [tẽjs], HABĒTĬS > havedes > haveis, FIDĒLĒS > fiéis, SŌLĒS > sóis, CĪVĪLĒS > civis, VADĬT > vai, FĪNĒS > ffis > fins > [fĩs]).

Additional Examples

SĒTA 'bristle' It: seta Sp: seda Ptg: seda Fr: soie 'silk'
COMŒDỊA 'play, comedy' It: commedia Sp: comedia Ptg:
comedia Fr: comédie (all learned forms) Eng: comedy
CŒNA 'dinner' It, Sp: cena Ptg: ceia
FŒNU 'hay' Sp: heno Ptg: feno (earlier feo) Fr: foin
FOEDU 'foul, abominable' It: fedo 'foul' Sp: feo Ptg: feio
'ugly'
VĒLŬ, -A 'sail' It, Sp: velo Ptg: veo Fr: voile (-A) (Eng:
veil)
MONĒTA 'coin' It: moneta Sp: moneda Ptg: moeda Fr:
monnaie (O.Fr: moneie) Eng: money, mint
PỸLU 'hair' It, Sp: pelo Fr: poil Eng: pile 'hair, down'
NỸGRU 'black' It: nero Sp: negro Fr: noir Eng: negro
MĒ, TĒ, SĒ Fr: moi, toi, soi (but note that unstressed, the
result is me, te, se [mə, tə, sə])
QUĒTU (for QUỊĒTU) 'quiet' It: cheto Sp, Ptg: quedo
Fr: coi Eng: coy
PĪSU, PỸSU 'pea' Fr: pois Middle Eng: pease (from this
form, mistaken for a plural, was derived a new singular
form: pea)
PỸPER 'pepper' It: pepe Sp: pebre Fr: poivre Eng: pepper
SĒRU 'late, evening' It: sera Fr: soir Eng: serein
'(meteorol.) a very fine rain falling from a clear sky after
sunset'
RĒ(G)E 'king' It: re Sp: rey Ptg: rei Fr: roi (Eng:
regent, royal)

Exercise

Opposite each of the words in Group A write down the number of its nearest cognate in Group B.

Group A
1. Eng: faith.... 2. Fr: poire... 3. It: secco....
4. Ptg: pescar.... 5. It: pece.... 6. Eng: pain....
7. It: sicuro.... 8. Eng: pepper.... 9. Sp: creencia....
10. It: nera.... 11. Fr: coi.... 12. Ptg: saber....
13. Fr: plein.... 14. Sp: pelo.... 15. Fr: moins....
16. Fr: soie.... 17. Ptg. veia.... 18. It: mese....
19. Fr: soirée.... 20. Sp: pared....

Group B
1. It: piano 2. Sp: sigo 3. Eng: peel 4. Fr: moi
5. Fr: fée 6. It: pera 7. Eng: vein 8. It: serata
9. Eng: saber 10. Fr: pain 11. Eng: peccary 12. Fr:
poil 13. Eng: pitch 14. Sp: veía 15. Eng: credence
16. Sp: mesa 17. Eng: sure 18. Sp: fe 19. Fr: sec

20. Fr: mois   21. Fr: paroi   22. Eng: quite   23. Sp: seda
24. Fr: poivre   25. Eng: quay   26. Fr: savoir   27. Sp:
lleno   28. Fr: noire   29. Sp: nuera   30. It: pena   31. Sp:
feo   32. Eng: minus   33. Fr: crainte   34. Fr: pois
35. Sp: misa   36. Fr: avoine   37. It: cheto   38. Eng:
part   39. Fr: pêcher   40. Sp: saco

RULE 14

‑ĔRE

Rule: Latin verbs whose infinitives bore the accent on their stem or root vowel always shifted this accent to the ending in Spanish and Portuguese. Italian almost invariably kept the original dactylic accentuation, as did French, but there the loss of the unstressed Ĕ could give rise to some curious consonant groups.

	Italian	Spanish	Portu‑guese	French	English cognate
SCRĪBĔRE 'to write'	scrívere	escribir	escrevir	écrire	scribe
FACĔRE 'to do'	fare	hacer	fazer	faire	affair
CRĒDĔRE 'to believe'	crédere	creer	crer	croire (O.Fr: creidre)	creed
FRĪGĔRE 'to fry'	fríggere	freír	frigir	frire	fry
TRAHĔRE 'to draw'	trarre, tràggere (poet.)	traer	trazer	traire	tractor, attract
MŎLĔRE 'to grind'	((macinare))	moler	moer	moudre (O.Fr: moldre)	molar
RESŎLVĔRE 'to resolve'	risólvere	resolver	resolver	résoudre (O.Fr: resoldre)	resolve
RŬMPĔRE 'to break'	rómpere	romper	romper	rompre	rupture
VĬNCĔRE 'to conquer'	víncere	vencer	venzer	vaincre	vanquish
VĒNDĔRE 'to sell'	véndere	vender	vender	vendre	vendor
TĬNGĔRE 'to dye'	tíngere	teñir	tingir	teindre	tinge, tincture

	Italian	Spanish	Portu-guese	French	English cognate
PŌNĔRE 'to put'	porre	poner	pôr	pondre 'lay (eggs)'	
CONSŬĔRE (*COSĔRE) 'to sew to-gether'	cucire	coser	coser	coudre (O.Fr: cosdre)	
PĔRDĔRE 'to lose'	pérdere	perder	perder	perdre	perdition
SŬRGĔRE 'to rise'	sórgere	surgir	surgir	sourdre	resurgent
CRĒSCĔRE 'to grow'	créscere	crecer	crescer	croître (O.Fr: creistre)	crescent
MĬTTĔRE 'to send'	méttere 'put'	meter 'put'	meter 'put'	mettre 'put'	emit
VĪVĔRE 'to live'	vîvere	vivir	viver	vivre	revive

Note. There are a few French and Italian verbs which have shifted their accent to -ĒRE or -ĪRE as in Spanish and Portuguese:

CADĔRE, *CADĒRE Sp: caer Ptg: cair Fr: choir (O.Fr: chadeir) It: cadére
SAPĔRE, *SAPĒRE Sp: saber Ptg: saber Fr: savoir It: sapére
RECĬPĔRE, *RECIPĒRE Sp: recibir Ptg: receber Fr: recevoir but It: ricépere
CŬRRĔRE, *CURRĪRE Sp: correr Ptg: correr Fr: courir but It: córrere
CŎLLĬ(G)ĔRE Sp: coger Ptg: colher Fr: cueillir but It: cógliere
JACĔRE, *JACĒRE Sp: yacer Ptg: jazer Fr: gésir but It: giácere

Additional Examples

DĪCĔRE 'to say' It: dire Sp: decir Ptg: dezir Fr: dire Eng: diction
CŎQ(Ṷ)ĔRE 'to cook' It: cuócere Sp: cocer Ptg: cozer 'boil' Fr: cuire Eng: cook
LĒGĔRE 'to read' It: léggere Sp: leer Ptg: ler Fr: lire Eng: legible
PLANGĔRE 'to weep' It: piángere Sp: plañir Ptg: prantear (*PLANCTĬDĬĀRE) Fr: plaindre 'complain' Eng: complain

FĬNGĔRE 'to mould, invent' It: fíngere Sp: heñir 'to knead'
(fingir 'to feign') Ptg: fingir Fr: feindre Eng: feign
JŬNGĔRE 'to join, yoke' It: giúngere Sp: uncir Por:
jungir Fr: joindre
CONSTRĬNGĔRE 'to constrict' It: costríngere Sp: constreñir
Ptg: construngir Fr: contraindre Eng: constrain
EXTĬNGĔRE 'to put out' Fr: éteindre (Sp: extinguir is
learned) Eng: extinguish
PĬNGĔRE 'to paint' It: píngere Fr: peindre (Sp, Ptg: pintar
*PINCTĀRE) Eng: pigment
NASCĔRE 'to be born' It: nascere Sp: nacer Ptg: nascer
Fr: naître Eng: renaissance
PASCĔRE 'to graze' It: páscere Sp: pacer Ptg: pascer
Fr: paître Eng: pasture
COGNOSCĔRE 'to know' It: cognóscere Sp: conocer Ptg:
conhecer Fr: connaître (O.Fr: conoistre)
PARESCĔRE 'to become visible' Ptg, Sp: parecer Fr: paraître
'to seem' Eng: appear
ESSĔRE (for ESSE) 'to be' It: éssere Fr: être (O.Fr: estre)
(Note that SS'R > str, while S'R, as in *CÓS(Ĕ)RE (for
CONSŬĔRE), gave sdr: O.Fr: cosdre.)

Exercise

Opposite each of the words in Group A write down the number of its nearest cognate in Group B.

Group A
1. Sp: crecer.... 2. Fr: coudre.... 3. It: resólvere....
4. Fr: croire.... 5. Fr: naître.... 6. Sp: leer....
7. Fr: peindre.... 8. Fr: cueillir.... 9. Eng: feign....
10. Fr: être.... 11. It: giúngere.... 12. Sp: freír....
13. Ptg: jazer.... 14. It: sapere.... 15. Ptg: pôr....
16. Ptg: moer.... 17. sórgere.... 18. Fr: teindre....
19. Ptg: venzer.... 20. Sp: conocer

Group B
1. Sp: teñir 2. Sp: coger 3. Fr: cuiller 4. Sp: hacer
5. It: giácere 6. Fr: croître 7. Sp: por 8. Eng: leer
9. Fr: sourdre 10. Eng: grow 11. It: crédere 12. Fr:
feindre 13. It: píngere 14. Ptg: ler 15. Sp: cocer
16. Fr: connaître 17. Sp: mover 18. It: cadere 19. Eng:
put 20. Fr: vaincre 21. Eng: attain 22. Sp: parecer
23. Ptg: coser 24. Fr: moudre 25. Eng: read 26. Fr:
résoudre 27. It: cuócere 28. It: náscere 29. Ptg: frigir
30. Eng: sapper 31. Sp: poner 32. Eng: sorghum 33. It:
éssere 34. It: piángere 35. Sp: henchir 36. Fr: joindre
37. Eng: advance 38. Fr: savoir 39. Ptg: meter 40. Sp:
ser

RULE 15

F-, -F-

Rule: The initial f- of the other Romance languages is represented in Spanish by a formerly aspirated, but now silent h-. Unaffected are learned words and words beginning with fue- and (sometimes) fie-.

	Italian	Spanish	Portu-guese	French	English cognate
FABA 'bean'	fava	haba	fava	fève	
FACĔRE, FACĒRE 'to do'	fare	hacer	fazer	faire	
FARĪNA 'flour'	farina	harina	farinha	harine	farinaceous
FENDĔRE, FENDĒRE 'to cleave'	fendere	hender	fender	fendre	fend
FĔRRU 'iron'	ferro	hierro (in American Sp: also fierro)	ferro	fer	ferrous
FĪCU 'fig'	fico	higo	figo	figue (s.l.)	fig
FĪCĀTU (JĒCUR) 'liver stuffed with figs'	fegato 'liver'	hígado 'liver'	figado 'liver'	foie 'liver'	
FĪLĬA 'daughter'	figlia	hija	filha	fille	filial
FĪLU 'thread'	filo	hilo	fio	fil	file
FĔLLE 'gall'	fiele (*FĔLE)	hiel	fel	fiel (*FELE)	

62

	Italian	Spanish	Portu-guese	French	English cognate
FŬRCA 'pitchfork'	forca	horca	forca	fourche	fork
FŬRNU 'oven'	forno	horno	forno	four	furnace
FŎLJA 'leaves'	foglia	hoja	folha	feuille	foliage
FŌRMA 'form'	forma	horma 'mould'	forma	forme	form
FORMĪCA 'ant'	formica	hormiga	formiga	fourmi	formic

Note 1. Examples of learned influence are fama, favor, fervor (but also hervor), defender (but dehesa), sofocar (but ahogar), fumar (but humo), fastidiar 'annoy' (but hastío), fecha 'date' (but hecho), fondo (but hondo), fijo FĪXU (but hito *FĪCTU), forma (but horma), fe, fin, fino, difunto. Examples with ie, ue: fiero FĔRU 'wild' fiesta, fiel FĬ(D)ĒLE 'faithful', fiebre 'fever', fieltro 'felt', fue FŬIT, fuente FŎNTE, fuerte FŎRTE, fuego FŎCU (but hogar), fuero FŎRU 'law'.

Note 2. In compound words whose constituent parts were once recognized, Spanish treated medial -f- as initial:

ADFAUCĀRE Sp: ahogar 'to asphyxiate, drown'
DĒFENSA Sp: dehesa 'enclosed field'
SŬBFŪMĀRE Sp: sahumar 'to fumigate'
SŬBFŬNDĀRE Sp: zahondar 'to dig; sink down'
SŬBFĔRĪRE Sp: zaherir 'to censure, reproach'
CANNAFERŬLA Sp: cañaherla (bot.) 'common fennel-giant'
CONFĪNJU Cohiño (near Santander)
REFŪSĀRE Sp: rehusar 'to decline'

Otherwise, medial -f- became -v- or -b- as in

TRĬFŎL(J)U 'three leaves' It: trifoglio Sp: trébol Ptg: trevo (via trevoo) Fr: trèfle 'clover'
TRĬFĪNJU 'three boundaries' Sp: Treviño
PROFĔCTU 'advantage' Sp: provecho

Additional Examples

FĀME 'hunger' It: fame Sp: hambre (FĀMINE) Ptg: fome Fr: faim Eng: famine
FĒMĬNA 'female' It: femmina Sp: hembra Ptg: fêmea Fr: femme Eng: feminine

FOENU 'hay' It: fieno Sp: heno Ptg: feno Fr: foin
*FENŬCŬLU (for FENĬCŬLU) 'fennel' It: finocchio Sp: hinojo
 Ptg: funcho Fr: fenouil Eng: fennel
FŪSU 'spindle' It: fuso Sp: huso Ptg: fuso Fr: fuseau
 (FŪSELLU)
FAGU, *FAGĘA 'beech tree' It: faggio Sp: haya Ptg: faia
FŪGĪRE 'to flee' It: fuggire Sp: huir Ptg: fugir Fr: fuir
 Eng: fugitive
FŪMU 'smoke' It: fumo Sp: humo Ptg: fumo Fr: fumée
 (FŪMĄ̄TA) Eng: fume
FŬNDĔRE 'to pour out; melt' It: fóndre Sp: hundir Ptg:
 fundir Fr: fondre Eng: founder, foundry
FĔRĪRE 'to strike, wound' It: ferire Sp: herir Ptg: ferir
FŬNGŲ 'fungus' Sp: hongo 'mushroom'
FĔRVĔRE 'to boil' Sp: hervir Ptg: ferver
FOETĒRE 'to stink' Sp: heder Ptg: feder Eng: fetid
FŎCĀLE 'pertaining to the hearth' Sp: hogar 'hearth, home'
FŎCĀCĘA 'pertaining to the hearth' It: focaccia 'bun'
 Sp: hogaza 'large loaf' Ptg: fogaça 'cake' Fr: fouace
 'griddle cake'
FOCĀRIU, -A 'pertaining to the hearth' Sp: hoguera 'bon-
 fire' Fr: foyer 'hearth'
FORMŌSU 'shapely' Sp: hermoso Ptg: formoso
FĬBRA 'fibre' Sp: hebra Ptg: febra
FŬRTU 'theft' It: furto Sp: hurto Ptg: furto Eng: furtive
FŬNDU 'deep' It: fondo Sp: hondo Ptg: fundo Fr: pro-
 fond Eng: profound
FĪLĮU DE ALIQUO(D) O.Sp: fi(jo)dalgo Sp: hidalgo 'noble-
 man' Ptg: fidalgo
FŬSTĬGĀRE 'to cudgel' Sp: hostigar Ptg: fustigar
*FĬBĔLLA (for FĬBŬLA) 'clasp, buckle' Sp: hebilla Ptg:
 fivela
FŎDĮU 'excavation' Sp: hoyo Ptg: fojo
FŎSSA 'ditch, trench' It: fossa Sp: huesa 'grave' Ptg:
 fossa Fr: fosse Eng: fossil
FŪMĬGĀRE 'to fumigate' Sp: humear Ptg: fumear
FASTĪDĮU 'disgust' Sp: hastío Ptg: fastio
FALCŌNE 'falcon' Sp: halcón Ptg: falcão
FABŬLĀRĪ 'to talk, chatter' Sp: hablar Ptg: falar
FASCE 'bundle' Sp: haz Ptg: feixe
FACĮE 'surface' Sp: haz Ptg: face
FAECE 'dregs' Sp: hez Ptg: fez
FALCE 'sickle' Sp: hoz Ptg: fouce
FAŲCE 'defile' Sp: hoz Ptg: foz
FĀTA 'Fates' It: fata Sp: hada Ptg: fada Fr: fée 'fairy'
FĪCTU (for FĪXU) 'fixed' Sp: hito Ptg: fito
FACTU 'done' It: fatto Sp: hecho Ptg: feito Fr: fait

Exercise

Opposite each of the words in Group A write down the number of its nearest cognate in Group B.

Group A
1. Sp: hongo.... 2. Fr: feuille.... 3. Eng: furtive....
4. Ptg: feito.... 5. Sp: hígado.... 6. Ptg: fossa....
7. It: faggio.... 8. Eng: fiber 9. Sp: heder....
10. Fr: faire... 11. It: fuggire.... 12. Sp: hada....
13. Ptg: feixe.... 14. Eng: fumigate..... 15. Ptg:
formosa.... 16. Fr: foyer.... 17. It: formica....
18. Sp: halcón.... 19. It: fémmina.... 20. Sp:
provecho....

Group B
1. Sp: huerto 2. Eng: famine 3. Sp: humear 4. Sp:
hueso 5. Sp: fiebre 6. Eng: Hades 7. Sp: huir
8. Sp: hoya 9. Sp: hombre 10. Sp: hija 11. Fr: je fusse
12. Sp: hoguera 13. Fr: heurter 14. Sp: haz 15. Eng:
hair 16. Sp: huesa 17. Eng: provocation 18. Ptg: fazer
19. Eng: feather 20. Sp: hambre 21. Eng: fade 22. Sp:
hermosa 23. Eng: fungus 24. Eng: fetid 25. Eng: heir
26. Sp: hormiga 27. Eng: profit 28. Sp: fiel 29. Sp:
hembra 30. Sp: hurtar 31. Ptg: falcão 32. Fr: foie
33. Sp: hecho 34. Sp: horno 35. Ptg: fito 36. Sp: hoja
37. Sp: hebra 38. Fr: prouve 39. Sp: haya 40. Fr: fée

RULE 16

H

Rule: H fell silent in Latin and has left no trace except in learned spellings.

	Italian	Spanish	Portu-guese	French	English cognate
HŌRA 'hour'	ora	hora	hora	heure	hour
HABET 'has'	ha	ha	hà	a	
HĪSPĀNĮA 'Spain'	Spagna	España	Espanha	Espagne	Spain
HĪBĔRNU 'winter (adj.)'	inverno	invierno	inverno	hiver	hibernate
HŎDĮE 'today'	oggi	hoy	hoje	aujourd'<u>hui</u>	
HĔRBA 'grass'	erba	hierba	erva	herbe	herb
HONŌRE 'honor'	onore	honor, honra	honra	honneur	honor
HĔDĔRA 'ivy'	édera	hiedra	hera	lierre (l'hierre)	
COHORTE 'enclosure; cohort'	corte 'court'	corte 'court'	corte 'court'	cour 'court'	court
APPREHENDERE 'apprehend'	appréndere 'learn'	aprender 'learn'	aprender 'learn'	apprendre 'learn'	apprehend, apprentice

Note 1. Mediaeval scribes, stretching the Latin alphabet to accommodate new sounds of Romance, Germanic, and Arabic origin, such as [tš], [ds], [dž], [dz], [š], [x], [θ], [ɟ], [ɣ], exploited the fact that h no longer had a sound of its own by combining it with other letters to represent new phonetic values. Ch, gh, lh, nh, sh, th have been used at various times in different languages; indeed, most of them are still used today, but there is no uniformity of meaning. For example, ch represents [tš] in English and Spanish, [š] in French and in Portuguese, [k] in Italian and [x] in German.

Note 2. Latin H must not be confused with later Germanic h- (now silent also) that prevents 'liaison' in haut, haine, honte, hache, hâter, hanche, hardi, hasard, hareng, homard, haie, halle, halte, hanter, hameau, harangue, havre, houe, houx, huche, houseau, hotte and many other French words. The other Romance languages ignore Germanic h entirely (It: aringa Sp, Ptg: arenque 'herring'), though the h- may appear in Spanish spelling (hacha 'axe, hatchet', pronounced [atša]).

Additional Examples

IOHANNE 'John' It: Giovanni Sp: Juan Ptg: João Fr: Jean Eng: John

RULE 17

Ī

Rule: In the stressed or initial positions, Latin Ī survives unchanged in Romance. Final -Ī, however, is preserved only in Italian, which keeps all final vowels. The other languages treat it like final -E, -AE, -Ē, and -Y̆, which become -e or disappear. In falling, however, -Ī inflects the [ę] of ā preceding syllable and closes it to i̯ (FĒCĪ Sp: hice˙ Ptg: fiz Fr: fis). In hiatus -Ī may form a diphthong (-Ā(V)Ī It: -ai Sp: (-ai > -éi >) -é, Ptg: -ei Fr: -ai).

	Italian	Spanish	Portu-guese	French	English cognate
VĪTA 'life'	vita	vida	vida	vie	vitality
MĪLLE 'thousand'	mille	mil	mil	mille	mil
VĔNĪRE 'to come'	venire	venir	vir	venir	convention
AMĪCU 'friend'	amico	amigo	amigo	ami	amicable
FĪNE 'conclusion'	fine (f.)	fin (m.)	fim (m.)	fin (f.)	final
HĪBĔRNU 'winter'	inverno	invierno (O.Sp: invierno)	inverno	hiver	hibernate
CĪV(Ĭ)TĀTE 'state'	città	ciudad	cidade	cité	city
RĪP(Ŭ)ĀRĮA 'bank (adj.)'	riviera	ribera	ribeira	rivière	river, Riviera
FĒCĪ 'I did'	feci	hice	fiz	fis	
VĒNĪ 'I came'	venni	vine	vim	vins	

	Italian	Spanish	Portu-guese	French	English cognate
VĬCĪNU 'neighbor'	vicino	vecino	vezinho	voisin	vicinity
VĪGĬNTĪ 'twenty'	venti*	veinte (formerly veînte*)	vinte	vingt	vigesimal
HĔRĪ 'yesterday'	ieri	ayer	((ontem))	hier	
CANTĀ(V)Ī 'I sang'	cantai	canté	cantei	chantai	chant

*In VĬCĪNU, VĪGĬNTĪ, which had two I's, the first one dissimilated to e, hence Sp: vecino Ptg: vezinho Fr: voisin; It: venti Sp: veinte.

Note 1. Spanish reír RĪDERE, decir DĪCERE, freír FRĪGERE 'to fry' (but not vivir, escribir), have changed their stem vowel to e by confusion with the vastly more numerous verbs in e...ír (like SENTĪRE sentir).

Additional Examples

SĪC 'thus, so yes' It: si Sp: sí Ptg: sim Fr: si ((oui)) 'yes'
SCRĪPTU It: scritto Sp: escrito Ptg: escrito Fr: écrit
VĪLĬTĀTE 'vileness' It: viltà Sp: vildad Ptg: vildade Fr: vilté
QUAESĪ Sp: quise Ptg: quis 'I wished (to), tried'
PRĒSĪ 'I took' Fr: pris
RUĪNA 'ruin' It: rovina Sp: ruina Fr: ruine (Eng: ruin)
RĒGĪNA 'queen' It: reína Sp: reina (O.Sp: reína) Ptg: rainha Fr: reine (Eng: Regina)
VAGĪNA 'sheath' It: guaína Sp: vaina (O.Sp: vaína) Ptg: bainha Fr: gaine. (The It and Fr forms show contamination with Gmc: w-. See Rule 42. From the Sp dimin. vainilla 'pod' is borrowed Eng: vanilla.)
DĪCIT It: dice Sp: dice Ptg: diz Fr: dit
LĪMĬTĀRE Sp, Ptg: lindar 'to border (on)'
ĬLLĪS Sp: les Ptg: lhes '(to) them'
DĪXĪ It: dissi Sp: dije Ptg: disse Fr: dis
NATĪVU 'natural, simple' Fr: naïf Eng: naïve
VĪNU 'wine' It, Sp: vino Ptg: vinho Fr: vin

Exercise

Opposite each of the words in Group A write down the number of its nearest cognate in Group B.

Group A
1. It: ieri.... 2. Fr: ami.... 3. Ptg: vida.... 4. Sp: ribera.... 5. It: città.... 6. Fr: voisin... 7. Sp: hice.... 8. Ptg: vim.... 9. Fr: écrit.... 10. It: dissi.....

Group B
1. Sp: cita 2. Fr: vide 3. It: scritto 4. Eng: eerie 5. It: venni 6. Sp: voz 7. Fr: hier 8. Fr: citer 9. Fr: dix 10. Sp: ciudad 11. It: feci 12. Sp: amo 13. Fr: rivière 14. Sp: dije 15. Sp: veces 16. Fr: vie 17. Eng: dice 18. It: amico 19. Fr: fils 20. Ptg: vezinho

RULE 18

J-, Ǵ-, DY-, GY-

Rule: Classical Latin J-, Ǵ-, DY-, GY- all gave Vulgar Latin yod [j]. This yod survives in Italian as [dž] (spelled ǵ- or gi-) and in Portuguese and French as [ž] (spelled ǵ- or j-). Spanish shows three developments: before e, a, the result is y [j] if that vowel is stressed, but if it is unstressed, then the yod falls. Before o, u, stressed or not, the result is j [x].

	Italian	Spanish	Portu-guese	French	English cognate
JAM 'already'	già [dža]	ya [ja]	jà [ža]	(déja, jadis, jamais)[ža]	
JACĬT 'lies'	giace [džatse]	yace [jaθe]	jaz [žaž]	gît (via *gieist)[ži]	gist
GEMMA 'bud, gem'	gemma	yema	gema	gemme	gem
GYPSUM 'plaster'	gesso	yeso	gêsso	gypse (l.)	gypsum
GĔNĔRU 'son-in-law'	género	yerno	genero (l.)	gendre	
JEN(Ŭ)ĀRĬU, JAN(Ŭ)ĀRĬU 'January'	gennaio	enero	janeiro	janvier	January
JUNĬPĔRU, *JENĬP(Ĕ)RU 'juniper'	ginepro 'juniper, 'gin'	enebro 'juniper'	zimbro 'juniper' genebra 'gin' (l.)	genièvre 'juniper, gin'	juniper, gin
GERMĀNU 'own brother'	germano 'own brother'	hermano (O.Sp: ermano)	irmão (O. Ptg: germão)	germain 'own (brother), first (cousin)'	german(e)
GĬNGĪVA 'gum'	gengiva	encía	gengiva	gencive	gingivitis

71

	Italian	Spanish	Portu-guese	French	English cognate
GĔNŬC(Ŭ)LU (for GĔNĬC(Ŭ)LU) 'knee'	ginocchio	hinojo (O.Sp: inojo)	joelho (met. from *geolho)	genouillère (*GENUC(U)-LĀRĮA 'knee-cap'	genuflexion
JŎCU 'game'	giuoco	juego	jûgo	jeu	joke
JŪNĮU 'June'	giugno	junio (s.l.)	junho	juin	June
JŪSTU 'just'	giusto	justo	justo	juste	just
JŬNCTU 'joined'	giunto	junto	junto	joint	joint
JŬVĔNE 'young'	giovane	joven	joven	jeune	juvenile
DIŬRNĀLE 'daily'	giornale	jornal	jornal	journal	journal
*GĘORGĮU 'George'	Giorgio	Jorge	Jorge	Georges	George

Note 1. Some of the exceptions to the foregoing rules for Spanish are popular jamás JAM MAGĪS (though ya JAM is regular); also learned género, gente (formerly yente), gesto, Jesús, gemir, general, jacinto HYACINTHU. The infinitive yacer (O.Sp: azer) owes its y- to analogy with yáce, yácen. Yugo JŪGU 'yoke', yunta JŬNCTA 'yoke of oxen', and uncir (uñir) JŬNGĔRE 'to yoke' are presumed to be dialectal in origin.

Additional Examples

GĔLU 'frost' It: gelo 'frost' Sp: hielo (properly yelo) 'ice'
Ptg: gêlo 'ice' Fr: gel 'frost'
DĮARĮA 'a day's ploughing' Ptg: geira 'acre'
GĔLĀRE 'to freeze' It: gelare Sp: helar (O.Sp: elar) Ptg: gelar Fr: geler Eng: congeal
*JECTĀRE (for JACTĀRE) 'to throw' It: gettare Sp: echar Ptg: ditar (DĒIECTĀRE) Fr: jeter Eng: projectile
*GEMĔLLĪCĮU (for GEMĔLLU) O.Sp: emellizo Sp: mellizo 'twin'
GENĔSTA '(bot.) genista, broom' It: ginestra Sp: hiniesta Ptg: giesta Fr: genêt
JŪDĬCĀRE 'to judge' It: giudicare Sp: juzgar Ptg: julgar Fr: juger Eng: judge
JŪDĬCĮU 'judgment' It: giudicio Sp: juicio Ptg: juizo

JŪDĀEU 'Jew' Sp: judío Ptg: judeu Fr: juif (*JŪDĪVU)
JO(H)ANNE 'John' Sp: Juan Ptg: João Fr: Jean (regard-
ing the Italian Giovanni, cp. RUĪNA It: rovina 'ruin',
VĪDUA It: védova 'widow')
JEJŪNU (*JAJŪNU) 'fasting' It: digiuno Sp: ayuno Ptg:
jejum Fr: jeûne Eng: jejune
HIERONYMU (<˙ Greek, lit. 'holy name') It: Gerólamo Sp:
Jerónimo (l.) Fr: Jérome

Exercise

Opposite each of the words in Group A write down the number of its nearest cognate in Group B.

Group A
1. Eng: joint.... 2. Fr: janvier..... 3. Sp: yerno....
4. It: giuoco.... 5. Ptg: jaz.... 6. Eng: gypsum....
7. Fr: déjeuner..... 8. Sp: echar.... 9. Pt: João....
10. It: gelare.... 11. Eng: judge 12. Sp: hermano....
13. It: gemma.... 14. Ptg: juizo.... 15. Eng: June....
16. Sp: judío.... 17. Fr: genièvre.... 18. Sp: hielo....
19. It: ginocchio.... 20. Sp: encía....

Group B
1. Sp: helar 2. It: giugno 3. Sp: enojo 4. Eng:
germane 5. Sp: yugo 6. It: giunto 7. Eng: gambler
8. Ptg: joelho 9. Fr: fâcher 10. Sp: enero 11. Eng:
yearn 12. It: giulio 13. Sp: desayunar 14. It: género
15. Fr: déjà 16. Eng: yell 17. Sp: yace 18. Fr:
gencive 19. It: giù 20. Eng: jute 21. Fr: jeter 22. Sp:
yema 23. It: giovane 24. Sp: enebro 25. Eng: juice
26. Fr: juif 27. Fr: juger 28. Eng: gypsy 29. It: già
30. Sp: yeso 31. Eng: Geneva 32. It: giudicio 33. Sp:
jugo 34. Fr: jeu 35. Fr: gel 36. It: giusto 37. Eng:
joy 38. Sp: haz 39. It: Giovanni 40. Eng: ounce

RULE 19

-J-, -Ǵ-, -DY-, -GY-

Rule: Classical Latin -J-, -Ǵ-, -DY-, -GY- all gave Vulgar Latin yod [j]. This yod frequently developed in Italian to gg(i) [ddž], but before accented é or í it usually fell. Zz [ddž], an alternative development for -DY-, is the result of an early erudite pronunciation that retained and reinforced -DY- while the unschooled said [j]. Spanish loses intervocalic yod in contact with e or i. (Cp. mayor with peor, ensayo with correa.) In Portuguese, DY and GY normally give j [ž] (words like meio, raio are semi-learned or else borrowed from Spanish), and G disappears. In French, the yod of Vulgar Latin usually remained to diphthongize with the preceding or following vowel.

	Italian	Spanish	Portu-guese	French	English cognate
MAJU 'May'	maggio	mayo	maio	mai	May
MAJŌRE 'greater'	maggiore	mayor	mór, maior (s.l.)	majeur, maire (MÁJOR)	major, mayor
PĚJŌRE 'worse'	peggiore	peor	peor	pire (PĚJOR) (via *pieire)	pejorative
LĒGE 'law'	legge	ley*	lei	loi	legal, loyal, law
FŪGĪRE 'to flee'	fuggire	huír	fugir	fuir	fugitive
SĬGĬLLU 'seal'	suggello	sello (O.Sp: seello)	sêlo	sceau (O.Fr: sel)	seal
DĬGĬTU 'finger'	dito	dedo	dedo	doigt (O.Fr: deit)	digit

	Italian	Spanish	Portuguese	French	English cognate
PLANTĀGĬNE 'plantain'	piantaggine	llantén	chantagem	plantain	plantain
MAGĬS 'more'	mai	más	mais	mais	
MAGĬSTRU 'master, teacher'	maestro	maestro, maestre	mestre**	maître	master
PAGĒ(N)SE 'country (adj.)'	paese	país	país	pays	peasant
RĒGĪNA 'queen'	reîna	reina (form. reína)	rainha	reine (form. reíne)	Regina
RADĮU 'spoke; ray; radius'	raggio, razzo	rayo	raio	rayon (-ŌNE)	ray, radius
VĬDĘO 'I see'	veggio	veo	vejo	vois	video, evident
MĚDĮU 'middle'	mezzo	medio (l.)	meio	mi (midi, parmi, demi) (via *miei)	medium
PŎDĮU 'podium'	poggio	poyo 'hill'	poyo 'stone seat'	pôjo 'jossing block'	puy 'cone-shaped hill'	podium
HŎDĮE 'today'	oggi	hoy	hoje	aujourd'hui	
FAGĘU, FAGĘA 'beech'	faggio	haya	faia	((hêtre))	
CORRĬGĮA 'strap, belt'	coreggia	correa	correa	courroie	
EXAGĮU	saggio	ensayo	ensaio	essai	essay

*Via *le(g)e; cp. BŎVE 'ox' > *bue(v)e > buey.
**-e due to influence of Old French or Provençal.

Note 1. In Spanish, (consonant +) DY gi̶ves z [θ] or [s]: *VĪRDĮA 'greenery' berza 'cabbage', HORDĘŌLU orzuelo, VERĒCŬNDIA vergüenza, GAŲDĮU gozo 'joy'. (Cp. AŲDĮO Ptg: ouço 'I hear'.) In French, RDY, NG, NGY, and RGY produced a [ž]: *VĪRDĮĀRĮU verger 'orchard', HORDĘU 'barley' orge, ÁNGĚLU 'messenger' > 'angel' ange, ĬNGĚNĮU 'cleverness, genius' engin 'engine', GĘORGĮUS Georges.

Additional Examples

RAJA 'ray (the fish)' It: razza (by confusion with RADĮA)
Sp: raya Ptg: raia Fr: raie Eng: ray

CŪJU 'whose' Sp: cuyo Ptg: cujo
PERFĪDJA 'treachery' Sp: porfía 'obstinacy'
SAGĬTTA 'arrow' It: saetta Sp: saeta Ptg: seta
VAGĪNA 'sheath' It: guaína Sp: vaina (form. vaína) Ptg:
bainha Fr: gaine (The Italian and French forms show con-
tamination with Germanic w-. See Rule 42.)
SEXAGĬNTĪ 'sixty' It: sessanta Sp: sesenta (O.Sp:
sessaenta) Ptg: sessenta Fr: soixante
QUADRAGĒSĬMA 'Lent' It: quarésma Sp: cuaresma Ptg:
quaresma Fr: carême
FASTĪDJU 'loathing' Sp: hastío Ptg: fastio (< Sp.)
SĒDEAT Sp: sea Ptg: seja 'be'
VADEAM Sp: vaya 'go'
VIGĬNTĪ 'twenty' It: venti Sp: veinte (form. veínte) Ptg:
vinte Fr: vingt (O.Fr: vint)
FRĬGĬDU 'cold' It: freddo Sp: frío (O.Sp: frido) Ptg: frio
Fr: froid (O.Fr: freit)
ADJŪTĀRE 'to help' It: aiutare Sp: ayudar Ptg: ajudar
Fr: aider Eng: aid
*APPŎDJĀRE 'to support' It: appoggiare Sp: apoyar Ptg:
apoiar Fr: appuyer
GLADJOLU 'little sword' Fr: glaïeul '(bot.) gladiolus'
MŎDJU 'an old dry measure' It: mozzo, moggio Sp: moyo
Ptg: moio Fr: muid
RĒGJA 'royal' It: reggia 'palace'
REGĬŌNE 'region' It: reggione Sp: región Ptg: regiào
Fr: région Eng: region
LĔGJŌNE 'legion' Sp: León Fr: Lyon (It: legione, Sp:
legión, Fr: légion are learned)
FŪGJO 'I flee' Sp: huyo (yet FŪGĪRE huir) (Note: huyes,
huye (FŪGĬS, FŪGĬT) owe their -y- to analogy with huyo
(FŪGJO).)
PŪLĒGJU '(bot.) pennyroyal' It: puleggio Sp: poleo Ptg:
poejo

Exercise

Opposite each of the words in Group A write down the number of its nearest cognate in Group B.

Group A
1. It: oggi.... 2. Sp: mayor.... 3. Ptg: dedo...
4. Fr: maître... 5. It: paese.... 6. Sp: vaina....
7. Fr: fuir.... 8. Sp: mayo.... 9. Ptg: vinte....
10. It: peggiore.... 11. Eng: seal.... 12. Ptg: vejo....
13. Sp: saetta.... 14. It: poggio.... 15. Eng: medium....
16. Sp: correa.... 17. Fr: raie.... 18. It: saggio....
19. Eng: plantain.... 20. Sp: ley....

Group B
1. Fr: assez 2. Ptg: seta 3. It: cui 4. Fr: moi 5. Fr:
meilleur 6. Sp: cuyo 7. Eng: essay 8. It: piantaggine
9. Sp: viejo 10. Fr: courroie 11. Sp: mío 12. Fr: paix
13. It: maestro 14. Sp: mejor 15. Fr: plante 16. Sp:
seda 17. It: sette 18. Fr: sage 19. Ptg: peor 20. Sp:
raya 21. Eng: currier 22. Fr: puy 23. Ptg: bainha
24. Fr: pays 25. Fr: loi 26. It: fuggire 27. Sp: veo
28. Fr: lai 29. Eng: ditto 30. It: mezzo 31. Sp: veinte
32. Fr: majeur 33. Eng: pace 34. Sp: sea 35. Sp: sello
36. Ptg: peojo 37. Eng: digit 38. Fr: mai 39. Eng: vain
40. Sp: hoy

RULE 20

-L-

Rule: Portuguese alone among the Romance languages lost single L and single N between vowels. As part of this same tendency, Portuguese weakened -LL- to -l- and -NN- to -n-. See Rules 10 and 24.

	Italian	Spanish	Portu- guese	French	English cognate
VOLŬNTĀTE 'will'	voluntà	voluntad	vontade	volonté	voluntary
CŎLŌRE 'color'	colore	color	côr	couleur	color
DŎLŌRE 'grief'	dolore	dolor	dôr	douleur	dolorous
VŎLĀRE 'to fly'	volare	volar	voar	voler	volatile
*CŎLŎBRA 'snake' (for CŎLŬBĔR)	colubro	culebra	cobra (earlier coovra)	couleuvre	cobra
PŎPŬLU 'people'	pópolo	pueblo	povo (via poboo)	peuple	people
MŎBĬLES '(lit.) movables'	móbili	muebles	móveis	meubles 'furniture'	mobile
PERĪCŬLU 'danger'	perícolo	peligro	perigo	péril	peril
AQŬĬLA 'eagle'	ácquila (s.l.)	águila (s.l.)	águia (s.l.)	aigle (s.l.)	eagle
SŌLU 'alone'	solo	solo	só	seul	sole
CAELU 'sky'	cielo	cielo	céu	ciel	celestial
FĪLU 'thread'	filo	hilo	fio	fil	file

78

Note 1. When in Portuguese the L became final, it was retained: SŌLE sol, PŎRTU CALE Portugal, but PŎRTU
CALE(N)SE português.

Additional Examples

AVĮŎLU 'little grandfather' Sp: abuelo Ptg: avô 'grand-
father' Fr: aïeul 'ancestor'
PALŬMBU 'dove' Sp: paloma Ptg: pombo
*MŎLĒRE (for MŎLĔRE) 'to grind' Sp: moler Ptg: moer
Fr: moudre (MŎL(Ĕ)RE)
PALU 'stick, cudgel, stake' It, Sp: palo Ptg: pau Fr: pal
(Eng: pale 'picket fence, boundary, limit')
MALU 'bad' It, Sp: malo Ptg: mau Fr: mal
PĪLA 'pillar' It: pila 'foot, pier' Sp: pila 'pile, fountain'
Ptg: pia 'fountain' Fr: pile 'heap, pier (of a bridge)'
Eng: pile
SALŪTĀTE 'greeting' Ptg: saudade 'longing'
SALŪTE 'health' It: salute Sp: salud Ptg: saúde Fr: salut
*VŎLU 'flight' It: volo Sp: vuelo Ptg: vôo Fr: vol
CALENTE 'hot' Sp: caliente Ptg: quente
PALA 'shovel' It, Sp: pala Ptg: pá 'shovel' Fr: pale 'oar-
blade'
AFFĪLĀTU 'sharpened' It: affilato Sp: afilado Ptg: afiado
Fr: affilé
SALĪRE 'to leap' It: salire 'rise' Sp: salir 'to depart, go
out' Ptg: sair 'go out'
DŎLĒRE 'to grieve' It: dolére Sp: doler Ptg: doer
SŎLĒRE 'to be wont to' It: solére Sp: soler Ptg: soer
VĬGĬLĀRE 'to stay awake, watch' It: vegliare (< Prov.?)
Sp: velar Ptg: vigiar Fr: veiller
ŪMBĬLĪCU 'navel' It: bellico Sp: ombligo Ptg: embigo
MŎLĪNU 'mill' It: molino Sp: molino Ptg: moinho Fr: moulin
TRĬFŎLU '(three-leafed) clover' It: tréfolo 'tangle of thread'
Sp: trébol 'clover' Ptg: trevo (via trévoo) Fr: trèfle
'clover' (Eng: trefoil)
DĮABŎLU 'devil' It: diavolo Sp: diablo Ptg: diavoo > diavo
Fr: diable (Eng: devil, diabolical)
ANGĔLU 'angel' It: angelo Sp: ángel Ptg: angeo > anjo
Fr: ange (Eng: angel)
PALĀTĮU 'palace' It: palazzo Sp: palacio (1.) Ptg: paço
Fr: palais (Eng: palace)
COLORĀTU 'colored' Sp: colorado 'ruddy' Ptg: corado
'colored'
*CALESCĒRE Sp: calecer Ptg: (a)quecer 'to heat'
RECELĀRE 'to distrust, fear' Sp: recelar Ptg: recear
MŪLU 'mule' It, Sp: mulo Ptg: mú Fr: mulet (-ĬTTU)
MŪLA 'she-mule' It, Sp: mula Ptg: mua Fr: mule
TĒLA 'web, cloth' It, Sp: tela Ptg: têa, teia Fr: toile

Exercise

Opposite each of the words in Group A write down the number of its nearest cognate in Group B.

Group A
1. Sp: caliente....   2. Ptg: sair....   3. Fr: moulin....
4. Eng: color....   5. Sp: abuelo....   6. Fr: veiller....
7. Ptg: cobra....   8. Fr: peuple....   9. Ptg: moer....
10. Sp: voluntad....   11. Fr: trêfle....   12. Ptg: mú.....
13. Eng: palace....   14. Ptg: corar....   15. Sp:
peligro....   16. It: affilare....   17. Ptg: pombo.....
18. It: bellico.....   19. Ptg: anjo....   20. Ptg: fio....

Group B
1. Fr: moudre   2. Sp: cuero   3. Ptg: paço   4. Fr: fils
5. Ptg: perigo   6. Sp: paloma   7. Ptg: belo   8. Ptg: afiar
9. Eng: mole   10. Eng: veil   11. Ptg: bondade   12. Sp:
calor   13. Sp: calavera   14. It: volere   15. Ptg: embigo
16. Sp: correr   17. Fr: fil   18. Ptg: quente   19. Eng:
anger   20. Sp: culebra   21. Ptg: vigiar   22. Sp: ángulo
23. Ptg: povo   24. Fr: plomb   25. Ptg: minho   26. Eng:
treble   27. Sp: mudo   28. It: salire   29. Fr: cor   30. Ptg:
moinho   31. Sp: colorar   32. Ptg: passo   33. Ptg: avô
34. It: angelo   35. Ptg: vontade   36. Sp: trébol   37. Sp:
ahijado   38. It: mulo   39. Ptg: côr   40. It: figlio

RULE 21

L (PLUS CONSONANT)

Rule: L (plus consonant) remains unchanged in Italian but regularly vocalizes to u̱ in French. In popular words, Latin AL (plus consonant) develops via *au̱ (plus consonant) to Portuguese ou̱, Spanish o, French au̱ or o̱, pronounced [o].* In ŬLT, the L̄ vocalizes ī n Spanish to i̱, g̱iving uch (compare NŎCTE > noite > Sp: noche).**

	Italian	Spanish	Portu-guese	French	English cognate
ALT(Ĕ)RU 'other'	altro	otro	outro	autre [otr]	alternate
FALCE 'scythe'	falce	hoz.	foice (orig. fouce)	faux [fo]	
CALCE 'heel'	in calce 'at the foot'	coz 'kick'	couce 'kick'	chausser (CALCEĀRE) 'to shoe' [s̆ose]	recalcitrant, lit. 'kicking back'
TALPA 'mole'	talpa	topo	toupeira (-ĀRĮA)	taupe [top]	
MŬLTU 'much'	molto	mucho, muy	muito	((beaucoup))	multitude
A(Ų)SCŬLTĀRE 'to listen'	ascoltare	escuchar	escutar	écouter	scout
CŬLTĔLLU 'little knife'	coltello	cuchillo	cutelo ((faca))	couteau	cutlass

*The popular development ALTĀRĮU Ptg: outeiro, Sp: otero 'mound', SALTU 'grove', Ptg: souto, Sp: s̆oto is not as common, however, as the semi-learned one which preserves the L, as in alba, alto, balde, caldo, calvo, etc. It is to be noted, furthermore, that in Romance groups, the L vocalized too late for the resulting au̱ to monophthongize to o̱, hence CAL(Ĭ)CE > cal'ce > Sp: cauce 'river-b̄ed', SAL(Ĭ)CE > sal'ce > Sp: sauce 'willow'.

**This development was arrested when the fall of the following unstressed vowel created a Romance group, e.g. VŬLT(Ŭ)RE > vuit're > buitre 'vulture', or when ŬLT became final, as in MŬLT(U) > O.Sp: muy(t) > Sp: muy 'very'.

81

Note 1. In Old French, the suffix -ĔLLA with its final vowel [ə] remained as -elle, whereas in -ĔL(LU) the loss of final U (Rule 1, Note 3) caused the L to vocalize before the initial consonant of the following word, e.g. (ĬL)LU BĔL(LU) CAMPU Fr: le beau champ, but (ĬL)LU BĔL(LU) ARBŎRE Fr: le bel arbre. In nouns the suffix has been standardized as -eau whether the next word begins with a consonant or not: CASTĔLLU château, VĬTĔLLU veau. The a or -eau is a transitional or 'glide' vowel that developed between the e and u due to a habit in Old French of drawling the ending. In later French, this triphthong eau or iau was reduced in pronunciation to au and finally to o, though the spelling -eau persists to this day.

Note 2. French final -x, as in les beaux chevaux, harks back to a time when final -us was written with a scribal flourish that was mistaken for an x. For example, les biax chevax would stand for les biaus chevaus (ĬL)LŌS BEL(LŌ)S CABAL(LŌ)S. Later, when the meaning of this -x had been forgotten, the u was reinserted and the -x came to be regarded as just a substitute for final -s. So today we often find -x for -s in words which never did have -us, such as PACE paix VŌCE voix.

Additional Examples

*SALTA (for SALTU) 'leap' O.Sp: sota, xota Sp: jota 'dance' (Sp: salto 'leap' is l.)
ALTU 'high, deep' It, Sp, Ptg: alto Fr: haut (with h- by contamination with Germanic hoh 'high' > Gm: hoch)
FALSU 'false' It, Sp, Ptg: falso Fr: faux
CAL(Ĭ)DU 'hot' It: caldo 'hot' Sp: caldo 'broth' Ptg: caldo 'hot' Fr: chaud
SALVĮA '(bot.) sage' It, Sp: salvia Ptg: salva Fr: sauge Eng: sage
MŬT(Ĭ)LĀRE 'to cut off' > *mol'tare > Sp: mochar 'to cut, lop off' Eng: mutilate
CŬLMĬNE 'summit' Sp: cumbre Ptg: cume
SŬLPHŬRE 'sulphur' Sp: azufre Ptg: enxofre
ĬNSŬLSU 'unsalted' Sp: soso Ptg: ensosso 'tasteless, insipid'
SALSA 'salted' Sp: salsa Fr, Eng: sauce
*ALBĀRĮU (< ALBU 'white') Sp: overo Fr: aubère 'dapple-grey (of horses)'
PALPĀRE 'to stroke, caress' Ptg: poupar 'to save, spare' Sp: popar 'to fondle'
CŌL(Ă)PHU 'blow' It: colpo Sp, Ptg: golpe Fr: coup
FĔLTRU 'felt' It: feltro Sp: fieltro Ptg: feltro Fr: feutre Eng: felt
PŪL(Ĭ)CE 'flea' It: púlice Fr: puce (*PŪLĬCA > Sp, Ptg: pulga)

SALVĀRE 'to save' It: salvare Sp, Ptg: salvar Fr: sauver
Eng: save
CALVU 'bald' It, Sp, Ptg: calvo Fr: chauve
VAL(Ĕ)T 'is worth' Fr: vaut
PŬLV(Ĕ)RE 'dust' It: pólvere Fr: poudre Eng: powder
(PŬLVU Sp: polvo)
FŬLGŬRE 'lightning' It: folgóre Fr: foudre
RESŎLV(Ĕ)RE 'to resolve' Fr: résoudre
MŎL(Ĕ)RE 'to grind' Fr: moudre
MAL(Ĕ)DĪCTU 'accursed' Sp, Ptg: maldito Fr: maudit
ĬL(LŌ)S O.Fr: els, eus Fr: eux 'them'
A(D)(Ĭ)L(LŌ)S O.Fr: als, aus Fr: aux 'to the (plur.)'
DĒ(Ĭ)L(LU) O.Fr: del, deu (before a consonant) Fr: du
'(masc.) of the' (Note that before a word beginning with a
vowel, the l does not vocalize: de l'homme, de l'arbre.)
MĔLĬ(Ŭ)S 'better' O.Fr: mielz, mieus Fr: mieux
CALMĀRE 'to calm, cease' Fr: chômer 'to cease work, to be
idle or unemployed'

Exercise

Opposite each of the words in Group A write down the number of its nearest cognate in Group B.

Group A
1. Eng: scout.... 2. Fr: chauve.... 3. Sp: salvia....
4. Ptg: golpe.... 5. It: falce.... 6. Eng: multitude....
7. Sp: mochar.... 8. Fr: maudir.... 9. Ptg: alto....
10. It: folgore.... 11. Fr: couteau.... 12. Eng: felt....
13. Sp: buitre.... 14. Ptg: martelos.... 15. It: caldo....
16. Fr: puce.... 17. Ptg: calmar.... 18. Fr: coupable....
19. Eng: veal.... 20. Ptg: couce....

Group B
1. Sp: cuchillo 2. Fr: fausse 3. It: pulice 4. Sp:
escudero 5. Fr: marteaux 6. Fr: beurre 7. Fr: chômer
8. Eng: culprit 9. Ptg: maldito 10. Sp: llave 11. Fr:
foudre 12. Eng: saliva 13. Sp: hiel 14. Fr: chaud
15. Ptg: falcão 16. Eng: sage 17. Fr: se moucher
18. It: ascoltare 19. Eng: fulcrum 20. Sp: vale 21. It:
pollice 22. Sp: muchedumbre 23. Eng: calf 24. Sp: cauce
25. Eng: mutilate 26. Sp: colmar 27. Fr: mouchoir 28. It:
colpo 29. Fr: veau 30. Ptg: calvo 31. Sp: coz 32. It:
altero 33. Sp: hoz 34. Sp: vela 35. Eng: cold 36. Eng:
vulture 37. Fr: feutre 38. Fr: couper 39. Ptg: salvar
40. Fr: haut

RULE 22

LY

Rule: LY develops into gli [ʎ] in Italian, j [x] in Spanish, lh [ʎ] in Portuguese, and il(1) [:j] in French. In other words, L̄Y gives the same results as C'L (see Rule 7) in all but Italian, where C'L becomes cchi [kj].

	Italian	Spanish	Portu-guese	French	English cognate
FĪLɅA 'daughter'	figlia [fiʎa]	hija [ixa]	filha [fiʎɐ]	fille [fi:j]	filial
PALɅA 'chaff, straw'	paglia	paja	palha	paille	paillasse 'straw mattress'
FOLɅA 'leaves'	foglia	hoja	folha	feuille	foliage, tinfoil
ALLɅU 'garlic'	aglio	ajo	alho	ail	
MILɅU 'millet'	miglio	mejo	milho	mil	millet
MĒLɅŌRE 'better'	migliore	mejor	melhor	meilleur	ameliorate
CONSĬLɅU 'advice'	consiglio	consejo	conselho	conseil	counsel
TALɅĀRE 'to cut'	tagliare	tajar, tallar (s.l.)	talhar	tailler	tailor, entail
CŎLLɅ(G)ĒRE 'to collect'	cogliere	cojer	colher	cueillir	coil, i.e. 'gather'
MŬLɅĒRE 'woman'	moglie	mujer	mulher	(O.Fr: moillier)	

Note 1. In Spanish, semi-learned words show ll [ʎ]. Besides maravilla and tallar, we find humillar HŮMÍLĮĀRE 'humiliate', muralla MŪRĀLĮA 'rampart', batalla BATT(Į)ĀLĮA 'battle', vitualla VICTUĀLĮA 'victuals', San Millán SANCTĪ (AE)MILĮĀNĪ. Concilio, julio, etc., are learned.

Note 2. In Old French, the pronunciation of ail, fille was [aʎ], [fiʎə]. If this [ʎ] came to stand before an s, it depalatalized to l and developed a transitional t between itself and the s (cp. SĀLSA 'salted' > [saltsə] > Fr, Eng: sauce (instead of *sause)): MĒLĮ(U)S O.Fr: mielz > [mjɛlts] > Fr: mieux [mjɛys] > [mjø] (for l > u before a consonant, see Rule 21). VEC'LUS O.Fr: vielz [vjɛlts] Fr: vieux [vjɛys] > [vjø]. After ĪÌ the l disappeared through assimilation: FĪLĮ(U)S 'son' O.Fr: filz [filts] > [fits] (Eng: Fitz- as in Fitzgerald, Fitzwilliam) > Fr: fils [fis]. LĪLĮ(O)S 'lilies' Fr: lis [lis].

Additional Examples

MOLLĮĀRE 'to soften' Sp: mojar Ptg: molhar Fr: mouiller 'to wet, dampen'

SĪMĪLĮARE 'to liken' It: somigliare Sp: semejar Ptg: semelhar Eng: similar

CĪLĮU 'eyelid' It: ciglio Sp: ceja 'eyebrow' Ptg: sobrancelha 'eyebrow' Fr: cil 'eyelash' Eng: supercilious

MĪRABILĮA (*MARABILĮA) It: meraviglia Sp: maravilla (s.l.) Ptg: maravilha Fr: merveille Eng: marvel

JŪLĮU 'July' It: luglio Sp: julio (l.) Ptg: julho Fr: juillet

ERVĪLĮA 'type of pea' Sp: arveja Ptg: ervilha

ŎLĘA 'oil' Fr: huile Eng: oil

VĪRĪLĮA Sp: verija Ptg: virilha 'groin'

ALĮĒNU 'alien, belonging to another' Sp: ajeno Ptg: alheio

ALĮŌRU Fr: ailleurs 'elsewhere, besides'

MALLĘĀRE 'to hammer' Sp: majar Ptg: malhar 'to pound, bruise, break in a mortar'

(DES) plus SPOLĮARE 'to rob, plunder' It: spogliare 'spoils' Sp: despojar Fr: dépouiller Eng: spoil, despoil

SŎLĮU 'seat' (confused with SŎLU 'ground') O.Fr, Eng: soil

CONCILĮU 'council' It: concilio (l.) Sp: concejo Ptg: concelho Fr: concile Eng: council 'municipal court'

CANĀLĮA (from CANE 'dog') Fr: canaille 'rabble' (Sp: canalla is semi-learned or borrowed from French)

CANĀLĮA (from CANĀLE 'canal') Ptg: calha 'millrace'

PECŪLĮĀRE Sp: pegujar or pegujal 'small privately owned farm'

Exercise

Opposite each of the words in Group A write down the number of its nearest cognate in Group B.

Group A
1. Sp: consejo.... 2. Ptg: palha.... 3. Fr: dépouille.....
4. It: ciglio.... 5. Eng: alien.... 6. Sp: hijo....
7. It: cogliere.... 8. Ptg: mulher.... 9. Fr: feuille....
10. Eng: council.... 11. Eng: affiliated.... 12. It:
somiglia.... 13. Fr: ail.... 14. Ptg: molhado....
15. Eng: tailor.... 16. It: meraviglia.... 17. Fr: huile....
18. Sp: tajo.... 19. Ptg: melhor.... 20. Fr: juillet....

Group B
1. Fr: cueillir 2. Sp: mujer 3. Fr: pâle 4. It: taglio
5. Eng: pail 6. Fr: aile 7. Sp: ajo 8. Sp: majo 9. Sp:
despojo 10. Eng: counsel 11. Sp: ojo 12. It: figlio
13. Fr: sommeil 14. Sp: mayor 15. Eng: tuile 16. It:
luglio 17. Fr: mouillé 18. It: togliere 19. Ptg: concelho
20. Fr: foule 21. Sp: majar 22. Fr: cil 23. Sp: muralla
24. Eng: oil 25. It: paglia 26. Eng: distill 27. Fr:
tailleur 28. Eng: collier 29. Sp: ahijado 30. Fr: ailleurs
31. Sp: ajeno 32. Eng: mail 33. Sp: mejor 34. Sp: hoja
35. Eng: toil 36. Eng: gullet 37. Sp: semeja 38. Eng:
soil 39. Fr: merveille 40. Sp: fijo

RULE 23

M'N (MB, M'C, M'L, MPS, MPT, M'R, M'T)

Rule: (1) M'N regularly turns into Spanish mbr and French mm or m. (2) If the intervening vowel dropped out before the -T- had voiced, then M'T regularly became nt in Romance; if the -T- had already voiced, then it became nd. (3) In Spanish, the group MB reduced to m.

	Italian	Spanish	Portuguese	French	English cognate
FĒMĬNA 'female'	fémmina	hembra	fêmea	femme	feminine
SĔMĬNAT 'shows'	sémina	siembra	semea	sème	disseminate
NŌMĬNAT 'names'	nómina	nombra	nomea	nomme	nominate
HŎMĬNE 'man'	uomo (HŎMO) (plur. uómini (HŎMĬNES))	hombre	homem	homme	homicide
CŎM(Ĭ)TE 'king's companion'	conte	conde (O.Sp: also cuende)	conde	comte [kɔ̃:t]	count
SĒM(Ĭ)TĀRĬU 'path'	sentiero	sendero	senda (SĒM(Ĭ)TA)	sentier	
PALŬMBA 'dove'	palomba	paloma	pombo	palombe	
PLŬMBU 'lead'	piombo	plomo	chumbo	plomb	plumb line, plumber
LŬMBU 'loin'	lombo	lomo 'loin, back, ridge'	lombo	lombes 'loins'	loins

Note 1. In Spanish, M'N first dissimilated to m'r, which then, together with original M'R, developed a b by way of a 'glide' consonant. Examples of M'R: HŬMÉRU⁻'shoulder' Sp: hombro, CŬCŬMÉRE Sp: cogombro Fr: concombre Eng: cucumber, CAMĚRA Fr: chambre Eng: chamber, NŬMÉRU Fr: nombre Eng: number. M'R could also give French ndr: GĒMÉRE 'to sigh, groan' Fr: geindre (O.Fr: gembre), *CRĒMÉRE for TREMÉRE 'to fear' Fr: craindre (O.Fr: creindre, crembre).

Note 2. M'L gives Fr: mbl: CŬMŬLĀRE 'to heap' Fr: combler Eng: accumulate (Sp, Ptg: colmar show metathesis); SĬMŬLĀRE Fr: sembler 'to seem' (cp. Sp: semblante 'countenance'); HŪMĬLE Fr, Eng: humble Eng: humility; TRĚMŬLARE Fr: trembler Sp: temblar (Eng: tremble).

Note 3. M'C gives French nc̣: PŬMĬCE 'pumice stone' Fr: ponce; RŬMĬCE 'sorrel' Fr: ronce 'bramble'. MPS gives ns: CAMPSARE 'to return' It: cansare 'to remove' Sp, Ptg: cansar 'to tire'; ASSŪMSĪ 'I assumed' It: assunsi. MPT gives nt: CŎMPŬTAT 'calculates' It: conta Sp: cuenta Ptg: conta Fr: compte [kõ:t]; PRŌMPTU It, Sp, Ptg: pronto 'ready, quick'; ASSŪMPTU 'matter (taken up)' It: assunto Sp: asunto Ptg: assunto; EXEMPTU 'exempt' It: esente Sp: exento (l.) Ptg: isento Fr: exempt [egzã].

Additional Examples

FAMĬNE 'hunger' Sp: hambre
NŌMĬNE 'name' Sp: nombre (It, Ptg: nome Fr: nom are from the nominative form NŌMĚN)
STAMĬNE 'warp; thread; cloth' Sp: estambre 'worsted, woolen yarn'
EXAMĬNE 'swarm, crowd' It: sciame Sp: enjambre Ptg: enxame Fr: essaim 'swarm (esp. of bees)'
AERĀMĬNE 'copperware' Sp: alambre Ptg: arame 'wire' It: _rame 'copper'
VĪMĬNE 'osier, twig' Sp: mimbre 'wicker'
LŪMĬNE 'light' Sp: lumbre
FERRŪMĬNE 'rust' Sp: herrumbre
LEGŪMĬNE 'vegetable' Sp: legumbre (It, Ptg: legume Fr: légume)
*CO(N)S(Ụ)ETŪMĬNE (for -ŪDĬNE) Sp: costumbre (It, Ptg: costume Fr: coutume Eng: custom)
*MULTĬTŪMĬNE (for -ŪDĬNE) Sp: muchedumbre 'multitude, rabble' (Ptg: multidão (-ŪDĬNE > O.Ptg: -om (by influence of -ŌNE) > Ptg: -ão (by confusion with -ĀNŪ)). See Rule 24.)
*CERTITŪMĬNE (for -ŪDĬNE) Sp: certidumbre (s.l.) Ptg: certidão (see example above)
CULMĬNE 'summit' Sp: cumbre (Ptg: cume)

*PŮTRŸTŪMŸNE (for -ŪDINE) 'rottenness' Sp: podredumbre
*SERVITŪMŸNE (for -ŪDINE) 'servitude' Sp: servidumbre
(s.l.) 'servitude; staff of servants'
LĪMŸTĀRE Sp, Ptg: lindar 'to border'; LĪMITĀLE O.Fr: lintel
(Eng: lintel Sp: dintel) Fr: linteau 'lintel (of a door)'
PRĪMU TĔMP(U)S Fr: printemps 'spring'
AMŸTA 'father's sister' O.Fr: ante (Eng: aunt) Fr: tante
DOMŸTĀRE 'to tame' O.Fr: danter (Eng: daunt) Fr: dompter
(Eng: indomitable)
REDEM(P)TĮŌNE 'repurchase' Sp: redención (s.l.) Fr: rançon
Eng: ransom
LAMBĒRE 'to lick' Sp: lamer Ptg: lamber (It: leccare Fr:
lécher are from a Gmc: *LIKK- Cp. Cm: lecken Eng: lick)

Exercise

Opposite each of the words in Group A write down the number of its nearest cognate in Group B.

Group A
1. Sp: plomo..... 2. fêmea.... 3. It: conte....
4. Fr: trembler.... 5. Eng: cucumber.... 6. Sp:
nombra.... 7. Fr: palombe..... 8. Ptg: isento....
9. It: sciame..... 10. Eng: number.....

Group B
1. Sp: cumbre 2. Fr: exempt 3. Fr: nomme 4. Eng:
encumber 5. Eng: scheme 6. Fr: comte 7. Sp: ausente
8. It: fémmina 9. Fr: nombre 10. Eng: plump 11. Ptg:
conta 12. Sp: enjambre 13. Eng: thimble 14. Fr: ombre
15. Eng: shame 16. Fr: concombre 17. Eng: member
18. Sp: paloma 19. It: piombo 20. Sp: temblar

RULE 24

-N-

Rule: In Portuguese, single intervocalic N disappeared during the tenth century, after first nasalizing the preceding vowel. The principal vowel combinations resulting from the loss of -N- developed as follows: -ĀNA contracted to -ã [ẽ]. -ĀNU, -ĀNE, -ŌNE, though in the plural respectively -ãos [-ẽús], -ães [-ẽĩs], -ões [-õĩs], were in the singular confused, the ending -ão serving for all three. (Thus cão 'dog' but cães 'dogs', lição 'lesson' but lições 'lessons'.) -ĒNA and -ĒNU gave -eia, -eio. -ĪNE gave -im [-ĩ]. -ŎNU gave -om [-õ]. -ĪNA and -ĪNU, after becoming -ĩa, -ĩo, developed a palatalized nasal to give -inha [-iɲɐ], -inho [-iɲú]. A similar nasalization of the preceding vowel, followed by loss of the N itself, occurred in French, too, but only if the N came to be final in a word or syllable (chien, chanter). Thus, for example, une bonne paysanne autrichienne [yn bɔn pejzan otriʃjɛn] but in the masculine un bon paysan autrichien [œ̃ bɔ̃ peizã otriʃjɛ̃].

	Italian	Spanish	Portuguese	French	English cognate
SANU 'healthy'	sano	sano	são	sain [sɛ̃]	sane
MANU 'hand'	mano	mano	mão	main [mɛ̃]	maintain
VANU 'vain'	vano	vano	vão	vain [vɛ̃]	vain
CANE 'dog'	cane	can ((perro))	cão	chien [ʃjɛ̃]	canine
PANE 'bread'	pane	pan	pão	pain [pɛ̃]	
LEŌNE 'lion'	leone	león	leão	lion [ljɔ̃]	lion

90

	Italian	Spanish	Portu- guese	French	English cognate
SAPŌNE 'soap'	sapone	jabón	sabão	savon [savɔ̃]	soap
PŬLMŌNE 'lung'	polmone	pulmón	pulmão	poumon [pumɔ̃]	pulmonary
PLANA 'flat ground'	piana	llana	chã	plaine [plɛ:n]	plain
LANA 'wool'	lana	lana	lã	laine [lɛ:n]	
PLĒNU 'full'	pieno	lleno	cheio	plein [plɛ̃]	plenary
VĒNA 'vein'	vena	vena	veia	veine [vɛ:n]	vein
CATĒNA 'chain'	catena	cadena	cadeia	chaîne [šɛ:n]	chain
VENĪRE 'to come'	venire	venir	vir	venir [v(ə)nir]	convention
TENĒRE 'to hold'	tenere	tener	ter	tenir [tənir]	tenacious, tenet
FĪNE 'end'	fine	fin	fim [fĩ]	fin [fɛ̃]	final
TONU 'sound'	tono (1.)	tono (1.)	tom [tɔ̃]	ton [tɔ̃]	tone
BONU 'good'	buono	bueno	bom [bɔ̃]	bon [bɔ̃]	bonbon
VĪNU 'wind'	vino	vino	vinho [viʸu]	vin [vɛ̃]	wine
CAMĪNU 'road'	camino	camino	caminho	chemin [š(ə)mɛ̃]	chimney
FARĪNA 'flour'	farina	harina	farinha	farine [farin]	farinaceous
VĪCĪNU 'neighbor'	vicino	vecino	vizinho	voisin [vwazɛ̃]	vicinity
MOLĪNU 'mill'	molino	molino	moinho	moulin [mulɛ̃]	mill, molar
VAGĪNA 'sheath'	guaina	vaina	bainha	gaine [gɛ:n]	vagina
SPĪNA 'thorn'	spina	espina	espinha	épine [epin]	spine
COCĪNA (for COQUĪNA) 'kitchen'	cucina	cocina	cozinha	cuisine [kʷizin]	kitchen

Note 1. The confusion between -ĀNE, -ŌNE, and -ĀNU also affected a few other words, like SANCTU 'saint' > San(to) > Ptg: São, NŌN 'not, no' Ptg: não.
Note 2. Portuguese pena, semana, castelhano, etc., are borrowings from Spanish. Menor, menos, feno 'hay' were reconstructed from Old Portuguese meor, meos, and feo, the latter perhaps in order to avoid confusion with meos MĒOS 'my (plur.)' and feo FOEDU 'ugly'. Words like fortuna, humano, tribuna, unir, and fenecer are erudite.
Note 3. In liaison, French final n̲ is preserved in addition to nasalizing the foregoing vowel, e.g. un bon ami [œ̃ bõ nami], on en est sûr [ɔ̃ nã nɛ sy:r].

Additional Exampl٤s

GERMĀNU 'brother' Sp: hermano Ptg: irmão
GERMĀNA 'sister' Sp: hermana Ptg: irmã
VERĀNU 'spring (adv.)' Sp: verano Ptg: verão 'summer'
MANE 'morning' plus -ĀNA Sp: mañana Ptg: manhã
RANA 'frog' Sp: rana Ptg: rã
AVELLANA 'hazelnut' Sp: avellana Ptg: avelã
(POMA) MATTĬĀNA 'type of apple' Sp: manzana Ptg: maçã
ARĒNA 'sand' Sp: arena Ptg: areia
CĒNA 'dinner' Sp: cena Ptg: ceia
CĔNTĒNU 'rye' Sp: centeno Ptg: centeio
PERSŌNA Sp: persona Ptg: pessoa
SŎNAT 'rings' Sp: suena Ptg: soa
PERDŌNAT Sp: perdona Ptg: perdoa
MONĒTA It: moneta Sp: moneda Ptg: moeda 'coin' Fr: monnaie Eng: money, mint
ANĔLLU 'ring' It: annello Sp: anillo Ptg: elo (via aelo)
GENĔSTA '(bot.) genista, broom' It: ginesta Sp: hiniesta Fr: genêt but Ptg: giesta
SĬNU 'fold, bosom' It, Sp: seno Ptg: seio Fr: sein [sɛ̃]
FĒMĬNA Sp: hembra Ptg: femea
SĔMĬNAT 'sows' Sp: siembra Ptg: semea
VANĬTŌSU 'conceited' Sp: vanidoso (s.l.) Ptg: vaidoso (s.l.)
*PANATĀRĬU Sp: panadero Ptg: padeiro 'baker'
PANĀTA (< PANE 'bread') Ptg: pada 'two or three loaves of bread sticking together, a batch'
GĔNĔRĀLE Sp: general Ptg: geral
GĔNĔRATĬŌNE Sp: generación Ptg: geração
VĔNĔRIA (< VENUS) Ptg: vieira 'shell, scallop'
CŬNĬCŬLU 'rabbit' Sp: conejo Ptg: coelho Eng: coney
LŪNA 'moon' Sp: luna Ptg: lua
FRAXĬNU '(bot.) ash' Sp: fresno Ptg: freixo
SŎNU 'sound, tune' Ptg: som
(E)LISĬPŌNE Ptg: Lisboa
BŎNA 'good (f.)' Sp: buena Ptg: boa
MAJ(Ŏ)RĪNU 'bailiff' Sp: merino Ptg: meirinho

GALLĪNA 'hen' It, Sp: gallina   Ptg: galinha   (O.Fr: geline,
cp. GALLU 'cock' O.Fr: gel)

Exercise

Opposite each of the words in Group A write down the number of its nearest cognate in Group B.

Group A
1. Fr: venir.... 2. Ptg: lição..... 3. Sp: manzana....
4. Fr: chaîne.... 5. It: pieno.... 6. Ptg: sabão....
7. Fr: laine.... 8. Ptg: fim.... 9. Ptg: manhã....
10. Eng: money.... 11. Fr: voisin.... 12. It: guaina....
13. Sp: cena.... 14. Ptg: verão.... 15. Eng: general....
16. Ptg: cão.... 17. Eng: vanity.... 18. Ptg: padeiro....
19. Sp: siembra.... 20. Ptg: fêmea....

Group B
1. Eng: scene 2. Ptg: lã 3. Fr: chien 4. Ptg: geral
5. Sp: sabían 6. Eng: five 7. Sp: maña 8. Ptg: cadeira
9. Fr: nous verrons 10. Sp: ver 11. Fr: semble 12. Ptg:
cheio 13. Sp: hombre 14. Fr: panier 15. Ptg: vir
16. Fr: maison 17. Sp: sábado 18. Ptg: ceia 19. Fr:
moine 20. Sp: fino 21. Ptg: semea 22. Sp: liceo 23. Eng:
canoe 24. Sp: jabón 25. Eng: fin 26. Sp: verano
27. Ptg: vaidade 28. Sp: mañana 29. Fr: veine 30. Eng:
lesson 31. Sp: panadero 32. Ptg: vizinho 33. Ptg:
cadeia 34. Eng: final 35. Sp: hembra 36. Ptg: moeda
37. Ptg: cem 38. Ptg: maçã 39. Ptg: lua 40. Ptg:
bainha

RULE 25

NS, PS, RS

Rule: That the changes NS > S [z] and PS, RS > SS [s] occurred very early is attested in numerous Roman inscriptions
and by the concordance of results in Modern Romance. In the
case of NS, the loss of the N was generally balanced by a closing of the preceding vowel.

	Italian	Spanish	Portu-guese	French	English cognate
MENSE 'month' (MĒSE)	mese [meẓe]	mes	mês	mois	mensual
INSŬLA 'island' (ĪSOLA)	isola [íẓola]	isla	ilha	île	isle
PRE(H)ENSU 'caught' (PRĒSU)	preso [prezo]	preso	preso	pris	apprehended
PAGENSE 'country (adj.)' (PAGĒSE)	paese [paeze]	país	país	pays	peasant
PENSĀRE 'to weigh' (PĒSĀRE)	pesare	pesar	pesar	peser	
CONSTĀRE 'to cost' (COSTĀRE)	costare	costar	custar	coûter	cost
METÍPSIMU 'self-same' (MĒTES(S)IMU)	medésimo	mismo (O.Sp: mesmo)	mesmo	même	
GYPSU 'plaster' (YESSU)	gesso	yeso	gesso	gypse (l.)	gypsum

94

	Italian	Spanish	Portu-guese	French	English cognate
PRŌRSA 'straight-forward (words)' (PRŌSA)	prosa	prosa	prosa	prose	prose
PERSĬCA 'Persian fruit, i.e. the peach' (PESSĬCA)	pesca	albérchigo*, prisca (met.)	pêssego	pêche	peach

*Albérchigo reached Spanish via Arabic, which does not differentiate between <u>p</u> and <u>b</u>. <u>Al</u>- is the Arabic definite article: 'the'.

Additional Examples

SPONSA 'betrothed' It: sposa Sp, Ptg: esposa Fr: épouse
  Eng: spouse
COHORTENSE 'courtly' It: cortese Sp: cortés Ptg: cortês
  Fr: courtois Eng: courteous
PENSU 'weight' It, Sp: peso Ptg: pêso Fr: poids (The <u>d</u>
  of poids is learned spelling based on a fancied derivation
  from PONDUS 'weight'.)
CONS(U)ĒRE 'to sew together' It: cucire Sp, Ptg: coser
  Fr: coudre (O.Fr: cosdre) Eng: suture
MENSA 'table' Sp, Ptg: mesa
MŎNSTRĀRE 'to show' It: mostrare Sp, Ptg: mostrar (but
  Fr: montrer, s.l.)
TRANS 'across, exceeding' It: tra Sp: tras 'after, beyond'
  Fr: très 'very'
(AD+) TRANSVERSĀRE 'to cross' Sp: atravesar Fr: traverser
  Eng: traverse
TRANSPASSĀRE 'to pass over' Fr: trépasser 'to pass away,
  die' Eng: trespass
*CONS(UE)TŪMĬNE (for -ŪDINE) 'habit' It: costume Sp:
  costumbre Ptg: costume Fr: coutume (Eng: custom)
*CONS(Ŭ)TŪRA (from CONSUTU 'sewn') It, Sp: costura
  'seam, stitch' Fr: couture 'sewing, seam' Eng: suture
MĬNĬSTĒRĬU 'employment, service' O.Fr: mestier Fr: métier
  'trade, occupation' (> It: mestiero)
CAPSA or CAPSĘA 'box' It: cassa Sp: caja Ptg: caixa Fr:
  caisse (Eng: case, capsule)
ĬPSU It: esso Sp: eso 'that'
ĬSTE plus ĬPSU 'that same' It: stesso 'same'
PERSŌNA Ptg: pessoa 'person'
ŬRSU Sp: oso 'bear'
VĔRSŪRA (from VERRĔRE 'to sweep') Sp: basura 'dirt,
  rubbish'
TRANSVĔRSU Sp: travieso 'transverse, (fig.) mischievous'
  (Eng: travesty is from TRANSVĔRSĬTĀTE)

MANSIŌNE 'dwelling' Fr: maison 'house' (> Sp: mesón 'tavern')
SENSU 'sense, feeling' Sp: seso 'brain'
TĔNSU Sp: tieso 'stiff, taut'
REVERS(Į)U It: rovescio Sp: revés Eng: reverse
(DĒ+) SŬRSU 'on top of' It: su Fr: dessus (O.Sp: suso)
DĔŌRSU (*DEŪRSU) 'under' It: siù (O.Sp: yuso)
DŌRSU 'back' Fr: dos Eng: dorsal, endorse

Exercise

Opposite each of the words in Group A write down the number of its nearest cognate in Group B.

Group A
1. It: medésimo.... 2. Fr: épouse.... 3. Eng: dorsal....
4. Sp: travieso..... 5. It: îsola... 6. Fr: pêché....
7. Ptg: cortês..... 8. It: peso.... 9. Sp: yeso....
10. Eng: reverse....

Group B
1. Sp: época 2. It: pesca 3. Fr: soleil 4. Sp: pecho
5. It: sposa 6. Eng: medicine 7. Ptg: costume 8. Fr:
dos 9. Sp: peso 10. Fr: courtois 11. Eng: gypsum
12. Ptg: preso 13. Sp: isla 14. Fr: coûter 15. Sp:
mismo 16. Ptg: pessoa 17. Sp: revés 18. Eng: transverse 19. It: corto 20. Sp: pecado

RULE 26

NY-, -GN- (MN, MNY)

Rule: Latin GN, NY gave in all four languages the sound [ɲ], spelled gn in Italian, ñ in Spanish, nh in Portuguese, and gn or ign in French. However, when [ɲ] came to be final in Old French, it reduced to [ẽ].

	Italian	Spanish	Portu-guese	French	English cognate
PŬGNU 'fist'	pugno	puño	punho	poing [pwẽ]	pugnacious
SĬGNU, SĬGNA 'sign'	segno 'sign'	seña 'sign'	senha 'sign'	seing 'signature' [sẽ]	sign, signal
ĬNSĬGNĀRE 'to show'	ensegnare	enseñar	ensinar (s.l.)	enseigner	ensign
DĬSDĬGNĀRE 'to scorn'	sdegnare	desdeñar	desdenhar	dédaigner	deign, disdain
SĔNĮŌRE 'older'	signore	señor	senhor	seigneur*	senior, sire, sir
HĬSPĀNĮA 'Spain'	Spagna	España	Espanha	Espagne	Spain
CASTĀNĘA 'chestnut'	castagna	castaña	castanha	châtaigne ((marron))	castanets
*ARANĘU, ARANĘA 'spider'	ragno	araña	aranha	araignée (ARANĘĀTA)	arachnid
BA(L)NĘĀRE 'to bathe'	bagnare	bañar	banhar	baigner	
BA(L)NĘU 'bath'	bagno	baño	banho	bain [bẽ]	

	Italian	Spanish	Portu-guese	French	English cognate
JŪN̯IU 'June'	giugno	junio (1.)	junho	juin [žyɛ̃]	June
CŬN̯EU 'wedge'	cúneo (1.)	cuño	cunha	coin [kwɛ̃]	coin
STANN̯EU 'lead and silver alloy'	stagno	estaño	estanho	étain [etɛ̃]	

*French, English sire derives from the nominative SĚN̯OR.

Note 1. MNY gives [ɣ] in Italian and Spanish: OMN̯IA 'all' It: ogna; OMNE > onne (see Note 2) > ogni (before a vowel at first, then generally); SŎMN̯IU 'dream' It: sogno Sp: sueño Ptg: sonho; CALŬMN̯IA 'slander' O.It: calogna Sp: caloña 'damage for slander'. In French the result is [~ž]: SŎMN̯IU Fr: songe; (LL) DŎM(Ῐ)N̯IŌNE 'stronghold' Fr: donjon Eng: dungeon; CALŬMN̯IA 'slander' O.Fr: chalonge Eng: challenge.

Note 2. MN gives n̲n̲ in Italian, ñ in Spanish, n̲ in Portu-guese, and m̲(m̲) in French: SŎMNŪ 'sleep' It: sonno Sp: sueño Ptg: sono Fr: sommeil (*SŎMNῙC(Ŭ)LU); DAMNU 'in-jury, loss' It: danno Sp: daño Ptg: dano Fr: dommage (*DAMNATῙCU); DŎMNA (for DŎMῙNA) 'mistress' It: donna Sp: dueña (doña when unstressed) Ptg: dona Fr: dame (DAMNA) Eng: dame; AŬTŬMNU It: autunno (s.l.) Sp: otoño Ptg: outono (Fr: automne [otɔn] is learned); SCAMNU 'stool' It: scanno Sp: escaño 'bench'

Semi-learned are Sp, Ptg: condenar CONDEMNĀRE. Sp: himno, alumno, columna are, of course, learned.

Additional Examples

IMPREGNĀRE 'to impregnate, fertilize' It: impregnare Sp: empreñar Ptg: emprenhar Fr: imprégner
LῙGNA 'firewood' It: legna Sp: leña Ptg: lenha
COGNĀTU 'related' It: cognato Sp: cuñado Ptg: cunhado 'brother-in-law'
COGN(Ῐ)TU 'known' O.Fr: coint(e) 'pleasing, pretty' Eng: quaint 'pleasantly strange or odd' (Note the reversal in meaning.)
TAM MAGNU 'so big' Sp: tamaño Ptg: tamanho 'size'
(MELO) COTON̯EU 'Cydonian apple tree' It: melo cotogno 'quince' Sp: melocotón 'peach' Fr: coing 'quince' (Eng: quince is taken from the O.Fr: plural)
PῙN̯EA 'pine (adj.)' It: pigna Sp: piña Ptg: pinha Fr: pigne 'pine cone'
CICŌN̯IA 'stork, crane' It: cicogna Sp: cigüeña Ptg: cegonha Fr: cigogne

*CANĘA (< CANE 'dog') It: cagna 'bitch'
*(L.L.)CATALONĮA It: Catalogna Sp: Cataluña Ptg: Cata-
lunha Fr: Catalogne (Eng: Catalonia)
VĪNĘA 'vineyard' It: vigna Sp: viña Ptg: vinha Fr: vigne
TĔNĘO It: tegno (tengo) Sp: tengo (orig. *teño) Ptg: tenho
VĔNĮO It: vegno (vengo) Sp: vengo Ptg: venho
MANE 'morning' (+ -ANA)_ Sp: mañana Ptg: manhã (but It:
domani Fr: demain < DĒ MĀNE)
*RĒNĮŌNES (for RĒNĒS) 'the kidneys' Sp: riñones (but It:
reni Ptg: rins Fr: reins < RĒNĒS)
LŬSCĪNĮŌLA 'nightingale' It: uscignuolo Sp: ruiseñor Ptg:
rouxinol Fr: rossignol
*ŬNĮŌNE (for ŪNĮŌNE) Fr: oignon Eng: onion
NĔ(C)ŪNU 'not one' ne uno > nįuno > It: gnuno 'nobody'

Exercise

Opposite each of the words in Group A write down the number of its nearest cognate in Group B.

Group A
1. Ptg: senhor.... 2. It: bagnare.... 3. Fr: coin....
4. Sp: araña.... 5. Eng: dame.... 6. Ptg: sonho....
7. It: danno.... 8. Sp: otoño.... 9. Fr: pigne....
10. Ptg: cunhado.... 11. It: legna.... 12. Eng: onion....
13. Sp: cigüeña.... 14. Fr: poing.... 15. Ptg: manhã....
16. It: uscignuolo.... 17. Eng: challenge.... 18. It:
giugno..... 19. It: impregnare.... 20. Sp: escaño....

Group B
1. Sp: dueña 2. Sp: caloña 3. Ptg: lenha 4. It: ogni
5. Sp: mañana 6. Eng: manna 7. Fr: danger 8. It:
signore 9. Ptg: emprenhar 10. Eng: ping-pong 11. Sp:
cuño 12. Eng: pin 13. Sp: empeñar 14. Fr: rossignol
15. Eng: malignant 16. Sp: puño 17. Eng: manner
18. It: scanno 19. Sp: caliente 20. It: ragno 21. Ptg:
tamanho 22. Fr: juin 23. Ptg: pinha 24. Sp: cuna
25. It: sono 26. Sp: sueño 27. Fr: chaleur 28. It:
gnuno 29. Ptg: banhar 30. Fr: somme 31. It: cognato
32. Fr: oignon 33. Eng: scan 34. Sp: arena 35. Ptg:
outono 36. Eng: join 37. Fr: cigogne 38. Sp: mano
39. Eng: quaint 40. Ptg: dano

RULE 27

Ŏ (VL ǫ)

Rule: In open syllables, an accented ǫ diphthongized to uó in Italian, to ue in Spanish, and eu, oeu [ø, œ] in French, but in closed syllables it diphthongized only in Spanish. In Portuguese, ǫ (like ę) did not diphthongize at all.

	Italian	Spanish	Portu-guese	French	English cognate
ŎVU (for ŌVU) 'egg'	uovo	huevo	ôvo	oeuf	ovum, ovary
NŎVU 'new'	nuovo	nuevo	novo	neuf	novel
MŎRĬT(UR) 'dies'	muore	muere	morre	meurt	mortal
JŎCU 'game'	giuoco	juego	jôgo	jeu	joke
PRŎBA 'proof'	prova (form. pruova)	prueba	prova	preuve	proof
BŎVE 'ox'	bue (plur. buoi)	buey	boi	boeuf	beef
MŎVET 'moves'	muove	mueve	move	meut	moves
PŎTĔT 'can'	può	puede	pode	peut	potential
MŎRDĬT 'bites'	morde	muerde	morde	mord	mordant
CŎRPU(S) 'body'	corpo	cuerpo	corpo	corps	corpse
ŎSSU 'bone'	osso	hueso	ôsso	os	ossified
CŎMPŬTAT 'calculates'	conta	cuenta	conta	compte	counts

Italian	Spanish	Portu- guese	French	English cognate
HŎSPĬTE 'guest, host'	óspite	huésped	hospede	hôte*	host
NŎCTE 'night'	notte	noche	noite	nuit (via *nueit)	nocturnal
FŎLĬA 'leaves'	foglia	hoja	folha	feuille	foliage
HŎDĬE 'today'	oggi	hoy	hoje	aujourd'hui (via *huei)	
CŎLLĬ(G)IT 'picks, plucks'	coglie	coge	colhe	cueille	culls
CŎRĬU 'leather, hide'	cuoio	cuero (via *coero)	coiro	cuir (via cueir)	excoriate, lit. 'to flay'
SŎMNĬU 'dream'	sogno	sueño	sonho	songe	
FŎRTĬA 'strength'	forza	fuerza	força	force	force

*For the final -e, see Rule 13, Note 7.

Note 1. In Spanish, but not in French, a yod of various types would 'close' the ǫ to ọ before it could break (noche, hoja, hoy, etc.) Exceptions to this are the yods that produced Spanish ñ and Spanish z (sueño, fuerza).

Note 2. In Italian, ǫ did not break after i (PLŎVET piove 'it rains'), nor before ggi or gli (HŎDĬE oggi, FŎLĬA foglia), nor generally in words stressed on the antepenult, such as ópera, pópolo.

Note 3. Not only does the u of Italian uó regularly disappear after consonant + r (pr(u)ova), but in all other cases uó and o are used interchangeably, e.g. b(u)ono, m(u)ove, n(u)ovo.

Note 4. In French, an ǫ would combine with a following yod to give first uei, then ui: NŎC(Ĕ)RE nuire 'to harm', CŎQ(ĬĔ)RE cuire 'to cook', ŎLĔA huile 'oil', ŎSTRĔA huître 'oyster', ŎCTŌ huit 'eight', CŎRĬU cuir 'leather'. The Spanish cuero is not a diphthongization of the ǫ (for the yod closed it to ọ, see Note 1) but the result of ọ + i was ói > óe > ué. See Rule 28.

Note 5. The Roman writer Priscian described as rustic a habit of saying FUNTES for FONTES, FRUNDES for FRONDES. This rustic trait of closing the ǫ before a nasal consonant survives in Italian (conta, conte, ponte, monte, fronte, compera, risponde, etc.), but in Spanish there is hesitation, e.g. contra, compra, monte, conde, respondo, hombre versus cuenta, fuente, puente.

Note 6. The stress pattern of the Latin present indicative and subjunctive (stem--stem--stem, ending--ending--stem) persists in Romance. When the stem vowel was ę or ǫ, the different development of stressed and unstressed forms is often striking. Compare Spanish quiére with querémos, cuélgo with colgámos. Oppositions of this type, common in Old French (quier:querons, fiert:ferons, prueves:pruvez), have in many cases been eliminated in Modern French by analogical levelling. Thus prueves became prouves by analogy with prouvóns, prouvér. But many so-called irregular verbs have resisted levelling to the present day. For example, tu viens but vous venez, j'acquiers but nous acquérons, je m'assieds but nous nous asseyons, vous mouvez but ils meuvent, je meurs but nous mourons, nous voulons but ils veulent.

Note 7. CŎLŎBRA culebra, FRŎNTE frente, FLŎCCU fleco 'fringe' have lost the labial element of their diphthong in Spanish due to dissimilation from another labial (b or f) in the same word.

Note 8. In Rumanian, ǫ often gives oa: ŎVE Rum: oae 'sheep', HŎMĬNE(S) Rum: oámeni 'men', HŎSPE(S) Rum: oaspe 'guest', HŎSTE Rum: oaste 'host, army', NŎCTE Rum: noapte 'night'; but ŎCTŌ Rum: opt 'eight'.

Additional Examples

LŎCU 'place' It: luogo 'place' Sp: luego 'then' Fr: lieu 'place' (by dissimilation from *lueu)

FŎCU 'hearth' It: fuoco Sp: fuego Ptg: fogo Fr: feu 'fire'

RŎTA 'wheel' It: ruota Sp: rueda Ptg: roda Fr: roue (RŌTA) Eng: rotate

NŎVEM 'nine' It: nove (dial. also nuove) Sp: nueve Ptg: nove Fr: neuf

CŎLŎBRA (for CŎLŬBER) 'snake' It: colubro Sp: culebra (via *culuebra) Ptg: cobra Fr: couleuvre

ŎPĔRA 'work' It: ópera Sp: obra, huebra '(agric.) a day's ploughing' Ptg: obra Fr: oeuvre

DŎLU 'grief' It: duolo Sp: duelo Fr: deuil (DŎLĮU)

ŎRPHĂNU 'orphan' Sp: huérfano but It: órfano Ptg: órfão Fr: orphelin

PŎPŬLU 'people' It: pópolo Sp: pueblo Ptg: povo Fr: peuple (s.l.)

JŎVĬS (DIĒS) 'Thursday' It: Giovedì (because the ǫ is unstressed) Sp: jueves Fr: jeudi

HŎMO 'man' It: uomo; HŎMĬNES 'men' It: uómini

SŎRŎR 'sister' (O.It: suoro) It: suora Fr: soeur

CŎR 'heart' It: cuore Fr: coeur (O.Sp: cuer) Ptg: de cor 'by heart' (Sp: corazón is from *CŎRATĮŌNE)

SŎCĔRA 'mother-in-law' It: suócera Sp: suegra Ptg: sogra

PŎS(Ĭ)TU 'placed' Sp: puesto

NŎRA (for NŬRU) 'daughter-in-law' It: nuora Sp: nuera

Exercise

Opposite each of the words in Group A write down the number of its nearest cognate in Group B.

Group A
1. It: muove..... 2. Fr: meurt.... 3. Ptg: boi...
4. Sp: huevo.... 5. Eng: joke.... 6. It: óspite....
7. Fr: peut.... 8. Ptg: cobra.... 9. Sp: cuenta....
10. Fr: feuille.... 11. It: coglie... 12. Ptg: roda
13. Sp: fuerza.... 14. Fr: soeur.... 15. It: suócera.....
16. Ptg: coiro.... 17. Fr: deuil.... 18. Sp: huérfano....
19. Ptg: nove..... 20. It: ópera....

Group B
1. Ptg: folha 2. Fr: neuve 3. Eng: force 4. It: fuoco
5. Sp: suegra 6. Fr: oeuvre 7. Sp: cobre 8. Eng: folly
9. Sp: mueve 10. Fr: comte 11. Sp: nuevo 12. It: duolo
13. Eng: buoy 14. Sp: hoy 15. Fr: boeuf 16. Ptg: órfão
17. Eng: sir 18. Sp: socio 19. It: suora 20. Fr: oeuf
21. Sp: hija 22. Sp: puede 23. It: cuore 24. Fr: cueille
25. Ptg: fogo 26. Sp: cuero 27. Ptg: povo 28. It: muore
29. Sp: jugo 30. Eng: hospital 31. Fr: neuf 32. Ptg: jogo
33. Eng: copra 34. Sp: huésped 35. Eng: boy 36. It:
ruota 37. Fr: coeur 38. Sp: culebra 39. Eng: devil
40. Fr: compte

RULE 28

Ō, Ŭ (VL ǫ)

Rule: In French, VL ǫ́ becomes eu [œ, ø] in open syllables, but in closed syllables o or ou [u]. The other three languages all show o.

	Italian	Spanish	Portu- guese	French	English cognate
FLŌRE 'flower'	fiore	flor	flor	fleur	flower
HŌRA 'hour'	ora	hora	hora	heure	hour
SŌLU 'alone'	solo	solo	só	seul	sole
FAMŌSU 'famous'	famoso	famoso	famoso	fameux	famous
GŬLA 'throat'	gola	gola	guela (*GŬLĔLLA)	gueule	gullet
ŬLMU 'elm'	olmo	olmo	olmo	orme	elm
ŬNDA 'wave'	onda	onda	onda	onde	undulate
BŬCCA 'mouth'	boca	boca	bôca	bouche	buccal
MŬSCA 'fly'	mosca	mosca	môsca	mouche	mosquito
FŬRNU 'oven'	forno	horno	forno	four	furnace
*CŌRTE 'court'	corte	corte	côrte	cour	court
PRŌRSA 'straightfor- ward (words)' as opposed to VERSA 'turned (words)'	prosa	prosa	prosa	prose	prose

Note 1. Free VL ǫ́ combined with a following n to give French -on [õ]: SAPŌNE 'soap' It: sapone Sp: jabón Ptg: sabão (see Rule 24) Fr: savon; RATIŌNE It: ragione Sp: razón Ptg: razão Fr: raison; DŌNU ;gift' Fr: don.

Note 2. VL ǫ́ combined with a following yod to give French oi: ANGŬSTIA angoisse 'anguish'; PARŌCHIA paroisse 'parish'; CŪNEU coin 'wedge'. In Spanish, ǫ́ + i̯ at first gave ói also, but this was later assimilated by the very common diphthong ué. Examples: A(U)GŬRIU 'omen' Sp: agüero Ptg: agoiro, agouro; SAL MŬRIA 'brine, pickle' Sp: salmuera Ptg: salmoira, salmoura; DŌRIU Sp: Duero.

Note 3. Before the accent, VL ǫ and ọ both give French ou or o: ŎPĔRĀRIU ouvrier; CŎRTĒSE courtois; SŬB(Ī)TĀNU soudain 'sudden'; GŬBĔRNĀRE gouverner 'to govern'; *SŬPĔRĀNU souverain 'sovereign'; *OBLĪTĀRE 'to forget' Fr: oublier; OBSTĀRE 'to thwart, prevent' Fr: ôter 'to remove'; OFFĔRĪRE Fr: offrir; ORATIŌNE 'speech' Fr: oraison 'oration'.

Additional Examples

MĔLIŌRE 'better' It: migliore Sp: mejor Ptg: melhor
Fr: meilleur
ĬMPĔRATŌRE 'emperor' O.Fr: empere(d)our Fr: empereur
Sp: emperador
NĔPŎTE 'grandchild, nephew' It: nipote Fr: neveu (Sp: nieto Ptg: neto come from a contracted *NĔPTU)
PA(V)ŌRE It: paúra Fr: peur 'fear'
(IL)LŌRU 'their' It: loro Fr: leur
PASTŌRE 'shepherd' It: pastore Sp, Ptg: pastor Fr: pasteur
VŌTA 'vows' Sp, Ptg: boda 'wedding'
CŬBĬTU 'cubit, elbow' It: gómito Sp: cǫdo ((Ptg: cotovelo)) Fr: coude 'elbow'
GŬTTA 'drop' It: gotta 'gout' Sp: gota Ptg: gota Fr: goutte 'drop, gout' Eng: gout, gutter
RŬPTU 'broken' It: rotto Sp: roto Ptg: roto Fr: route (RŬPTA (VĪA)) 'broken road' hence 'direction, course') Eng: rout, route
PŬRPŬRA 'purple' It: pórpora Fr: purpre Eng: purple
CŌGĬTĀRE Sp: cuidar 'to take care of, mind'
PŬLLU 'chicken' It: pollo 'fowl' Sp: pollo 'chicken' Fr: poule (PŬLLA) 'hen' Eng: pullet

Exercise

Opposite each of the words in Group A write down the number of its nearest cognate in Group B.

Group A
1. Fr: four... 2. Sp: gola.... 3. Eng: sole....
4. Ptg: môsca.... 5. It: pollo..... 6. Fr: bouche...

7. Sp: codo....   8. Fr: meilleur...   9. It: nipote...
10. Eng: purple

Group B
1. Eng: code   2. Sp: boca   3. Fr: coude   4. It: pópolo
5. Eng: four   6. Fr: pourpre   7. Sp: pueblo   8. Fr:
mouche   9. Ptg: cada   10. Fr: neveu   11. Fr: poule
12. Sp: suelo   13. Fr: gueule   14. Eng: mosque   15. Sp:
boga   16. It: forno   17. Eng: soil   18. Sp: mejor   19. Fr:
seul   20. Eng: mayor

RULE 29

-P-, -B-, -V-

Rule: Between vowels, -B- and -V- both gave VL [β]. The sound persists in Spanish with both spellings. Everywhere else the result is [v]. P between vowels usually survives in Italian, but sometimes becomes v̱ as in French. The Peninsular languages developed -P- to ḇ.

	Italian	Spanish	Portu- guese	French	English cognate
SAPŌNE 'soap'	sapone	jabón	sabão	savon	soap
SAPĒRE 'to know'	sapere	saber	saber	savoir	savant
RĪPA 'bank, shore'	ripa, riva	riba 'embank- ment'	riba 'embank- ment'	rive 'bank'	
COPĔRTU 'closed'	coperto, coverto	cubierto	coberto	couvert	covert
EPĬSCŎPU 'bishop'	véscovo	obispo	bispo	evêque (via evésqueve)	Episcopalian
CAPŲ (for CAPŬT) 'head'	capo	cabo	cabo	chef* (O.Fr: chief)	chief, chef
CABALLU 'horse'	cavallo	caballo	cavalo	cheval	cavalry
FĀBA 'bean'	fava	haba	fava	fève	
PROBĀRE 'to prove'	provare	probar	provar	prouver	prove
HABĒRE 'to have'	avere	haber	haver	avoir	
DĒBĒRE 'to owe'	dovere	deber	dever	devoir	debt, debit
SCRĪBĔTĬS 'you write'	scrivete	escribís	escreveis	écrivez	scribe, script

107

Italian	Spanish	Portu-guese	French	English cognate
LAVĀRE 'to wash'	lavare	lavar	lavar	laver	lave, lavatory
VĪVĔRE 'to live'	vívere	vivir	viver	vivre	survive
NŎVU 'new'	nuovo	nuevo	novo	neuf*	novice
ŎVU 'egg'	novo	huevo	ôvo	oeuf*	oval
CLĀVE 'key'	chiave	llave	chave	clef*	clef

*Old French developed -P- > -b- > -v-, which, when final, always unvoiced to f.

Note 1. APOTHĒCA It: bottega 'shop', EPĬPHANĪA It: befanía 'Epiphany' illustrate the curious case of a consonant checked midway in its passage from P > v by the fall of the initial syllable.

Note 2. Occasionally, -V- shows a tendency to fall in Romance, especially in the common suffix -ĪVU. VACĪVU 'empty' Sp: vacío Ptg: vazio; RĪVU 'brook, river' It: rivo, rio Sp: río; AESTĪVU 'summer (adj.)' It: estivo, estio Sp: estío Ptg: estio; TARDĪVU 'tardy, late' Sp: tardío Ptg: tardio (but It: tardivo Fr: tardif); NATĪVU 'simple, natural' It: natio, nativo (but Fr: naïf Eng: naïve). In French, [v] sometimes disappeared in contact with a back vowel: *SAPŪTU 'known' O.Fr: soü, seü Fr: su; *DĒBŪTU O.Fr: deu Fr: dû; HABŪTU eu; MOVŪTU mu; PAVŌRE peur; CLĀVU clou (O.Fr: clo); PAVŌNE 'peacock' paon; *AĮVŎLU (for AVĮŎLU) aïeul 'grand-father, ancestor'; LŬPU 'wolf' O.Fr: leu (Mod: loup), but LŬPA 'she-wolf' Fr: louve; NOVĔLLU 'news, tidings' Fr, Eng: Noël.

Note 3. In Rumanian, both -B- and -V- tend to fall: CABALLU Rum: cal 'horse'; LAVĀBAT Rum: la 'washed'; JŪRĀBAT Rum: jurá 'swore'; ŎVE Rum: oae 'sheep'; CĪVĬTĀTE Rum: cetate 'city'.

Additional Examples

SAPŌRE 'taste' It: sapore 'taste (savore 'sauce') Sp, Ptg: sabor Fr: saveur Eng: savor
CAPĬLLU 'hair' It: capello Sp: cabello Ptg: cabelo Fr: cheveu Eng: disheveled
*PŌPĔRE (for PAUPĔRE) 'poor' It: póvero Sp, Ptg: pobre Fr: pauvre
CŪPA 'pail' Sp: cuba Fr: cuve
TRĬPĔDES 'trivet, tripod' Sp: trébedes 'three-legged stool' (In It: treppiede Fr: trépieds the accent shifted to the PĔD-, whose P was treated as initial.)

PRAEPŎS(Ĭ)TU 'superior' It: preposto (prevosto) Sp, Ptg: preboste** Fr: prévôt (Eng: provost Germ: Probst stem from a form PROPŎS(Ĭ)TU)
NĔPŌTE 'grandchild, nephew' It: nipote Fr: neveu (Sp: nieto Ptg: neto 'grandson' are from *NEP(O)T(U)
AP(ŬD H)ŎC O.Fr: avuec Fr: avec 'with'
GŬBĔRNĀRE 'to govern' It: governare Sp: gobernar Ptg: governar Fr: gouverner Eng: govern
CERĔBĔLLU 'brain' It: cervellò Fr: cerveau
HĪBĔRNU 'winter (adj.)' It: inverno Sp: invierno Ptg: inverno Fr: hiver Eng: hibernate
CŬBĪLE 'lair' It: covile Sp: cubil (1.)
AB ANTE It: avanti Fr: avant 'forwards, before'
AB ŎC(Ŭ)LU Fr: aveugle (s.1.) 'blind'
DĒBĬTA 'debt' Ptg: divida (s.1.)
DŪBĬTA 'doubt' Ptg: duvida (s.1.)
CAPTĪVU 'captive' It: cattivo 'bad, wicked' Sp: cautivo 'captive'
VĪVU 'alive, active' It, Sp, Ptg: vivo Fr: vif
JŎVĪS DIĒS 'Jupiter's day' It: Giovedî Sp: jueves Fr: jeudi 'Thursday'

**Question: How can we tell that Sp: preboste is borrowed from French?

Exercise

Opposite each of the words in Group A write down the number of its nearest cognate in Group B.

Group A
1. Sp: haber.... 2. Fr: fève.... 3. It: vivo....
4. Ptg: cabo..... 5. Sp: jabón.... 6. Fr: tardif....
7. Sp: huevo.... 8. Ptg: cabelo..... 9. It: sapore....
10. Fr: écrivez....

Group B
1. Fr: cheveu 2. Eng: saber 3. Fr: savon 4. It: cavallo
5. Sp: haba 6. Fr: cuve 7. Sp: escribís 8. Eng: tart
9. Fr: avoir 10. Fr: saveur 11. Eng: cable 12. It: vif
13. Fr: jambon 14. Eng: fief 15. Fr: oeuf 16. Eng: cavil
17. Ptg: tardio 18. Sp: bebo 19. Fr: avare 20. Eng: chief

RULE 30

PL - (CL-, FL-)

Rule: PL-, CL- FL- have developed i [j] for l in Italian.
In Spanish and Portuguese, the three result in ll- [ʎ] and ch-
[š], respectively. French shows no change.

	Italian	Spanish	Portu-guese	French	English cognate
PLĒNU 'full'	pieno	lleno	cheio	plein	replenish
*PLOVĒRE (for PLUERE) 'to rain'	piovere	llover	chover	pleuvoir	--
PLUVIA 'rain'	pioggia*	lluvia	chuva	pluie	pluvial
PLICĀRE 'to fold, fold one's sails'	piegar 'fold'	llegar 'arrive'	chegar 'arrive'	plier 'fold'	ply
PLANTA 'plant'	pianta	llanta 'cabbage; tire'	chanta 'vine-prop'	plante	plant
PLŌRĀRE 'weep, cry'	((piangere)) (PLANGĔRE)	llorar	chorar	pleurer	implore
PLANCTU 'weeping'	pianto	llanto	pranto (O.Ptg: chanto)	plainte (PLANCTA)	complaint, plaintiff
CLAMARE 'to call'	chiamare	llamar	chamar	clamer 'to shout'	clamor, claim
CLAVE 'key'	chiave	llave	chave	clef	
FLAMMA 'flame'	fiamma	llama	chama	flamme	flame

*For the -ggi, see Rule 32, note 3.

110

Note 1. While in Spanish and Portuguese this change occurs in certain popular words only, in Italian it is not only regular, but affects BL- and GL- also, e.g. It: bianco BLANCU 'white', ghiacciaio GLACIĀRIU 'glacier'. It even occurs medially, e.g. doppio DŬPLU 'double'; esempio EXEMPLU 'example'.

Note 2. In Portuguese, a consonant plus L quite often gives consonant plus r. For example, PLACĒRE Sp: placer Ptg: prazer 'pleasure'; PLATEA 'street' Sp: plaza Ptg: praça 'square'; PLAGA 'wound' Sp: llaga Ptg: praga; *PLATTA Sp: plata Ptg: prata 'silver'; ĬMPLĬCARE Sp: emplear Ptg: empregar 'to employ'; DŬPLU 'double' Sp: doble Ptg: dobre; *ECLĒSIA (for ECCLĒSIA) Sp: iglesia Ptg: igreja 'church' (but note FIDĒLE ECLĒSIAE 'parishioner' Sp: feligrés); BLANDU 'soft' Sp: blando Ptg: brando. BLANCU 'white' Sp: blanco Ptg: branco; GLŪTEN 'glue' Ptg: grude Fr: glu Eng: glue; RĒG(Ŭ)LA 'rule' Sp: regla (s.l.) Ptg: regra; CLĀVU 'nail' Sp: clavo Ptg: cravo Fr: clou; FLACCU 'weak' Sp: flaco Ptg: fraco. In general, this Portuguese development occurs in those same words which in Spanish do not result in ll-, i.e. in learned or semi-learned words.

Note 3. There are a few instances of FL-, GL- > l- in Spanish and Portuguese: FLACCĬDU 'limp' Sp: lacio; FLĀVIĀNA Sp: Laviana; GLATTĪRE 'to yelp' Sp, Ptg: latir but It: ghiattire Fr: glapir (*GLAPPĪRE); GLANDE or GLANDŬLA 'acorn; gland, tumor' Sp: landre Ptg: lande but It: ghianda Fr: gland; GLAREA 'gravel' Sp: glera (dial. lera) Ptg: leira 'flower bed' but It: ghiaia. There is at least one example of GL- > l- in French: GLĪRE or *GLĪRŌNE 'dormouse' It: ghiro Sp: lirón Ptg: lirão Fr: loir.

Additional Examples

PLAGA 'wound, sore' It: piaga Sp: llaga Ptg: praga Fr: plaie Eng: plague
PLANU 'flat' It: piano Sp: llano Ptg: chao Fr: plain Eng: plain
PLŬMBU 'lead' It: piombo Sp: plomo Ptg: chumbo Fr: plomb Eng: plumbing
PLŬV- 'rain' plus -ASCU It: piovasco Ptg: chubasco (> Sp: chubasco) 'shower, squall'
CLŎC (onomat.) 'a hen's cluck' It: chioccia Sp: llueca 'brooding hen' Ptg: choca 'bell-cow'
CLAŲSA 'enclosure' Sp: llosa 'fenced-in field' Ptg: chousa 'enclosed garden'
FLŌRE 'flower' O.Ptg: chor (but modern flor), *FLŌRŪTU 'flowery, opulent' Ptg: chorudo 'succulent'
FLAMMŬLA 'Little Flame' Ptg: Chamoa
FLAGRĀRE (for FRAGRĀRE) 'to smell' Ptg: cheirar 'to scent, smell' (cp. Ptg: cheiro 'scent, odor' Fr, Eng: flair 'keen olfactory sense')

AFFLĀRE, *FAFFLĀRE 'to sniff out' Sp: hallar Ptg: achar
'find' (Note that Sp: echar de menos 'to miss' is a corruption
of Ptg: achar menos 'to find missing'.)
PLŮTE̦A 'shed' Ptg: choça (> Sp: choza) 'hut, cottage'
Italian: chiesa (E)CLĒSIA 'church'; fiévole FLĒBĬLE 'feeble',
Fiandra 'Flanders', fiacco FLACCU 'flaccid, weak'; ghiaia
GLARE̦A 'gravel' (Sp: glera); fiume FLŪMEN 'river'; più
PLŪS 'more'; piuma PLŪMA 'feather'; pianeta PLANĒTA
'planet'; piazza PLATE̦A 'square'

Exercise

Opposite each of the words in Group A write down the number of its nearest cognate in Group B.

Group A
1. Sp: plomo.... 2. It: pieno.... 3. Fr: plume....
4. Sp: llano.... 5. Eng: plague.... 6. Ptg: chama....
7. Sp: lluvia.... 8. It: ghianda.... 9. Eng: example....
10. Ptg: achar.... 11. Eng: flair.... 12. Sp: plata....
13. Fr: pleurer.... 14. Eng: glacier.... 15. It: chiesa....
16. Fr: plus.... 17. Ptg: chegar.... 18. Ptg: fraco....
19. Eng: employ.... 20. Ptg: grude....

Group B
1. Eng: glass 2. Sp: llorar 3. Ptg: pranto 4. It: fiamma
5. Ptg: praça 6. Eng: glue 7. Sp: frac 8. Fr: clou
9. Eng: pliers 10. Ptg: chumbo 11. Fr: acheter 12. Eng:
cheese 13. Ptg: grande 14. Sp: lleno 15. Ptg: empregar
16. It: piaga 17. Fr: fiacre 18. Eng: prate 19. Fr: clef
20. It: esempio 21. Eng: plum 22. Sp: hallar 23. Eng:
gland 24. Ptg: prata 25. Ptg: chanta 26. Sp: llegar
27. Ptg: cheiro 28. It: pioggia 29. Eng: flock 30. It:
più 31. Eng: plain 32. Ptg: igreja 33. Sp: enjambre
34. It: piuma 35. It: ghiacciaio 36. Eng: shame 37. Sp:·
llanto 38. Fr: fleur 39. It: fiasco 40. Eng: clove

RULE 31

PT

Rule: Latin PT gives Italian t̲t̲, Spanish t̲ or u̲t̲ (s.l.), Portuguese t̲, i̲t̲, or u̲t̲, French p̄t, t̲t̲, or t̲ (all p̄ronounced [t]).

	Italian	Spanish	Portu-guese	French	English cognate
SĔPTEM 'seven'	sette	siete	sete	sept	septet
SCRĪPTU 'written'	scritto	escrito	escrito	écrit	script
RŬPTU 'broken'	rotto	roto	roto	route (RŬPTA VĬA)	route, rout, rupture
CAPTĪVU 'captive'	cattivo 'bad'	cautivo 'captive'	captivo (l.), cativo	chétif 'mean, worthless'	captive, caitiff
BAPTĬZARE 'to baptize'	battezzare	bautizar	O.Ptg: boutiçar	baptiser	baptize
RECEPTA 'receipt'	((ricevuta))	receta	receita	recette	receipt

Note: The Romance groups P'T, P'D, B'T, V'T give Spanish u̲d̲ or d̲. In French, the separating vowel generally dropped ou̲t before the T had a chance to voice between vowels, so the t̲ generally remains. Examples: CAPĬTĔLLU 'little chief' (O.Sp: cabdiello) Sp: caudillo; CAPĬTĀLE 'capital' (O.Sp: cabdal) Sp: caudal 'wealth' (O.Fr: chatel Norm.-Picard: catel) Eng: cattle, chattle 'goods and cattle, livestock'; RAPĬDĀLE 'rapids' Sp: raudal 'torrent'; CŬPĬDĬTĬA 'avarice, greed' (O.Sp: cobdiçia) Sp: codicia (cp. Mexican Sp: codo CŬPĬDU 'stingy'); DŬBĬTA 'doubt' (O.Sp: dubda) Sp: duda

113

Fr: doute; DĒBĬTA 'debt' (O.Sp: debda) Sp: deuda Fr: dette (the silent b of Eng: doubt, debt is an etymological spelling); CŬBĬTU 'elbow, cubit' Sp: codo Fr: coude; *SŬBĬTĀNU (for SŬBĬTĀNĘU) Fr: soudain Eng: sudden; LĒVĬTĀRE 'to leaven' Sp: leudar, lleudar; CĪVĬTĀTE 'state' (O.Sp: cibdat) Sp: ciudad Fr: cité Eng: city. MPT, MP'T give Romance nt TĔMPTĀRE It: tentare Sp, Ptg: tentar Fr: tenter 'to try; tempt'; CŎMP(Ŭ)TĀRE 'to calculate' It: contare Sp, Ptg: contar Fr: compter 'to count', conter 'to recount, tell'; PRŌMPTU 'ready, quick' It, Sp, Ptg: pronto Fr: prompt [prɔ̃].

Additional Examples

SĔPTĬMU 'seventh' Sp, Ptg: sétimo (L.) Fr: septième
CONCEPTU Ptg: conceito Eng: conceit
PRAECEPTU Ptg: preceito 'precept'
CAPTĀRE 'to take in (with the eyes)' Sp, Ptg: catar 'to examine'
AEGYPT(Į)ĀNU 'Egyptian' Sp: gitano Eng: gypsy
APTĀRE 'to adjust' Sp, Ptg: atar 'to tie'
NŬPTĮAE It: nozze Fr: noces 'wedding'
*NĔPTU (for NĔPŌTE) 'grandson, nephew' Sp: nieto Ptg: neto
SŬBTĪLE It: sottile Sp: sútil (l.) Fr: soutil Eng: subtle (with silent b)
SŬBTŬS 'under' It: sotto Fr: sous
BĬBĬTU 'drunk' (O.Sp: bebdo, beudo, béodo) Sp: beodo 'intoxicated' (but Ptg: bêbedo)
APŎTHĒCA 'storeroom' Ptg: adega 'cellar' (via abdega) (An alternative development was bodega 'canteen', as in Sp.)
ABSENTE 'absent' Sp: ausente

Exercise

Opposite each of the words in Group A write down the number of its nearest cognate in Group B.

Group A
1. Eng: script.... 2. Sp: deuda.... 3. Fr: cité.....
4. It: cattivo.... 5. Ptg: bêbedo.... 6. Fr: compter......
7. Sp: duda.... 8. Sp: caudal.... 9. Ptg: sete......
10. Eng: prompt....

Group B
1. It: contare 2. Eng: cite 3. Eng: chattle 4. It: coda
5. Sp: cita 6. Fr: écrit 7. Ptg: pronto 8. Sp: gato
9. Fr: sept 10. Eng: dude 11. Eng: vivid 12. Fr: doute
13. Sp: beodo 14. Eng: compost 15. Fr: chétif 16. Sp: imprenta 17. Eng: debt 18. It: védova 19. Sp: ciudad
20. Eng: chatter

RULE 32

PY, RY, SY (BY, MY, VY)

Rule: PY doubles in Italian to ppy, palatalizes in French to ch [š]. Spanish and Portuguese popularly transpose the yod to the preceding syllable, where it combines to form a diphthong (SAPIAM > *saipa > seipa > Sp: sepa). In the case of RY and SY, French joins Spanish and Portuguese in transposing the yod to the preceding syllable. (Note especially -ARIU Fr: -ier; -ORIU (> oiro) > Sp: -uero; -ASIU Ptg: -eijo; -ESIU Ptg: -ejo). Italian does not transpose. Instead, RY goes to y, SY palatalizes to gi [dž]. Cacio and bacio show irregular development. Chiesa goes back to a thirteenth and fourteenth century fashion for dropping the yod after l, n, r, and s, as in It: strano EXTRANEU 'strange' or vangélo EVANGELIU 'gospel'.

	Italian	Spanish	Portu-guese	French	English cognate
SAPIAM '(subjunct.) I know'	sappia	sepa	saiba	sache	
SEPIA 'cuttlefish'	seppia	jibia (s.l.)	siba (via *seiba)	seiche	sepia
APIU 'parsley, celery'	appio	apio (l.)	aipo (s.l.)	ache 'wild celery'	(bot.) apium
AREA 'surface, threshing floor'	aia	era	eira	aire	area
PRIMARIU 'first'	primaio ((primo))	primero	primeiro	premier	primer
OPERARIU 'worker'	operaio	obrero	obreiro	ouvrier	operator
CAL(I)DARIA 'cauldron'	caldaia	caldera	caldeira	chaudière (Eng. chowder)	cauldron

	Italian	Spanish	Portu-guese	French	English cognate
CŎRĮU 'leather'	cuoio	cuero	coiro, couro	cuir	excoriate, (lit.) to flay
(SAL) MŬRĮA 'brine, pickle'	moia	salmuera	salmoira, salmoura	saumure (via *salmuire)	
AŲGŬRĮU 'omen'	augurio (1.)	agüero	agoiro, agouro	-heur (as in bonheur, malheur)	augur
BASĮĀRE 'to kiss'	baciare	besar	beijar	baiser	
CASĘU 'cheese'	cacio	queso	queijo	((fromage FORMATĬCU))	cheese
*CERĔSĘA 'cherry'	ciliegia*	cereza	cereja	cerise	cherry
E(C)CLĔSĮA 'church'	chiesa	iglesia (s.l.) (O.Sp: eglisa, egrija)	igreja	église	ecclesiastical

*Ciriegio 'cherry tree'.

Note 1. In Spanish SAPĮAM sepa, CAPĮAM quepa, the yod jumped early enough to protect the P from voicing, whereas in Portuguese saiba, caiba, the jump occurred too late even to allow the resulting diphthong to go on to ei like the ai from -ARĮU or -ASĮU.

Note 2. French regularly develops BY, VY to ge [ž] and MY, MBY to nge [~ž]. Examples: RŬBĘU rouge; *RABĮA (for RABĮĒS) Fr, Eng: rage; Gmc: laubja Fr: loge Eng: lodge; TĪBĮA tige; CAVĘA cage; SALVĮA sauge Eng: sage; *LĒVĮĀRĮU léger; SĔRVĮENTE sergent Eng: sergeant; *DĪLŬVĮU déluge; SĪMĮA singe 'monkey'; VĪNDĒMĮA vendange; COMMĘĀTU congé 'leave'; CAMBĮARE changer Eng: change; PLŬMBĮĀRE plonger Eng: plunge.

Note 3. In Italian, just as PY doubles to ppy, so BY and VY (both [βj] in VL) double to bby and MY doubles to mmy: *RABĮA rabbia; HABĘAT abbia; LĀBĮA labbia; OBJECTU obbietto; CAVĘA gabbia; SĪMĮA scimmia; VĮNDĒMĮA vendemmia. After consonants, however, the groups remain: CAMBĮARE cambiare; SALVĮA salvia; COMMĘĀTU commiato. Forms with [ddž] like FOVĘA foggia 'pit, snare'; Gmc: laubja loggia; RŬBĘU roggio; *LĒVĮĀRĮU leggero; *PLŎVĮA pioggia are borrowings from Sicilian, Provençal, or French.

Note 4. Though in Spanish the popular development of BY and VY is to y (FŎVĘA hoya 'pit'; RŬBĘA roya '(bot.) rust, red blight'), examples are rare. In most cases VY, BY, and MY remain, but exert a closing influence on the preceding

vowel: LABĮU labio; RŬBĘU rubio; CAVĘA gavia; PLŬVĮA
lluvia; PRAEMĮU premio; VĪNDĒMĮA vendimia. SĒPĮA jibia,
CĒRĘU cirio 'wax taper' show the same phenomenon. But
Portuguese regularly transposes the yod of BY, VY and MY:
*RABĮA Ptg: raiva; RŬBĘU Ptg: ruivo; CAVĘA Ptg: gaiva;
VĪNDĒMĮA Ptg: vindima (cp. SĒPĮA > *seiba > siba).

Additional Examples

PROPĮU, PROPĮĀNU, ADPROPĮĀRE Fr: proche, prochain,
   approcher Eng: approach
GLARĘA 'gravel' It: ghiaia Sp: glera Ptg: leira 'flowerbed'
DŬRMĬTŌRĮU 'dormitory' Fr: dortoir
GLŌRĮA Fr: gloire 'glory'
HĬSTŌRĮA It: storia (s.l.) Fr: histoire 'history'
PĪSTŌRĮU It: Pistoia
PARĮA 'pairs' It: paia
MATĒRĮA 'timber' Sp: madera Ptg: madeira 'wood, timber'
STŌRĘA 'a rush mat' It: stoia Sp: estera (via *estuera
   influenced by -ĀRĮU)
DORĮU Sp: Duero
TONSĮŌNE 'shearing' Fr: toison 'fleece'
AMBROSĮU It: Ambrogio Fr: Ambroise Eng: Ambrose
OCCASĮŌNE It: cagione 'cause' (O.Fr: ochoison 'opportunity')
MA(N)SĮŌNE Fr: maison
Gmc. kausjan 'to choose' Fr: choisir
PREHENSĮŌNE, *PRĒSĮŌNE It: prigione 'prison, prisoner'
   Sp: prisión (s.l.) Fr, Eng: prison
CĒRVĪSĮA 'beer' It: cervigia Sp: cerveza Ptg: cerveja
   (O.Fr: cervoise)
(Low Latin) GŬBĮA 'gouge' Sp: gubia Ptg: goiva Fr, Eng:
   gouge
PE(N)SĮŌNE It: pigione 'rent'
PHASĮANA It: fagiana 'pheasant' Fr: faisan Eng: pheasant
ANASTASĮU It: Anastagio
SEGŪSĮU 'bloodhound' It: segugio Sp: sabueso Ptg: sabujo
NAŲSĘA O.Fr, Eng: noise
*FRAMBŌSĮA 'raspberry' Sp: frambuesa Fr: framboise

Exercise

Opposite each of the words in Group A write down the number of its nearest cognate in Group B.

Group A
1. Sp: caldera.... 2. Fr: sache..... 3. It: cervigia....
4. Ptg: aipo.... 5. Fr: faisan.... 6. It: seppia....
7. Sp: cambiar.... 8. Fr: baiser.... 9. Eng: Ambrose....
10. It: cacio.... 11. Sp: obrero.... 12. It: salvia....

13. Fr: cuir.... 14. Ptg: igreja.... 15. It: gabbia....
16. Fr: singe..... 17. Ptg: raiva.... 18. Fr: vendange....
19. It: ghiaia.... 20. Sp: frambuesa....

Group B
1. Fr: changer 2. Fr: chambre 3. Ptg: queijo 4. Fr:
ouvrir 5. Eng: rage 6. Sp: joya 7. Sp: selva 8. Sp:
sepa 9. Fr: cerveau 10. It: vendemmia 11. Eng: bandage
12. Sp: glera 13. Fr: seiche 14. It: cuore 15. Eng:
catch 16. It: operaio 17. Fr: rive 18. Ptg: cerveja
19. Fr: chaudière 20. Eng: queer 21. It: appio 22. Eng:
singe 23. Fr: cache 24. It: fagiana 25. Fr: framboise
26. It: cuoio 27. Sp: bajo 28. Fr: flambeaux 29. Fr:
église 30. Eng: egress 31. It: scimmia 32. Eng: base
33. Fr: sauge 34. Eng: jabber 35. Ptg: gaiva 36. Sp:
Amberes 37. Eng: vintage 38. It: Ambrogio 39. Eng:
gavel 40. Ptg: beijar

RULE 33

QU̯ (GU̯)

Rule: Latin QU̯, GU̯ may be regarded as velar consonants [k,g] combined with lip-rounding [w]. Lip-rounding was normally kept in Italian; Spanish and Portuguese normally retained it before the vowel a̱; French lost it entirely (qu = [k]). Between vowels, QU̯'s velar̄ element [k] voiced to [g] in Italian, Spanish, and Portuguese. The French treatment of QU̯ between vowels is irregular, though in Old French the result was usually v̱ (cp. VĬDU̯A 'widow' O.Fr: ve(d)ve Fr: veuve).

	Italian	Spanish	Portu-guese	French	English cognate
*QU̯ATTRO (for QUÁTTU̯OR) 'four'	quattro [kwa-]	cuatro [kwa-]	quatro [kwa-]	quatre [ka-]	
QU̯ANDO 'when'	quando	cuando	quando	quand	
QU̯ALE 'what kind of'	quale	cual	qual	quel	quality
QU̯ARTU 'quarter'	quarto	cuarto	quarto	quart	quart
QU̯ATT(U)ORDĔCĬM 'fourteen'	quattordici	catorce		catorze	quatorze
QŬADRAGĬNTA 'forty'	quaranta	cuarenta	quarenta	quarante	quarantine
QU̯ĪNDĔCĬM 'fifteen'	quindici	quince	quinze	quinze	
*CĪNQU̯A(G)ĬNTA (for QU̯ĪNQU̯AGĬNTA) 'fifty'	cinquanta	cincuenta (O. Sp: cinquaénta)		cinqüenta	cinquante
*CĪNQU̯E (for QU̯ĪNQU̯E) 'five'	cinque	cinco	cinco	cinq [sɛ̃k]	

	Italian	Spanish	Portuguese	French	English cognate
AEQŲALE 'equal'	eguale, uguale	igual	igual	égal (s.l.) (O.Fr: ivel)	equal
AQŲA 'water'	acqua (*ACQŲA)	agua	agua	eau (O.Fr: aigue, aive, eve)	aquatic
AQŲĀRĮU,-A (from ĄQUA 'water')	acquaio 'sink'	agüera 'irrigation ditch'	agüeiro 'gutter, drain'	évier 'sink'	aquarium
SEQŲENTE 'following'	seguente	siguiente	seguinte	suivant (O.Fr: sivant)	sequence
ĔQŲA 'mare'	((cavalla))	yegua	egua	(O.Fr: ive)	equestrian, equine
LĬNGŲA 'tongue'	lingua	lengua	lingua	langue	bilingual
SANGŲE 'blood'	sangue	sangre (-GŲĬNE)	sangue	sang	sanguinary
ŬNGŲENTU 'unguent'	unguento (1.)	ungüento (1.)	ungüento (1.)	onguent	unguent

Note 1. Latin QŲĪNQŲE 'five' and QŲĪNQŲE(G)ĬNTA 'fifty' lost the first of their two Ų's in VL times, due to dissimilation of the first of two identical sound groups. In QŲĪNDĔCĬM 'fifteen' the QŲ naturally remained.

Note 2. The Ų of QŲE, QŲI remained long enough to prevent palatalization of the k as in Rule 6.

Note 3. Except in Italian, the spellings qu, gu before front vowels (e or i) serve merely to indicate velar [k] and velar [g]. The u is not pronounced.

Note 4. Even more striking than the development in French of -QŲ- > [kv] > -iv- is the Rumanian -QŲ- > [kp] > p: AQŲA Rum: apa 'water'; ĔQŲA Rum: iapa 'mare'; ADAQŲO Rum: adap 'lead (animals) to water'; QŲATTRO Rum: patru 'four'; QŲADRAGĒSĬMAE Rum: parésemi 'Lent'.

Additional Examples

QŲĔM Sp: quien
ALĬQŲĔM Sp: alguien Ptg: alguêm
ALĬQŲOD Sp, Ptg: algo
QUĀ RĒ Fr: car 'for, because'
QŲĒTĀRE (for QŲIĒTĀRE) It: chetare 'to quiet' Sp: quedar 'to remain'
ŬNQŲA(M) (+ adverbial -s) O.Fr: onques 'ever'

DE U͜NQU͜A(M) Fr: donc 'therefore'
QU͜Ī 'who' It: chi Fr: qui
QU͜ĒTU (for QU͜IĒTU) 'quiet' It: cheto Sp, Ptg: quedo Fr:
  coi Eng: coy
*QU͜ATERNU 'set of four sheets' It: quaderno Sp: cuaderno
  Ptg: caderno O.Fr: quaier Fr: cahier 'notebook' Eng:
  quire 'set of 24 sheets of paper'
QU͜AERO 'I seek' Sp: quiero Ptg: quero
QU͜ĬD Sp, Ptg: que 'who, which'
NŪMQU͜A(M) Sp, Ptg: nunca
QU͜ĀSĬ 'as if' It: quasi 'almost, as if' Sp: cuasi casi 'almost'
  Ptg: quási 'almost'
QU͜ADRĬFU͜RCU 'crossroads (where four roads meet)' Fr:
  carrefour
QUŌMŎDŎ 'how' It: come 'how; like' Sp: como (O.Sp:
  cuomo) 'how; like' Ptg: como Fr: comme 'like'
QU͜ADRAGĒSĬMA 'Lent (period of 40 days)' It: quaresima
  Sp: cuaresma Ptg: quaresma Fr: carême
ANTĪGU͜A Sp: antigua Ptg: antigua, antiga O.Fr: antive
ĪNGU͜ĬNE 'groin' Sp: ingle

Exercise

Opposite each of the words in Group A write down the number of its nearest cognate in Group B.

Group A
1. It: quattordici.... 2. Fr: langue.... 3. Sp: quince.....
4. Ptg: quaresma.... 5. Fr: suivant.... 6. Eng: quire.....
7. Fr: qui,.... 8. It: acquaio.... 9. Ptg: alguêm.....
10. It: cheto....

Group B
1. Sp: cuaderno 2. Eng: key 3. It: chi 4. Sp: alguien
5. Eng: servant 6. Eng: long 7. It: quindici 8. Sp:
cuarenta 9. Ptg: catorze 10. Fr: évier 11. Sp: gato
12. Eng: coy 13. Eng: acquire 14. Eng: cheat 15. Sp:
siguiente 16. Sp: algo 17. Fr: carême 18. Eng: quince
19. It: lingua 20. Eng: languid

RULE 34

R (-RB-)

Rule: The following changes, though entirely too sporadic to be called rules, are yet sufficiently common to be worth noting: R ... R, by dissimilation, often loses one R or changes it to l. R ... L sometimes changes by metathesis to l ... r. Even single R is liable to change syllables or interchange with L (as in ULMU 'elm' It, Sp, Ptg: olmo but Fr: orme).

	Italian	Spanish	Portu-guese	French	English cognate
PRŌPRI̯U 'own'	propio	propio	proprio	propre	proper, property
ARĀTRU 'plough'	aratro	arado	arado	((charrue))	arable
CHĪRŪRGU 'surgeon'	chirurgo	cirujano	cirurgião	chirugien	surgeon
ARBŎRE 'tree'	álbero	árbol	árvore	arbre	arbor
MĔRCŬRI (DIĒS) 'Wednesday'	mercoledí	miércoles	((quarta-feira))	mercredi	Mercury
PEREGRĪNU 'stranger'	pellegrino	pelerino	peregrino (1.)	pélérin	pilgrim
MARMŎRE 'marble'	marmo	mármol	mármore	marbre	marble
BŎRSA 'moneybag'	borsa	bolsa	bôlsa	bourse	purse, bursary
ANCHŎRA 'anchor'	áncora	ancla	âncora	ancre	anchor
PAPȲRU 'papyrus'	papíro	papel	papel	papier	paper
PERĪC(Ŭ)LU 'danger'	perícolo	peligro	perigo	péril	peril

Italian	Spanish	Portu- guese	French	English cognate
PARĀB(Ŏ)LA 'word'	parola	palabra	palavra	parole	parabola, parable, parole
CRĔPĀRE 'to creak' 'to break'	crepare 'burst'	quebrar (O.Sp: crebar)	quebrar	crever 'burst'	decrepit

Note 1. The group RB gave Portuguese r̄v̄: HĔRBA 'grass' Ptg: erva (but It: erba Sp: hierba Fr: he͡rbe); ARBŎRE 'tree' Ptg: árvore (but It: álbero Sp: árbol Fr: arbre Eng: arbor, arboretum); CARBŌNE 'coal, charcoal' Ptg: carvão (but It: carbone Sp: carbón Fr: charbon Eng: carbon); TŪRBĬDU 'disturbed, muddy' Ptg: turvo (but Sp: turbio).

Note 2. When in French the group R (+ cons.) comes to be final through the fall of a final vowel, then the consonant generally falls also, at least in pronunciation. Here are some examples: RM: VERME ver 'worm'; RN: DĬŬRNU jour 'day' O.Fr: jorn, FŬRNU four 'oven, furnace', CŎRNU cor 'horn', CARNE chair 'flesh', HĪBĔRNU hiver 'winter', QŬATĔRNU cahier 'note-book', TŬRNU tour 'turn'; RC: QUADRĬFŬRCU carrefour 'crossroads', PŎRCU porc [pɔr] 'pork' (but O.Fr: and Eng: [pɔrk]); RS: VĒRSU vers [vɛ·r] 'verse', DĒ FORĪS dehors [dəɔr] 'outside'; RPS: CŎRPUS corps [kɔ·r] 'body'; RT: COHORTE cour 'court', FORTE fort [fɔ·r] 'strong', CŬRTU court [kur] 'short', ARTE art [a·r] 'art'; RD: TARDE tard [ta·r] 'late', LŬRDU lourd [lu·r] 'heavy'; -BŬRGU- bourg [bur] 'town, burgh'. The phenomenon is irregular, however. The -c̱ is pronounced in arc 'arch', for example; so is the -s̱ in moeurs 'morals', ours 'bear'.

Note 3. A sporadic but interesting phenomenon is the opening of pretonic e > a in contact with r in certain words. Examples: PER⁻ Fr: par, PERDŌNU ⁻Fr, Eng: pardon, PERFACTU Fr: parfait, MERCĀTU Fr: marché Eng: market, PĬGRĬTĬA Fr: paresse, FERŌCE Fr: farouche, REDEMPTĬŌNE Fr: rançon Eng: ransom; MĬRABĪLĬA Sp: maravilla Ptg: maravilha Eng: marvel, CAMĔRA Sp: cámara Ptg: camara, VĔRSŪRA Sp: basura Ptg: vassoira, VERRĒRE Sp: barrer, ERVĬLĬA Sp: arveja, RĒSĔCĀRE Sp, Ptg: rasgar, RĒGĪNA Ptg: r̄ainha, VERVACTU Sp: barbecho Ptg: barbeito, *EXTĔRRESCĒRE Ptg: estarrecer.

Additional Examples

FREDERĪCCU Sp: Federico
CREMĀRE 'to burn' Sp: quemar Ptg: queimar Eng: cremate

*CON FRATRE   Sp: cofrade 'member of a brotherhood'
CHRĪSTOPHŎRU   Sp: Cristóbal   Eng: Christopher
DĒ RĒTRO 'behind'   It: dietro (but Fr: derrière)
FRATRE '(eccles.) brother'   Sp: fraile 'friar', also Fray
  'Brother'.   Cp. It: fra, fratello 'brother'   Ptg: frade,
  where the second R has also disappeared.
PRESBYTER   It: prete   Sp, Ptg: preste   Fr: prêtre 'priest'
  Eng: priest, Prester (John)
AERAMĪNE 'copperware'   Sp: alambre   Ptg: arame 'wire'
  It: rame 'copper'
LŪSCĪNĮŎLA 'little nightingale'   It: uscignuolo   Sp: ruiseñor
  Ptg: rouxinol   Fr: rossignol 'nightingale'

RULE 35

S (PLUS CONSONANT)

Rule: S (+ consonant) remains in Italian, Spanish, and Portuguese. In the initial position, S (+ consonant) prefixed an e- in Spanish, Portuguese, and French, but in French the s itself then generally aspirated and fell (espi > *ehpi > épi) like French s (+ consonant) in other positions (forest > *foreht > forêt). Frequently, an acute (´) or a circumflex (^) marks the grave of s (+ consonant).

	Italian	Spanish	Portu-guese	French	English cognate
SCALA 'ladder, stair'	scala	escala	escada	échelle	scale
SCHŎLA 'school'	scuola	escuela	escola (s.l.)	école (s.l.)	school
SCRĪPTU 'written'	scritto	escrito	escrito	écrit	script
SCŪTU 'shield'	scudo	escudo	escudo	écu	escutcheon
*SMERALDU (for SMARAGDU 'emerald'	smeraldo	esmeralda	esmeralda	émeraude	emerald
SPĒRĀRE 'to hope'	sperare	esperar	esperar	espérer	
SPĪRĬTU 'spirit'	spîrito	espíritu (l.)	espirito (l.)	esprit	spirit
SPĪNA 'thorn, back-bone'	spina	espina	espinha	épine	spine
SPĀTHA 'sword'	spada	espada	espada	épee	
SPŌNSA 'bethrothed'	sposa	esposa 'wife'	esposa 'wife'	épouse 'wife'	spouse

125

	Italian	Spanish	Portu-guese	French	English cognate
SPĪCA 'spike, ear of grain'	spica	espiga	espiga	épi	spike
STĀTU 'stood, state'	stato	estado	estado	été	state, estate
STŪDĮĀRE 'to study'	studiare (1.)	estudiar (1.)	estudiar (1.)	étudier	study
STELLA, *STĒLA 'star'	stella	estrella*	estrella*	étoile	stellar, constellation
STRĬCTU 'narrow'	stretto	estrecho	estreito	étroit	strait, strict
STANNEU 'silver and lead alloy'	stagno	estaño	estanho	étain	stannous
AS(Ĭ)NU 'donkey'	asino	asno	asno	âne	ass, asinine
MŬSCA 'fly'	mosca	mosca	môsca	mouche	mosquito
PĬSCĀRE 'to fish'	pescare	pescar	pescar	pêcher	piscatory
CONSTĀRE 'to cost'	costare	costar	costar	coûter	cost
*G(W)ASTĀRE 'to waste, spoil, spend'	gastare	gastar	gastar	gâter 'to spoil'	waste
GŬSTU 'taste' relish'	gusto	gusto	gusto	goût	gusto
A(Ŭ)GŬSTU 'august, August'	agosto	agosto	agosto	août[u]	August
HŎSPĬTE 'host'	óspite	huésped	hospede	hôte	host
CASTĚLLU 'castle'	castello	castillo	castelo	château	castle
METĬPSĬMU 'same, self'	medésimo	mismo	mesmo	même	
*DESCARRĬCĀRE 'to discharge'	scaricare	descargar	descaregar	décharger	discharge

*The r of Sp: estrella Ptg: estrêla 'star' results apparently from confusion with CL ASTRŪM 'star'.

Note 1. Italian says la scuola, but in iscuola, reserving the right to prefix an i- if the preceding word does not end in a vowel.

Additional Examples

SCŪTĀRJU 'shield-bearer' It: scudiero Sp: escudero Ptg:
escudeiro Fr: écuyer Eng: squire
SPATŬLA 'ladle, shoulder blade' It: spalla Sp: espalda
Ptg: espadua Fr: épaule 'shoulder'
SPONGJA It: spugna Sp, Ptg: esponja Fr: éponge Eng:
sponge
STĔPHĂNU It: Stéfano Sp: Esteban Ptg: Estêvão Fr:
Étienne Eng: Steve, Stephen
Also Fr: étoffe 'stuff', étable 'stable', étandard 'banner,
standard', épeler 'to spell', échafaud 'scaffold', épars
'sparse', écureuil 'squirrel', épice 'spice'
HŎSPĬTĀLE 'of a host' It: ospedale Sp: hostal Fr: hôtel
Eng: hostel, hotel
MASC(Ŭ)LU It: maschio Sp, Ptg: macho Fr: mâle (Eng:
male)
DĪCĬT 'says' Fr: dit (O.Fr: dist)
JACĔT 'lies' Fr: gît (O.Fr: gist)
VĔSTĪRE 'to clothe' It: vestire Sp, Ptg: vestir Fr: vêtir
OSTRĘA 'oyster' Fr: huître Eng: oyster
ĪNSŬLĂ 'isle' It: ísola Sp: isla Fr: île Eng: isle
EPĬSCŎPU 'bishop' It: véscovo Sp: obispo Ptg: bispo
Fr: evêque (O.Fr: evésqueve)
DĔCĬMU 'tithe, tenth' Sp: diezmo 'tithe' O.Fr: disme
Eng: dime 'tenth of a dollar'
CRĒSCĔRE 'to grow' Fr: croître
MAGĬSTRU 'teacher, master' It, Sp: maestro Ptg: mestre
Fr: maître Eng: master
MĬSCŬLĀRE 'to mix' It: mescolare Sp: mezclar Fr: mêler
PRAESTĀRE 'to lend' It: prestare Sp: prestar Ptg:
emprestar Fr: prêter
ELĔĔMOSỲNA (*ALEMOSỲNA) 'alms' It: limosina Sp: limosna
Ptg: esmola Fr: aumone Eng: alms
IMPŎSĬTU 'tax' Sp: impuesto Fr: impôt 'impost'
ASPĔRU 'rough, harsh' Sp: áspero Ptg: áspero Fr: âpre
DĒPŎSĬTU 'deposit, dump' Fr: dépôt Eng: depot
NŎSTRU 'our' It: nostro Sp: nuestro Ptg: nosso Fr: nôtre
Also Fr: rôtir 'roast', pâte 'paste', baptême 'baptism', hâte
'haste', coutume 'custom', paître 'to pasture', prévôt 'provost',
dédaigner 'to disdain', mât 'mast', plâtre 'plaster', vêpres
'vespers', and many others.

Exercise

Opposite each of the words in Group A write down the number of its nearest cognate in Group B.

Group A
1. Fr: épée.... 2. Ptg: pescar.... 3. It: véscovo....
4. Sp: esposa.... 5. Eng: Stephen.... 6. It: smeraldo....
7. Ptg: castelo.... 8. Fr: nôtre.... 9. Fr: étroit.....
10. It: scudo... 11. Eng: squire.... 12. Ptg: agosto....
13. It: stagno.... 14. Sp: áspero.... 15. Fr: âne....
16. Ptg: espadua.... 17. Eng: dime.... 18. Fr: même.....
19. Ptg: macho..... 20. It: vestire....

Group B
1. Sp: espada 2. Fr: écu 3. It: medésimo 4. Ptg: ano
5. Fr: mâle 6. Eng: aghast 7. Sp: nuestro 8. Fr: épaule
9. Eng: stagnant 10. Eng: peach 11. Fr: épouse 12. Sp:
pecar 13. Eng: viscous 14. Fr: evêque 15. Sp: esmerado
16. Ptg: estreito 17. Sp: gusto 18. Sp: esquivo 19. Fr:
pêcher 20. It: mássimo 21. Fr: étain 22. Fr: mâchoir
23. Fr: demi 24. Fr: château 25. Sp: año 26. It: ásino
27. Fr: âpre 28. Eng: asp 29. Fr: vêtir 30. Eng: epic
31. Fr: août 32. Fr: châtier 33. Sp: diezmo 34. Eng:
match 35. Fr: émeraude 36. Fr: écouter 37. Fr: écuyer
38. Fr: écureuil 39. It: spero 40. Fr: Étienne

RULE 36

-T-, -D-

Rule: Between vowels, T usually remains in Italian but voices to d in Spanish and Portuguese. French has lost it altogether, the development being t > d > ꝺ >-. As for D between vowels, Italian maintains it, French and Portuguese drop it, Spanish vacillates.

	Italian	Spanish	Portu- guese	French	English cognate
VĪTA 'life'	vita	vida	vida	vie	vitality
MATŪRU 'ripe'	maturo	maduro	maduro	mûr	mature
PRATU 'meadow'	prato	prado	prado	pré	
RŎTA 'wheel'	ruota	rueda	roda	roue	rotate, rotary
CATĒNA 'chain'	catena	cadena	cadeia	chaîne	chain
PASSĀTU 'past'	passato	pasado	passado	passé	past
SALŪTĀRE 'to greet'	salutare	saludar	saudar	saluer	salute
MARĪTU 'husband'	marito	marido	marido	mari	marital
RŎTŬNDU 'round'	rotondo	redondo	redondo	rond (O.Fr: reond)	round, rotund
SCŪTU 'shield'	scudo	escudo	escudo	écu	
MŪTĀRE 'to change'	mutare, mudare	mudar	mudar	remuer	mutation
SŪDĀRE 'to sweat'	sudare	sudar	suar	suer	exude

129

	Italian	Spanish	Portu-guese	French	English cognate
VADU 'ford'	guado	vado	vao	gué	Gmc. cognate: Eng: wade Gm: waten
CRŪDU 'raw'	crudo	crudo	cru	cru	crude
NŪDU 'naked'	nudo	desnudo	nu	nu	nude
MERCĒDE 'reward'	mercede 'reward'	merced 'grace'	mercê	merci 'thanks'	mercy
RĪDĔRE 'to laugh'	ridere	reír	rir	rire	deride
CRŪDĒLE 'cruel'	crudele	cruel	cruel	cruel	cruel
VĬDĒRE 'to see'	vedere	ver (O.Sp: veer)	ver	voir	vision, video
CRĒDĔRE 'to believe'	credere	creer	crer	croire	creed
SEDĒRE 'to sit'	sedere 'to sit'	ser (O.Sp: seer 'to be')	ser 'to be'	asseoir 'to seat'	sedentary
PĔDE 'foot'	piede	pie	pé	pied [pje]	pedestrian, centipede
FĬDE 'faith'	fede	fe (O.Sp: fee)	fé	foi	faith

Note 1. When final in Spanish, as in usted, edad, verdad, Madrid, caridad, juventud, the -d is now so weak as to be almost inaudible: [usteᵈ] [edaᵈ]⁻[berdaᵈ] [Maḍriᵈ]. It is also very weak in the ending -ado, e.g. [pasaᵈo] [estaᵈo] [kontaᵈo] [soldaᵈo], and in certain common words like todo, modo, nada [toᵈo] [moᵈo] [naᵈa]. A popular (but not yet accepted) tendency is to relax this [ᵈ] altogether and say pasáo, soldáo, tóo, móo, náa, usté, verdá, Madrí.

Note 2. When preceded by the Latin diphthong AỤ, whose Ụ is in reality a semiconsonant, the T is preserved in Spanish and Portuguese: AỤTŬMNU 'autumn' Sp: otoño Ptg: outono; AỤ(C)TŌR(Ĭ)CĀRE 'to authorize' Sp: otorgar Ptg: outorgar.

Remark. The -th of Eng: faith reveals the fact that the Norman conquerors brought it to England just at the time when French had developed intervocalic d as far as [ð]. Like other voiced consonants in Old French, this [ð], when final, changed to its voiceless counterpart, in this case [θ]. Traces of a similar phenomenon can still be observed in English. Compare bathe [-ð] with bath [-θ], loaves [v] with loaf [f], houses

[z] with house [s]. German shows it even better: Wälder
[d] Wald [t], Weiber [b] Weib [p], Tage [g] Tag [x], Häuser
[z] Haus [s].

Additional Examples

PĔTĒRE 'to seek' Sp, Ptg: pedir 'ask for, solicit' Eng:
petition
ADVOCĀTU 'lawyer' Sp: abogado [abogaᵈo] Ptg: advogado
Fr: avoué Eng: advocate
APŎTHĒCA 'wine cellar' Sp, Ptg: bodega 'tavern' Also Ptg:
adega (via abdega) 'cellar'
QUADRĀTU 'square' It: quadrato Sp: cuadrado Ptg:
quadrado Fr: carré
*OBLĪTĀRE 'to forget' Sp: olvidar (met.) Fr: oublier
Eng: oblivion, obliterate
RŪTA '(bot.) rue' It: ruta Sp: ruda Ptg: arruda Fr, Eng:
rue
CĬTU 'quick' Ptg: cedo 'quickly'
*SĔDĔNTĀRE 'to seat' Sp: sentar Ptg: assentar
LĪMPĬDU 'clear, clean' Sp: limpio Ptg: limpo Eng: limpid
CADĒRE 'to fall' It: cadere Sp: caer Ptg: cair Fr: choir
(+) ((tomber))
LŪRĬDU 'sallow, pale yellow, wan, ghastly' Mexican Sp: lurio
'lovesick, crazy'
RADĪCE 'root' It: radice Sp: raíz Ptg: raiz Fr: rai- (as in
raifort 'horseradish') Eng: radish
AUDĪRE 'to hear' It: udire Sp: oír Ptg: ouvir Fr: ouïr
(+) ((entendre)) Eng: oyez! oyez! 'hear ye, hear ye!'
(Eng: audit, audible)
HĒRĒDĬTĀRE 'to inherit' It: ereditare Sp: heredar (O.Sp:
hereedar) Ptg: herdar Fr: hériter Eng: inherit
TRADĬTŌRE 'traitor' It: traditore Sp, Ptg: traidor Fr:
traitre (TRADITOR) Eng: traitor
FRĪGĬDU 'cold' It: freddo Sp: frío (O.Sp: frido) Ptg: frio
Fr: froid Eng: frigid
BĔNĒDĬCTU 'blessed' It: benedetto Sp: bendito (l.) Ptg:
bemdito, bento 'holy' Fr: bénit
BĔNĒDĬCTU 'Benedict' It: Benedetto Sp: Benito (l.) Ptg:
bemdito, bento 'holy' Fr: bénit
VŌTA 'vows' Sp, Ptg: boda 'wedding'
NATĪVU 'natural, simple' Fr: naïf Eng: naïve
CŬM ĒDERE 'to eat' Sp, Ptg: comer
TURBĬDU 'disturbed, muddy' Sp: turbio Ptg: turvo

Exercise

Opposite each of the words in Group A write down the number of its nearest cognate in Group B.

Group A
1. Sp: rueda.... 2. It: sudar.... 3. Fr: mûr.....
4. Eng: past.... 5. Ptg: prado.... 6. It: vita....
7. Sp: oír.... 8. Eng: crude.... 9. Ptg: vao....
10. Fr: voir.... 11. Sp: raíz.... 12. Eng: rue.....
13. Fr: pied..... 14. It: catena.... 15. Ptg: mercê.....
16. Sp: creer.... 17. Eng: nude.... 18. Fr: traitre....
19. Sp: olvidar..... 20. It: fede

Group B
1. Fr: croire 2. Eng: radish 3. Fr: noeud 4. It: ruota
5. Eng: suitor 6. Fr: vide 7. Sp: voy 8. Eng: chain
9. It: rotta 10. Sp: pie 11. Fr: voie 12. Eng: feather
13. Ptg: maduro 14. Eng: rice 15. Fr: vite 16. It: udire
17. Sp: hiede 18. Fr: foi 19. Sp: pasto 20. It: vedere
21. Sp: muro 22. Fr: pré 23. It: pasta 24. Fr: suer
25. Eng: route 26. Ptg: traidor 27. Fr: oublier 28. Sp:
pasado 29. Fr: ouvrir 30. Eng: kitchen 31. Fr: vie
32. Fr: chacun 33. Ptg: nu 34. Fr: cru 35. Sp: traer
36. It: merced 37. Fr: prier 38. It: ruta 39. Fr: pitié
40. Sp: vado

RULE 37

-T, -C, -D, -L, -M, -N, -R, -S

Rule: Latin final -T, -C, and -D regularly fell away in Romance, though in Old French -t̲ was retained for a while after a consonant, e.g. O.Fr: est̄, valt, dist DĪX(Ȳ)T, chantast CANTA(VȲ)SS(Ḗ)T (modern est [ɛ], vaut [vo], dit [di], chantât [šắta]). Final -M disappeared except in certain monosyllables where it survives as n̲ or as mere nasalization of the preceding vowel, e.g. CŬM It̄, Sp: con Ptg: com; TAM 'so' Sp: tan; QŲAM 'how' Sp: cuán; QŲḖM 'whom' Sp: quién 'who'; NḖ...RḖM 'not a thing' Fr: ne...rien 'nothing' MḖ(Ŭ)M Fr: mien 'mine'; *MŬM (unstressed form of MEŬM) Fr: mon. Final -N may remain (It: in Sp: en), disappear (It, Sp: no), or nasalize the preceding vowel (Ptg: em, não, Fr: en, non). As for final -S, Italian rejected it entirely, even forming its plurals in -e̲ and -i̲ where others used -s̲. Spanish and Portuguese preserve̲ the S, as did Old French, but in Modern French the S is silent.

	Italian	Spanish	Portu- guese	French	English cognate
VALĔT 'is worth'	vale	vale	vale	vaut (O.Fr: valt)	
CANTAT 'sings'	canta	canta	canta	chante	chant
CANTANT 'sing'	cántano	cantan	cantam	chantent	
SŬNT 'are'	sono	son	são	sont	
ĔST 'is'	è	es	es	est	
AŲT 'or'	o, od	o	ou	ou	
SĪC 'thus, so'	si	sí	sim	si	

	Italian	Spanish	Portu-guese	French	English cognate
(AD) ĬLLĪC (or ĬLLĀC) 'there'	lí	allí	alí	là	
DĪC 'say'	di	di	diz (*DĪCE)	dis	
AD 'to'	a	a	a	à	
QUĬD, QUOD 'that'	che	que	que	que	
JAM 'already'	già	ya	já	déja (DĒ JAM)	
SĔPTĔM 'seven'	sette	siete	sete	sept	
NŎVĔM 'nine'	nove	nueve	nove	neuf	
CRĒDAM 'I believe' (subjunctive)	creda	crea	crea	croie	creed
CANTĀBAM 'I sang'	cantava	cantaba	cantava	chantais	
NŌN 'no'	no	no	não	non	
ĬN 'in'	in	en	em	en	
TRĒS 'three'	tre	tres	três	trois	
SĔX 'six'	sei	seis	seis	six	
MAGĬS 'more, greater'	mai	más	mais	mais	
VĒNDĬS 'you sell'	vendi	vendes	vendes	vends	
VĒNDĒMUS 'we sell'	vendiamo	vendemos	vendemos	vendons	

Note. In Italian, where a number of Latin nominative forms survived, L and R were sometimes final. These were kept in monosyllables (CŎR cuore, FĔL fiele, MĔL miele), but in polysyllables they were dropped: FRATĔR frate 'monk'; CĬCĔR cece 'chickpea'; TRIBŪNAL tribuna 'platform'; MARMŎR marmo 'marble'; SŎRŎR O.It: suoro Modern suora 'sister'; PĬPĔR pepe 'pepper'.

Additional Examples

ĔT It: e Sp: y Fr: et [e]

VĬDĔT It: vede Sp, Ptg: ve O.Fr: veit Fr: voit [vwa]
AD HŪNC 'to this (time)' Sp: aún 'yet, still'
HŎC ĬLLE 'that is so' O.Fr: oïl, ouïl Fr: oui 'yes'
ĔCCE HŎC It: ciò 'that'
PER HŎC It: però 'however, therefore' Sp: pero 'but'
NŪMQŲAM 'never' Sp: nunca
(DĒ) ŪNQŲAM 'ever' O.Fr: onques 'ever' Fr: donc 'therefore'
DĔCEM 'ten' It: dieci Sp: diez Ptg: dez Fr: dix
*TŬM (for TŬŬM) Fr: ton 'your'
*SŬM (for SŬŬM) Fr: son 'his, her, its'
PLŪS 'more' It: più Fr, Eng: plus
MĬNŬS 'less' It: meno Sp: menos Ptg: menos (s.l.) Fr: moins [mwɛ̃]
(DĒ)SŪRSU 'above, over' It: su Fr: dessus (O.Sp: suso)

Compare It: li muri, le rose with Sp: los muros, las rosas, Ptg: os muros, as rosas, and Fr: les murs, les roses. Italian takes its plural from the nominative: ILLĪ MŪRI, ILLAE ROSAE; the others form theirs from the accusative: ILLŌS MŪRŌS, ILLĀS RŌSĀS.

RULE 38

-TĀTE (-TŪTE)

Rule: The Latin suffix -TAS, -TĀTE becomes Italian -tà, Spanish -tad or -dad, Portuguese -tade or -dade, French -té, and English -ty. All words with this suffix are feminine in all four languages.

	Italian	Spanish	Portu-guese	French	English cognate
LIBERTĀTE 'freedom'	libertà (l.)	libertad (l.)	libertade (l.)	liberté (l.)	liberty
VOLUNTĀTE 'will'	volontà	voluntad	vontade	volonté	voluntary
DIFFICULTĀTE 'difficulty'	difficultà (l.)	dificultad (l.)	dificultade (l.)	difficulté (l.)	difficulty
MAJESTĀTE 'majesty'	maestà	majestad	majestade	majesté	majesty
BONĬTĀTE 'goodness'	bontà	bondad	bondade	bonté	bounty
VERĬTĀTE 'truth'	verità (l.)	verdad	verdade	vérité	verity
VĪCĪNĬTĀTE 'neighborhood'	·vicinità (l.)	vecindad	vezindade ((vizinhança))	((voisinage))	vicinity
AEQUALĬTĀTE 'equality'	((eguaglianza))	igualdad	igualdade	égalité	equality
CĪVĬTĀTE 'state'	città	ciudad	cidade	cité	city
VANĬTĀTE 'vanity'	vanità (l.)	vanidad (l.)	vaidade	vanité (l.)	vanity
QUALĬTĀTE	qualità (l.)	c(u)alidad (l.)	qualidade (l.)	qualité (l.)	quality

	Italian	Spanish	Portu- guese	French	English cognate
CARĬTĀTE 'love'	carità (1.)	caridad (1.)	caridade (1.)	charité (s.l.)	charity
SOCIETĀTE 'society'	società (1.)	sociedad (1.)	sociedade (1.)	société (1.)	society
PRŌPRIETĀTE 'property'	proprietà	propiedad	propriedade	propriété	property, propriety

Note 1. The majority of these words show scholastic influence, especially in Italian and French. Their interest for us is small except to show the regular development of the suffix.
Note 2. The suffix -TŪTE, also feminine, gives It: -tù, Sp: -tud, Ptg: -tude, Fr: -tu: VIRTŪTE 'courage' It: virtù (s.l.) Sp: virtud (s.l.) Ptg: virtude (s.l.) Fr: vertu Eng: virtue; JŬVENTŪTE 'youth' It: gioventù Sp: juventud Ptg: juventude ((Fr: jeunesse (-ĬTĮA))).
Note 3. Earlier Italian had -tate or -tade, but the final syllable of -tade being mistaken for the preposition de, it was commonly dropped, particularly when the syllable occurred twice in succession in common phrases like la citta(de) de Roma, la bonta(de) de Cristo.
Note 4. Spanish and Portuguese have -tad(e) when Latin -TĀTE was preceded by a consonant, otherwise they have -dad(e) or -idad(e). The i is learned, since it represents unstressed Latin Ĭ (VL ę), and in an intertonic syllable at that. More popular words like bondad, verdad eliminated this syllable entirely.
Note 5. The development of MĔDĬĔTĀTE 'middle; half' It: metà Sp: mitad Ptg: metade Fr: moitié Eng: moiety 'half' is complicated and irregular. Sp: Navidad NATĪVĬTĀTE 'Nativity, Christmas' shows contraction from *nadividad due in part to the length of the word but more especially to dissimilation from the other two d's.

Additional Examples

AETATE 'age' It: età Sp: edad Ptg: edade O.Fr: eé (but Fr: âge (O.Fr: eage) AETĀTĬCU (Eng: age))
BELLĬTĀTE 'beauty' It: beltà Sp: beldad Ptg: beldade Fr: beauté Eng: beauty
HĔRĔDĬTĀTE 'inheritance' It: eredità Sp: heredad ((Ptg: herança)) Eng: heredity
GERMANĬTĀTE 'brotherhood' Sp: hermandad Ptg: irmandade
HŪMĬLĬTĀTE 'humility' It: umiltà Sp: humildad Ptg: humildade
TRĪNĬTĀTE 'Trinity' It: Trinità Sp: Trinidad Ptg: Trindade Fr: Trinité Eng: Trinity

ŪNĪVERSĪTĀTE 'the whole, the universe' It: università
Sp: universidad   Ptg: universidade   Fr: université   Eng:
university
CRŪDĒLĪTĀTE 'cruelty'   It: crudelità   Sp: crueldad   Ptg:
crueldade   Fr: cruauté (O.Fr: cruelté)   Eng: cruelty

A vast number of internationally current words, many of them
of recent origin, show the same correspondence in the Romance languages and in English: unity, immunity, activity,
ferocity, duplicity, reality, facility, amenity, fertility,
felicity, tranquility, longevity, sterility, agility, universality,
divinity, eternity, maternity, individuality, domesticity,
impossibility, equanimity, nasality, impurity, electricity,
conductivity, radioactivity, elasticity, sonority, and so on.

Exercise

Opposite each of the words in Group A write down the number of its nearest cognate in Group B.

Group A
1. Eng: bounty....   2. Ptg: beldade....   3. Sp: edad....
4. It: città.....   5. Fr: vérité.....

Group B
1. Ptg: vontade   2. Sp: verdad   3. Ptg: cidade   4. Eng:
variety   5. Sp: bondad   6. It: eredità   7. Sp: caridad
8. It: età   9. It: beltà   10. Ptg: virtude

RULE 39

-TR- (-PR-, -CR-)

Rule: Before R, T voices or remains in Italian, voices in Spanish and Portuguese, but regularly falls in French. P remains in Italian (Tuscan), voices in Spanish and Portuguese, gives v (seldom b) in French. C voices in Italian, Spanish, and Portuguese. In French the result was gr or r, often preceded by a yod.

	Italian	Spanish	Portu-guese	French	English cognate
PĔTRA 'rock, stone'	pietra	piedra	pedra	pierre	petrous, petrified
VĬTRU 'glass'	vetro	vidrio (VĬTRĘU)	vidro	verre	vitreous
*NŬTRĪCĮA (for NŬTRĪCE) 'wetnurse'	nutrice (l.)	nodriza	nutriz (l.)	nourrice	nurse, nourish
MĀTRE 'mother'	madre	madre	mai (via made)*	mère	maternal
PĀTRE 'father'	padre	padre	pai (via pade)*	père	paternal
LĀTRŌNE 'robber'	ladro (LĀTRO)	ladrón	ladrão	larron	larceny
CAPRA 'goat'	capra	cabra	cabra	chèvre	capricious
LĔP(Ŏ)RE 'hare'	lepre	liebre	lebre	lièvre	leveret
APRĪCU 'sunny'	aprico 'sunny'	abrigo 'shelter'	abrigo 'shelter'	abri 'shelter'	
APRĪLE 'April'	aprile	abril	abril	avril	April
ŎPĔRĀRĮU 'worker'	operaio	obrero	obreiro	ouvrier	operator

139

	Italian	Spanish	Portu- guese	French	English cognate
MACRU 'thin'	magro	magro	magro	maigre	meager
VĪN(U) ĀCRE 'bitter wine'	((aceto))	vinagre	vinagre	vinaigre	vinegar
LACRĬMA 'tear'	lágrima	lágrima	lágrima	larme	lacrimal

*These forms have been explained as arising by analogy with FRATRE
'brother' whose second R fell through dissimilation to give It: fra, fratello
'brother' Sp: fray Ptg: frade.

Note: In words showing learned influence T, P, C remain.
Compare It: sacrare 'to consecrate' with popular It: sagrare
'to curse', Fr: sacrament with Fr: serment (O.Fr: sair(e)ment
'oath', Fr: vitre 'windowpane' with Fr: verre 'glass', Sp: ópera
'opera' with Sp: obra 'work'.

Additional Examples

LATRĀTE It: latrare Sp, Ptg: ladrar 'to bark'
DĔRĔTRO It: dietro Fr: derrière 'behind'
ŎPĔRA It: ópera Sp: obra Ptg: obra Fr: oeuvre 'work'
CŬPRU Sp, Ptg: cobre Fr: cuivre 'copper'
LŬCRĀRE Sp, Ptg: lograr 'to succeed in, obtain'
SŎCRU Sp: suegro Ptg: sogro 'father-in-law'
SĒCRĔTU It: secreto (1.) segreto (pop.) Sp, Ptg: secreto
  (1.) Fr: secret (1.) 'secret'
PŬTRĪDU 'rotten' It: putrido Sp: podrido Ptg: podre,
  podrido Fr: purri Eng: putrid
ĬTĔRĀRE 'to wander' (< ĬTĔR 'journey') Fr: errer 'to wander'
PĬPĔRE 'pepper' It: pepe (PĬPĔR) Sp: pebre 'a red pepper
  sauce' Fr: poivre 'pepper' Eng: pepper

Exercise

Opposite each of the words in Group A write down the number of its nearest cognate in Group B.

Group A
1. Fr: larron.... 2. It: vetro.... 3. Eng: nurse....
4. Sp: madre.... 5. Ptg: lebre.... 6. Fr: chèvre....
7. It: operaio.... 8. It: dietro.... 9. Sp: lágrima....
10. Fr: pourri....

Group B
1. Ptg: magra 2. Sp: viejo 3. Fr: mer 4. Fr: nuire
5. Ptg: cabra 6. Sp: cifra 7. Fr: mère 8. Sp: libra
9. Eng: alarm 10. Sp: ladrón 11. Eng: matter 12. Fr:
larme 13. Eng: putrid 14. Sp: nodriza 15. Fr: louvre
16. Ptg: obreiro 17. Fr: derrière 18. It: lepre 19. Fr:
lèvre 20. Fr: verre

RULE 40

TY (CY)

Rule: CY and TY both result in Modern Spanish ć, z̄ (both pronounced [θ] in Castile and [s] in Spanish America).⁻ In Portuguese, the regular development of TY was to z̄ [z], but more often it was confused with CY, which gave ç̄ [s]. Italian developed CY to cci [tš] but TY to zz [ts] or [dz]. In French, CY, (cons. +) CY͵ and (cons. +)⁻ TY all produced Old French [ts], Modern French [s], variously spelled c͵, ç͵, ss or s (when final). TY gives is, the s of which is [z̄] between vowels (poison) but which at the end of a word is now silent (puits, palais).

	Italian	Spanish	Portu-guese	French	English cognate
PŬTĘU 'well'	pozzo	pozo	poço	puits [pɥi]	
TĪTĮŌNE 'firebrand'	tizzone	tizón	tição	tison	
ACŪTĮĀRE 'to sharpen'	aguzzare	aguzar	aguçar	aiguiser	acute
TRĪSTĬTĮA 'sadness'	tristezza	tristeza	tristeza	tristesse	
RĪCC+ĬTĮA 'power, wealth'	ricchezza	riqueza	riqueza	richesse	rich
DŪRĬTĮA 'hardness'	durezza	dureza	dureza	duresse	duress
MARTĮU 'March'	marzo	marzo (O.Sp: março)	março	mars (O.Fr: marz [marts])	March
SPĒRĀNTĮA 'hope'	speranza	esperanza (O.Sp: esperança)	esperança	espérance	

141

	Italian	Spanish	Portu-guese	French	English cognate
ALTIĀRE	alzare	alzar (O.Sp: alçar)	alçar	hausser	altitude
DĪRECTIĀRE 'to straighten, prepare'	dirizzare	aderezar	adereçar	dresser	dress, dressing
CŬMĬNĬTIĀRE 'to initiate, begin'	comenzare	comenzar (O.Sp: començar)	começar	commencer	initiate, commence
BRA(C)CHIU 'arm'	braccio	brazo	braço	bras (O.Fr: braz)	brace
FACIE, *FACIA 'face'	faccia	haz	face	face	face
MĬNĀCIA 'threat'	minaccia	amenaza	ameaça	menace	menace
LAQ(U)EU 'noose, snare'	laccio	lazo (> Eng: lasso)	laço	(O.Fr: laz)	lace
ACIĀRIU 'steel'	acciaio	acero (O.Sp: azero)	((aço))	acier	
ŬNCIA 'ounce, inch'	oncia	onza (O.Sp: onça)	onça	once	ounce, inch
LANCEA 'lance, spear'	lancia	lanza (O.Sp: lança)	lança	lance	lance

Note 1. In Old Spanish, TY, CY gave z̄ [dz] when alone, ç [ts] when preceded by a consonant, but in Modern Spanish, both sounds have become [θ] (in America, [s]). (See the bird's eye view of Spanish sibilants given at the front of this manual.)

Note 2. By the fourth century A.D., Vulgar Latin TY had become [ts], while in the fifth and sixth centuries, CY went to [tš] or [ts]. That the two sounds were confused is attested not only in Roman inscriptions but by the Romance languages themselves. For example, PLATEA gives It: piazza but Fr, Eng: place, O.Sp: plaça Sp: plaza. MATEA gives It: mazza but O.Sp: maça, Fr: masse Eng: mace. The forms SŌLĀTIU and SŌLĀCIU, coexistent in Latin, gave It: sollazzo and O.Fr: solaz (Eng: solace), respectively. Italian derives both comenzare and cominciare from CŬMĬNĬTIĀRE. In French, the suffix -ĬTIA, confused with -ĪCIA, gives now -ice (JŪSTĬTIA justice), now -esse (TRĪSTĬTIA tristesse).

Note 3. In Italian, TY and SY were often confused. Witness PRĒTĮU prezzo pregio, PALATĮU palazzo palagio, RATĮŌNE ragione, STATĮŌNE stagione. CTY and PTY were also mixed up, giving at random [tts] or [ttš]: *DĪRECTĮĀRE dirizzare, *DUCTĮĀRE docciare, FACTĮONE fazzone, SŬSPĒCTĮŌNE sospeccione sospezzone, CAPTĮĀRE cacciare, NŬPTĮAE nozze, *CORRŬPTĮĀRE corrucciare 'to enrage'.

Note 4. In Old Spanish, (cons. +) DY gave ç [ts], modern z [θ], just like (cons. +) TY or (cons. +) CY: *VĪRDĮA 'greenery' Old Sp: verça 'cabbage', HORDEŎLU 'barley' Sp: orzuelo '(med.) sty; trap, snare', VERĒCŬNDIA Sp: vergüenza, GAŲDĮU Sp: gozo (> Ptg: gôzo).

Note 5. The groups SCY, STY, and SSY fell together in French and Italian to give Italian [š], French [įs]: FASCĮA 'bundle of faggots' It: fascia O.Fr: faisse; PĪSCĮŌNE Fr: poisson 'fish'; ANGŬSTĮA It: angoscia Fr: angoisse Eng: anguish; PŎSTĘA 'afterwards, then' It: poscia Fr: puis; *BĪSTĮA (for BESTĮA) O.Fr: bisse 'hind'; ŪSTĮU (for ŌSTĮU) It: uscio; *ŪSTĮĀRĮU Fr: huissier Eng: usher; *MŬSTĮŌNE (from MŬSTU 'new wine, must') Fr: moisson 'harvest, crop'; *RĒVĒRSĮU *RĒVESSĮU (see Rule 25) It: rovescio, CAPSĘA *CASSĘA (Rule 25) Sp: caja Fr: caisse; BASSĮĀRE Sp: bajar Fr: baisser.

Note 6. It: -zione (lezione, nazione), Sp: -ción (lección, nación), Fr: -tion (action, nation) are learned, as are also, for example, Sp: precio, gracia, palacio, servicio, vicio, espacio, justicia; It: servizio, pigrizia, prazia, spazio; Fr: grace, espace, service, justice.

Note 7. In Spanish, TY, CY palatalized too early to close the preceding vowel (witness veza, cabeza, pieza, lienzo, fuerza). Spanish also palatalized too early to permit the CT of CTY to become ch, as we see from AD+ *DĪRECTĮĀRE Sp: aderezar 'to prepare', or from COLLACTĘU 'one who shares milk' (just as COMPANĮŌNE is 'one who shares bread', hence 'companion') Sp: collazo 'farmhand'.

Additional Examples

PALATĮU It: palazzo Sp: palacio Ptg: paço Fr: palais
  Eng: palace
VĪTĮU It: vezzo O.Sp: bezo Ptg:vêzo 'habit, custom'
*JŬVĔNĬTĮA Fr: jeunesse
GRANDĪTĮA It: grandezza Sp: grandeza
RATĮŌNE It: ragione Sp: razón Ptg: razão Fr: raison
  Eng: reason
SATĮŌNE 'sowing-time' Sp: sazón Ptg: sazão Fr: saison
  Eng: season
POTĮŌNE Fr: poison Eng: poison, potion
LĪGATĮŌNE 'a binding' Fr: liaison

LĒCTĮŌNE   It: lezione (1.)   Sp: lección (1.)   Ptg: lição
Fr: leçon   Eng: lesson
FACTĮŌNE   It: fazzone   Sp: facción   Ptg: façao   Fr: façon
Eng: fashion
VĬNDĬCANTĮA   Sp: venganza   Ptg: vingança   Fr, Eng:
vengeance
FLŌRENTĮAE 'Florence'   It: Firenze (older Fiorenze)
*GLACĮA (for GLACĮE) 'ice'   It: ghiaccia   Fr: glace   Eng:
glacier, glass
PRĒTĮU   It: prezzo pregio   Sp: precio (1.)   Ptg: preço (yet
PRĒTĮĀRE Ptg: prezar 'to prize')   Fr: prix   Eng: price,
prize
PĬGRĬTĮA 'laziness'   It: pigrizia (1.)   Sp: pereza   Ptg:
preguiça (met.)   Fr: paresse
MALĬTIA 'badness'   It: malizia (1.)   Fr: malice 'malice' but
Sp: maleza 'weeds, underbrush'
CANTĮŌNE   It: canzone   Sp: canción (1.)   Ptg: canção   Fr:
chanson 'song'
CAPTĮĀRE   It: caciare   Sp: cazar   Ptg: caçar   Fr: chasser
(O.Fr: chacier)   Eng: chase, catch
*NOPTĮAE *NOPTĮAS (for NŬPTĮAE)   It: nozze   Fr: noces
Eng: nuptials
VENĒTĮA   Ptg: Veneza 'Venice'
JŪSTĬTĮA   It: giustezza   Ptg: justiça   Fr: justice   Eng:
justice
*CAPĬTĮA (for CAPUT)   Sp: cabeza   Ptg: cabeça
CŬPĬDĬTĮA 'greed'   It: covidigia cupidigia   Sp: codicia (s.l.)
VENATĮŌNE 'hunting'   O.Fr: venaison, veneson   Eng: venison
BĔNĔDĬCTĮŌNE   O.Fr: beneison   Eng: benison 'blessing'
TRADĬTĮŌNE   Fr: trahison   Eng: treason
ORATĮŌNE 'speech'   Fr: oraison 'oration'
REDEMPTĮŌNE 'a buying back'   Fr: rançon   Eng: ransom
NĔPTĮA 'granddaughter, niece'   Fr: nièce   Eng: niece
FŎRTĮA   It: forza   Sp: fuerza   Ptg: força   Fr, Eng: force
FŬRNACĘA 'oven'   Sp: hornaza   O.Fr, Eng: furnace
*CORTĬCĘA 'bark'   It: corteccia   Sp: corteza   Ptg: cortiça
TĔRTĮU 'third'   It: terzo   Sp: tercio (1.) Tierzo (place name)
Ptg: terço   Fr: tier   Eng: tierce, tercet
*PĔTTĮA 'piece'   It: pezzo   Sp: pieza   Ptg: peça   Fr: pièce
Eng: piece
*LĔNTĘU (for LĪNTĘU) 'linen'   Sp: lienzo   Ptg: lenço 'cloth,
canvas'   It: lenzuolo (*LĔNTĘŎLU) 'sheet, shroud'   Fr:
linceul (LĪNTĘŎLU) 'shroud'
ERĪCĮU 'hedgehog'   It: riccio   Sp: erizo   Ptg: ouriço   Fr:
hérisson (*ERĪCĮŌNE)
VĬCĮA '(bot.) vetch'   It: veccia   Sp: veza   ((Ptg: ervilhaca))
Fr: vesce (the s is a whim of spelling)   Eng: vetch
LĪCĮŌS 'warp-thread'   It: licci   Sp: lizos   Ptg: liços   Fr:
lices (LĪCĮĀS) 'warp'

SPECĮA 'kind' Fr: épice Eng: spice (It: spezie Sp, Ptg: especie Fr: espèce and Eng: species are learned) CALCĘĀRE It: calciare 'to kick' Sp: calzar 'to shoe' Ptg: calçar 'to shoe' Fr: chausser (O.Fr: chalcier) 'to shoe'

Exercise

Opposite each of the words in Group A write down the number of its nearest cognate in Group B.

Group A
1. It: aguzzare.... 2. Ptg: poço..... 3. Sp: haz.....
4. Eng: menace.... 5. It: braccio.... 6. Fr: saison....
7. It: prezzo.... 8. Ptg: lição.... 9. It: ghiaccia....
10. Eng: chase..... 11. It: acciaio.... 12. Sp: fuerza....
13. Fr: façon... 14. Eng: justice.... 15. Sp: lazo....
16. It: palazzo.... 17. Fr: angoisse.... 18. Ptg: tição
19. Sp: hornaza.... 20. It: dirizzare...

Group B
1. It: angoscia 2. Eng: prison 3. It: giustezza
4. Eng: lace 5. Fr: menage 6. It: lasciare 7. Fr: poison
8. Eng: furnace 9. Sp: brazo 10. Fr: hausse 11. Eng: sauce 12. Sp: acero 13. Fr: aiguiser 14. Eng: place
15. It: fazzone 16. Fr: chaise 17. Sp: cazar 18. It: piazza 19. Fr: faux 20. It: pozzo 21. Fr: tison 22. Eng: furnish 23. Ptg: sazão 24. Eng: glass 25. Fr: farce
26. Eng: derision 27. Eng: face 28. Sp: ansioso 29. Fr: force 30. Eng: gas 31. Fr: tige 32. Eng: hornet 33. It: minaccia 34. Fr: place 35. Eng: lesson 36. Fr: dresser
37. Sp: acción 38. Fr: prix 39. Eng: lease 40. Fr: palais

RULE 41

Ū

Rule: Tonic or pretonic Ū remains u̱ in Romance but in French is pronounced [y] or [ɥ].

	Italian	Spanish	Portu- guese	French	English cognate
MŪRU 'wall'	muro	muro	muro	mur [myr]	mural
TŪ 'you (sing.)'	tu	tú	tu	tu [ty]	Eng: thou, Gm: du
LŪNA 'moon'	luna	luna	lua	lune [lyn]	lunar
DŪRU 'hard'	duro	duro	duro	dur	durable
SŪDĀRE 'to sweat'	sudare	sudar	suar	suer	exude
MŪTĀRE 'to change'	mutare	mudar	mudar	remuer 'to stir, move'	commute, mutation
SĒCŪRU 'safe'	sicuro	seguro	seguro	sûr	sure, secure
VĬRTŪTE 'courage'	vertù	virtud	virtude	vertu	virtue
SCŪTU 'shield'	scudo	escudo	escudo	écu [eky]	escutcheon
MENSŪRA 'measure'	misura	mesura	mesura	mesure	measure
MATŪRU 'ripe'	maturo	maduro	maduro	mûr [myr] (O.Fr: meür	mature

Note. While Spanish and Portuguese formed the regular past participles of their verbs with -ado (-ATU) and -ido (-ĪTU), French and Italian favored VL -ŪTU. This suffix accounts for French bu, battu, couru, connu, cru, dû, eu, fallu, lu, mu, moulu, paru, perdu, plu, pu, su, tu, vu, valu, vécu, vaincu, vêtu, voulu, venu, vendu, and the rest. Some of the Italian counterparts of these are bevuto, creduto, dovuto, avuto, perduto, saputo, veduto (or visto, as in Spanish), vestuto, voluto, venduto. There are scores of others.

Additional Examples

LEGŪM(ĪN)E 'vegetable' It: legume Sp: legumbre Ptg:
 legume Fr: légume Eng: leguminous
RŪGA 'furrow, rut; It, Sp: ruga 'rut' Ptg: rua 'street'
 Fr: rue 'street' Eng: corrugated (i.e. 'furrowed')
ACŪTU 'sharp' It: acuto Sp, Ptg: agudo Fr: aigu Eng:
 acute, ague
FRŪCTU 'fruit' It: frutto Sp, Ptg: fruto Fr, Eng: fruit
ŪSTĬĀRĮU (for ŌSTĬĀRĮU) 'janitor' (from ŌSTĮU 'door,
 entrance') It: usciere Fr: huissier Eng: usher Cp. It:
 uscio O.Sp: uço 'door'
VL ILLŪI '(dat.) (to) him' It: lui Fr: lui [lɥi]
CŪI '(dat.) (to) whom' It: cúi
FATŪTU 'ill-fated; i.e. deceased' Fr: feu 'deceased, late'
 (O.Fr: fe-ü)

Exercise

Opposite each of the words in Group A write down the number of its nearest cognate in Group B.

Group A
1. It: scudo.... 2. Fr: suer.... 3. Ptg: lua....
4. Sp: agudo..... 5. Eng: mature... 6. Ptg: fruto....
7. It: vestuto.... 8. Fr: dû...... 9. Eng: sure....
10. It: creduto....

Group B
1. Ptg: muto 2. Ptg: seguro 3. Fr: cru 4. It: sudare
5. Fr: matière 6. It: dovuto 7. Fr: lui 8. Fr: mûr
9. Sp: suegro 10. Fr: écu 11. Eng: frugal 12. It: acuto
13. Sp: luna 14. Eng: credit 15. Fr: vêtu 16. Fr: fruit
17. Eng: vest 18. Sp: dudo 19. Sp: madre 20. It: freddo

RULE 42

W- (OF GERMANIC ORIGIN)

Rule: Many of the Germanic words borrowed by the Romans during the latter days of the Empire began with [w-], a labio-velar sound that existed in Latin (AQŬA, LINGŬA) but which no longer occurred initially. The Romans solved this by exaggerating the velar constriction of the [w-], thus producing a momentary closure at the back of the mouth. The result was [gw-]. [gw-] survives in Italian, but in French only the [g] remains. Spanish and Portuguese generally maintain [gw] before a following a, but before the front vowels e and i the [w] was lost, as in French. Cp. Rule 33.

	Italian	Spanish	Portuguese	French	English cognate
Gmc. *want 'glove'	guanto	guante	guante ((luva))	gant	gauntlet
Gmc. *wardan 'to keep'	guardare	guardar	guardar	garder	ward, guard
Gmc. werra 'war'	guerra [gwe-]	guerra [ge-]	guerra [ge-]	guerre [ge-]	war
Gmc. wîsa 'manner'	guisa	guisa	guisa	guise	wise, guise
Gmc. wîtan 'to look after, direct'	guidare	guiar	guiar	guider	guide
Gmc. waidanjan 'to pasture, raise cattle' > 'gain'	guadagnare	ganar (O.Sp: gañar)	ganhar	gagner	win, gain
Gmc. warjan 'defend' > 'heal'	guarire	guarecer	guarecer	guérir	wary, garrison

148

	Italian	Spanish	Portu-guese	French	English cognate
Gmc. *warant 'guarantee'	garante	garante	garante	garant	guarantee, warrant
Gmc. Wilhelm 'William'	Guglielmo	Guillermo	Guilherme	Guillaume	William

Note 1. In France and Italy, where the Germans settled in greater numbers than in the Iberian peninsula, the influence of Germanic w- even affected the pronunciation of a few Latin words. For example, Latin VADU 'ford', influenced by the Germanic forerunner of English wade German waten, became guado in Italian and gué in French, though Sp: vado Ptg: vao were unaffected. Similarly, we find VAGĪNA 'sheath' giving It: guaína Fr: gaine but Sp: vaina Ptg: bainha. Latin VŬLPE 'fox', influenced by its cognate wolf 'wolf' in Germanic, yielded It: volpe or golpe and O.Fr: goupil. It is perhaps significant that Latin VASTARE 'to devastate, lay waste' was contaminated by its Germanic cognate wastjan even in the peninsula, which together with Italy, North Africa, and Gaul, was cruelly ravaged in the holocaust that followed the collapse of the Western Roman Empire. Thus, besides It: guastare and Fr: gâter 'to spoil', we find Sp, Ptg: gastar 'to waste, spend, wear out'.

Note 2. Later in the Peninsula, Arabic w- also gave Romance [gw-]. For example, Arabic wâdî 'river' appears as the first element in many Peninsular toponymics: Guadalquivir 'the big river' (Ar: kabîr 'big'), Guadalajara 'the river of the stony place', Guadarrama 'the river of sand', Guadalete, Guadiana, Guadalaviar and so on. Ar: al-wazîr 'the vizier' gave Sp: alguacil 'constable'.

Note 3. The reinforcement of [w-] to [gw-] remains a characteristic of Spanish popular speech to this day, e.g. pop. güevo, güeso, Guaxaca for standard huevo, hueso, Oaxaca. Native American words borrowed by the conquistadores in the sixteenth century underwent the same modification as earlier borrowings from Arabic or Germanic. Mexican guacamole, guajolote, aguacate, for example, all had w- in the original Náhuatl.

Additional Examples

Compare Latin AVĪSPA 'wasp' (It: vespa Sp: avispa Ptg: bespa) with Fr: guêpe Gm: Wespe Eng: wasp. Compare It: guíndolo 'reel' Sp, Ptg: guindar 'to hoist (on a pulley)' Fr: guindeau 'windlass' with Gm: winden Eng: wind. Compare It: guarnire Sp, Ptg: guarnecer Fr: garnir 'to prepare' with Gm: warnen Eng: warn. Compare It: guado Sp:

gualdo   Ptg: gauda (met.) Fr: guède 'woad' with Eng: woad.
Lastly, compare Fr: gager 'to bet' with Eng: wager; Fr:
guetter 'to watch for, wait (in ambush) for' with Eng: wait;
Fr: guichet 'turnstile' with Eng: wicket; It: guancia 'cheek'
with Gm: Wange 'cheek'; Fr: Gauthier with Eng, Gm: Walter;
Fr: Galles with Eng: Wales; It: guai!   Sp: guay! 'alas' with
Eng: woe!; Fr: guimpe 'nun's veil' with Eng: wimple; Fr:
guipon 'mop' with Eng: wipe; Fr: gare! 'look out!' with
Eng: beware!

Exercise

Opposite each of the words in Group A write down the number of its nearest cognate in Group B.

Group A
1. Fr: gâter...   2. Eng: William.....   3. It: guadagnare...
4. Ptg: guindar...   5. Fr: guêpe....

Group B
1. Eng: wind   2. Fr: guère   3. Fr: Guillaume   4. Eng:
wade   5. Eng: wasp   6. Sp: gato   7. Fr: gagner   8. Eng:
vast   9. Eng: waste   10. Fr: Gauthier

RULE 43

X

Rule: Latin -X- [ks] gave Italian ss [ss] or sce, sci [š],
Portuguese ss [s] or x [š], Spanish j [x], and (in popular
words) French is(s). In words beginning with EX- plus vowel,
however, Italian and Portuguese pronounced the X as [z].
Before a consonant, Latin X was popularly pronounced [s].

	Italian	Spanish	Portu- guese	French	English cognate
LŪXU 'luxury'	lusso [lusso]	lujo [luxo]	luxo [lušo]	luxe (l.) [lyks]	de luxe
FĪXĀRE 'to fix'	fissare	fijar	fixar	fixer (l.)	fix
DĪXĬT 'said'	disse	dijo	disse	dit (O.Fr: dist)	dictum
AXE 'axle, axis'	asse	eje	eixo	essieu (AXĔLLU)	axis
BŬXU 'box tree'	bóssolo (-ŬLU)	boj	buxa	buis (buisson) BUXONE 'bush'	box tree
SĔXAGĬNTA 'sixty'	sessanta	sesenta (through influence of seis)	sessenta	soixante	sexa- genarian

	Italian	Spanish	Portu-guese	French	English cognate
(DĒ+) LAXĀRE 'to loosen, let (go)'	lassare 'to loosen' lasciare 'leave, let'	dejar (DĒ (LA)XĀRE)	deixar (DĒ (LA)XĀRE) 'leave, let'	laisser 'to leave, let'	laxative, relax
VAXĔLLA (for VASCĔLLA) 'crockery' (from VAS 'vase')	vascello 'boat' vasellame 'crockery'	vajilla	baixel	vaisselle 'crockery' vaisseau 'ship'	vessel 'recepta-cle; ship'
*VEXĪCA (for VESSĪCA) 'bladder'	vescica	vejiga	bexiga	vessie	
EXĀMEN 'swarm (esp. of bees)'	sciame	enjambre (-AMĬNE)	enxame	essaim	
EXĔMPLU 'example'	esempio	ejemplo	exemplo	example (1.)	example
EXERCĬTU 'army'	esército	ejército	exército	((armée))	
EXERCĪTĮU 'exercise'	esercizio	ejercicio	exercício	exercice (1.)	exercise
EXTRĀNĔU 'strange'	strano	extraño	extranho	étrange (O.Fr: estrange)	strange, es-tranged

Note 1. In Spanish, the process was [ks] > [i̯š] > Old Spanish x [š], Modern Spanish j [x]. If the [i̯š] came to be final or stand before a consonant, the [š] depalatalized to [s]: SĔX It: sei Sp, Ptg: seis Fr: six (via *sieis); FRAXĬNU '(bot.) ash' It: frássino Sp: fresno (O.Sp: freisno) Ptg: freixo Fr: frêne; SĔXᵀMA 'a sixth' O.Sp: seisma Sp: sesma 'a former coin'. Sp: siesta, diestra 'right hand', mesta 'place where streams meet' are not directly from SĔXTA, DĔXTRA, and MĬXTA, but from VL forms with ST for XT.

Note 2. The yod given off by the X at the [i̯š] stage combined with a preceding a to give first ai, then ei (as in Portuguese), and finally Spanish e. Examples of this are AXE Ptg: eixo Sp: eje and TAXU Ptg: teixo Sp: tejo 'yew tree'.

Note 3. Spanish j is the result of the fusion of two sounds which Old Spanish distinguished: Old Spanish x [š] and Old Spanish j, ǵ [ž]. For the sources of Old Spanish [ž], see Rules 7, 18, 19, 22. The sources of Old Spanish and Portuguese x, besides Latin X, were the Latin groups PSY and SSY

and Arabic shin: CAPSEA 'box' O.Sp: caxa Ptg: caixa Fr:
caisse Eng: caisson; BASSIARE 'to lower' O.Sp: baxar Ptg:
baixar Fr: baisser; PASSIONE Ptg: paixão; RUSSEU 'red,
ruddy' O.Sp: roxo Ptg: roxo (Cp. It: rosso RÓSSU, Eng:
russet.) Of Arabic origin are Sp: ojalá Ptg: oxalá (Ar:
waŝa Allah 'Would to Allah...!'), O.Sp: axedrez Ptg: xadrez
'chess', and a great many other words with x and j.

Note 4. In learned words, Spanish has x, which is usually
pronounced [gs] but occasionally [s] before consonants: extra,
máximo, próximo, nexo, examen, auxilio, exhibir, exento,
excelente, exigir, etc.; extraño, extranjero, extender, ex-
cusado, extraordinario, etc.

Note 5. In a few words Latin X gave Spanish s, e.g.
*ADTOXICĀRE Sp: atosigar 'to poison', EXTĪRĀRE estirar
'to stretch out'.

Note 6. Like SSY and SCY (as in FASCIA Ptg: faixa, faxa
'band'), SC gives Portuguese x [š]: FASCE feixe 'faggot'
MĪSCĒRE mexer 'to mix', PĪSCE peixe 'fish'. In Spanish, SC
gave Old Spanish ç [ts], modern ç, z [θ]: haz, mecer 'to
rock', pez.

Note 7. Before a following consonant, the prefix EX- became
VL es-. The e- of this prefix was confused in Italy with the
vowel prefixed to words beginning with S (+ cons.) ((iscuola,
(i)spata, (i)stato) and with the latter it has disappeared in
Modern Italian (see Rule 35). Examples: It: scusa 'excuse',
schiudere 'to exclude', spiegare 'to explain' (Sp: explicar),
spesa 'expense', squisito 'exquisite', stendere 'to extend'.
Likewise affected were words like (H)ISPANIA It: Spagna
'Spain', (H)ISTŌRIA It: storia 'history', and the prefixes
DIS- and EXTRA- which became, respectively, s- and stra-.
Examples: sbarcare 'to disembark', scoperto 'discovered',
sdegnoso 'disdainful', sfavore 'disfavor', sgradévole 'disagree-
able', sleale 'disloyal', smontare 'to dismount, snudare 'to lay
bare', sprezzo 'contempt', staccato 'detached', sviluppo 'development'. (Note that the s- represents [z] before the
voiced consonants b, d, g, l, m, n, r, and v); strabello
'extremely beautiful', stracaro 'very expensive', straordinario,
stravagante, stranio 'strange' (EXTRANEU) and many others.

Additional Examples

RĪXA 'brawl, quarrel' It: rissa Sp: rija Ptg: rixa Fr:
   rixe (1.)
PROXĪMU 'next' It: próssimo (1.) Sp: prójimo (s.l.)
   '(biblical) neighbor' próximo (1.) 'next'
TRAXĪ 'I brought' (pret. of TRAHĒRE) It: trassi Sp: traje
   (a form *TRAXUI gave rise to Ptg: trouxe O.Sp: and dial:
   truxe, truje)
VEXĀRE 'to vex, torment' It: vessare Sp: vejar Ptg: vexar
   Fr: vexer (1.)

VĪXĪ 'I lived' It: vissi
TAXU 'yew tree' It: tasso Sp: tejo Ptg: teixo (Fr: if is of
Gmc. origin and akin to Gm: Eibe Eng: yew)
CŎXA 'hipbone' It: coscia Ptg: coxa Fr: cuisse 'thigh'
*CŎXU (from COXA) It: coscio 'leg of meat' Sp: cojo 'lame'
LĪXĪVĮA (*LĪXĪVA) 'lye' It: lisciva Sp: lejía Ptg: lixivia
Fr: lessive
REFLEXĀRE 'to reflect' Sp: reflejar
*ADNEXU (for ANNEXU) 'annex, appendix' Sp: anejo Eng:
annex
COMPLEXU 'complex' Sp: complejo Eng: complex
FĪXU 'fixed' Sp: fijo
ĔXĬT 'goes out' It: esce
TAXĬLLU 'small die' It: tassello 'plug' Eng: tassel
MAXĬLLA, MAXĔLLA 'jaw bone' It: mascella 'jaw' Sp: mejilla
'cheek' Eng: maxillary
EXAGĮU 'a weighing or balance' It: saggio Sp: ensayo
Ptg: ensaio Fr: essai Eng: essay
MAXĬMU 'maximum' It: mássimo (l.) Sp: máximo (l.)
TOXĬCU 'poisonous' It: tóssico (l.) 'poisonous' tosco 'poison'
Eng: toxic
EXEMPTU 'exempt' Ptg: isento It: esente Sp: exento (l.)
SAXU 'rock' It: sasso

Exercise

Opposite each of the words in Group A write down the number of its nearest cognate in Group B.

Group A
1. Eng: example.... 2. Fr: cuisse... 3. Ptg: eixo.....
4. Sp: mejilla..... 5. It: vascello..... 6. Fr: frêne.....
7. Eng: annex.... 8. It: sasso.... 9. Sp: lejía.....
10. Fr: vessie....
Group B
1. Fr: meilleur 2. Ptg: seixo 3. Sp: enjambre 4. Eng:
missile 5. Ptg: coxa 6. Sp: ejemplo 7. Eng: vex
8. It: frássino 9. Sp: freno 10. It: asse 11. Sp: vejiga
12. It: lusso 13. It: mascella 14. Ptg: cousa 15. Fr:
anneau 16. Sp: anejo 17. Eng: vassal 18. Fr: lessive
19. Ptg: seis 20. Fr: vaisseau

TABLE OF CROSS REFERENCES

For rule ...	See also rule ...
1	12 (ÁE)
2	32 (RY)
4	29 (-B-)
	10 (BB)
	30, notes 2, 3, 4 (BL)
	7, note 4 (B'L)
	11 (BR)
	31, note 1 (B'T)
	32, notes 2, 3, 4 (BY)
5	37 (-C)
	10 (CC)
7	30 (CL)
8	39 (CR)
9	40, notes 3, 7 (CT)
	40 (CY)
	36, 37 (D)
	10 (DD)
	43, note 7 (DIS-)
	7, note 4 (D'L)
11	18, 19 (DY)
13	12, note 6 (-ELLU)
14	43, note 7 (EX-, EXTRA-)
15	30 (FL)
	5 (Gª)
	18, 19 (Ĝ)
	30, notes 1, 2, 3 (GL)
	7, note 1 (G'L)
	26 (GN)
	11 (GR)
	33 (GU)
	18, 19 (GY)
17	13 (I)
21	10 (-LL-)

155

For rule ...	See also rule ...
22	37 (-M)
23	10 (-MM-)
	25, note 2 (MN)
	25, note 1 (MNY)
	32, notes 2, 3, 4 (MY)
24	37 (-N)
	19 (NG)
	7, note 3 (NG'L)
	10 (-NN)
28	13 (OE)
29	31, note 1 (P'D)
30	10 (-PP-)
	39 (-PR-)
	26 (-PS-)
	43, note 3 (PSY)
31	31, note 1 (P'T)
	30, note 3 (PTY)
34	10 (-RR-)
	26 (-RS-)
	32 (RY)
35	37 (-S)
	43, note 6 (ŚC)
	40, note 5 (SCY)
	10 (SS)
	40, note 5 and 43, note 3 (SSY)
	40, note 5 (STY)
	32 (SY)
38	7, note 4 (T'L)
41	28 (Ŭ)
	29 (-V-)
	31, note 1 (V'T)
	32, notes 2, 3, 4 (VY)

ANSWERS TO THE EXERCISES

Rule 1 (Å)
   1:6, 2:8, 3:3, 4:5, 5:4, 6:16, 7:11, 8:13, 9:18, 10:14

Rule 2 (-ĀRĮU)
   1:7, 2̂:27, 3:31, 4:14, 5:37, 6:18, 7:20, 8:5, 9:21,
   10:4, 11:35, 12:11, 13:39, 14:29, 15:30, 16:25, 17:34,
   18:2, 19:16, 20:9

Rule 3 (-ĀTỲCU)
   1:8, 2:10, 3:18, 4:4, 5:20, 6:13, 7:15, 8:2, 9:16, 10:5

Rule 4 (AŲ)
   1:4, 2:15, 3:32, 4:12, 5:20, 6:7, 7:22, 8:10, 9:19,
   10:38, 11:1, 12:34, 13:18, 14:29, 15:23, 16:25, 17:20,
   18:37, 19:28, 20:6

Rule 5 (C^a, Ga)
   1:35, 2:32, 3:11, 4:16, 5:30, 6:33, 7:12, 8:28, 9:22,
   10:15, 11:23, 12:26, 13:25, 14:24, 15:21, 16:17, 17:1,
   18:8, 19:10, 20:20

Rule 6 (Ć)
   1:26, 2:39, 3:37, 4:36, 5:32, 6:29, 7:14, 8:20, 9:31,
   10:3, 11:8, 12:21, 13:19, 14:16, 15:5, 16:30, 17:1,
   18:34, 19:10, 20:9

Rule 7 (C'L)
   1:17, 2:28, 3:10, 4:23, 5:32, 6:35, 7:2, 8:16, 9:8,
   10:26, 11:4, 12:5, 13:29, 14:11, 15:38, 16:30, 17:19,
   18:31, 19:18, 20:27

Rule 8 (C^{o,u})
    1:5, 2:8, 3:10, 4:4, 5:7

Rule 9 (C'T)
    1:15, 2:10, 3:21, 4:11, 5:31, 6:38, 7:19, 8:36,
    9:20, 10:39, 11:2, 12:28, 13:24, 14:23, 15:3,
    16:40, 17:34, 18:27, 19:13, 20:17

Rule 10 (Double consonants)
    1:15, 2:19, 3:13, 4:20, 5:11, 6:10, 7:14, 8:17, 9:8,
    10:12

Rule 11 (-DR)
    1:19, 2:7, 3:10, 4:11, 5:15, 6:2, 7:6, 8:4, 9:16, 10:17

Rule 12 (Ĕ)
    1:27, 2:12, 3:16, 4:2, 5:22, 6:11, 7:34, 8:32, 9:15,
    10:9, 11:40, 12:26, 13:33, 14:18, 15:25, 16:23, 17:3,
    18:5, 19:30, 20:29

Rule 13 (Ē)
    1:18, 2:6, 3:19, 4:39, 5:13, 6:30, 7:17, 8:24, 9:15,
    10:28, 11:37, 12:26, 13:27, 14:12, 15:32, 16:23, 17:7,
    18:20, 19:8, 20:21

Rule 14 (-ĔRE)
    1:6, 2:27, 3:26, 4:11, 5:28, 6:14, 7:13, 8:2, 9:12,
    10:33, 11:36, 12:29, 13:5, 14:38, 15:31, 16:24, 17:9,
    18:1, 19:20, 20:16

Rule 15 (F-)
    1:23, 2:36, 3:30, 4:33, 5:32, 6:16, 7:39, 8:37, 9:24,
    10:18, 11:7, 12:39, 13:14, 14:3, 15:22, 16:12, 17:26,
    18:31, 19:29, 20:27

Rule 17 (T̄)
    1:7, 2:18, 3:16, 4:13, 5:10, 6:20, 7:11, 8:5, 9:3, 10:14

Rule 18 (J-)
    1:6, 2:10, 3:14, 4:34, 5:17, 6:30, 7:13, 8:21, 9:39,
    10:1, 11:27, 12:14, 13:22, 14:32, 15:2, 16:26, 17:24,
    18:35, 19:8, 20:18

Rule 19 (-J-)
1:40, 2:32, 3:37, 4:13, 5:24, 6:23, 7:26, 8:38, 9:31,
10:19, 11:35, 12:27, 13:2, 14:22, 15:30, 16:10, 17:20,
18:7, 19:8, 20:25

Rule 20 (-L-)
1:18, 2:28, 3:30, 4:39, 5:33, 6:21, 7:20, 8:23, 9:1,
10:35, 11:36, 12:38, 13:3, 14:31, 15:5, 16:8, 17:6,
18:15, 19:34, 20:17

Rule 21 (L plus Consonant)
1:18, 2:30, 3:16, 4:28, 5:33, 6:22, 7:25, 8:9, 9:40,
10:11, 11:1, 12:37, 13:36, 14:5, 15:14, 16:3, 17:7,
18:8, 19:29, 20:31

Rule 22 (LY)
1:10, 2:25, 3:9, 4:22, 5:31, 6:12, 7:1, 8:2, 9:34,
10:19, 11:29, 12:37, 13:7, 14:17, 15:27, 16:39, 17:24,
18:4, 19:33, 20:16

Rule 23 (M'N)
1:19, 2:8, 3:6, 4:20, 5:16, 6:3, 7:18, 8:2, 9:12, 10:9

Rule 24 (-N-)
1:15, 2:30, 3:38, 4:33, 5:12, 6:24, 7:2, 8:34, 9:28,
10:36, 11:32, 12:40, 13:18, 14:26, 15:4, 16:3, 17:27,
18:31, 19:21, 20:35

Rule 25 (N̲S̲)
1:15, 2:5, 3:8, 4:18, 5:13, 6:2, 7:10, 8:9, 10:17

Rule 26 (N̲Y̲)
1:8, 2:29, 3:11, 4:20, 5:1, 6:26, 7:40, 8:35, 9:23,
10:31, 11:3, 12:32, 13:37, 14:16, 15:5, 16:14, 17:2,
18:22, 19:9, 20:18

Rule 27 (Ŏ)
1:9, 2:28, 3:15, 4:20, 5:32, 6:34, 7:22, 8:38, 9:40,
10:1, 11:24, 12:36, 13:3, 14:19; 15:5, 16:26, 17:12,
18:16, 19:31, 20:6

Rule 28 (Ō)
1:16, 2:13, 3:19, 4:8, 5:11, 6:2, 7:3, 8:18, 9:10, 10:6

Rule 29 (-P-)
    1:9, 2:5, 3:12, 4:20, 5:3, 6:17, 7:15, 8:1, 9:10, 10:7

Rule 30 (PL)
    1:10, 2:14, 3:34, 4:31, 5:16, 6:4, 7:28, 8:23, 9:20,
    10:22, 11:27, 12:24, 13:2, 14:35, 15:32, 16:30, 17:26
    18:39, 19:15, 20:6

Rule 31 (PT)
    1:6, 2:17, 3:19, 4:15, 5:13, 6:1, 7:12, 8:3, 9:9, 10:7

Rule 32 (PY)
    1:19, 2:8, 3:18, 4:21, 5:24, 6:13, 7:1, 8:40, 9:38,
    10:3, 11:16, 12:34, 13:26, 14:29, 15:35, 16:31, 17:5,
    18:10, 19:12, 20:25

Rule 33 (QU)
    1:9, 2:19, 3:17, 4:17, 5:15, 6:1, 7:3, 8:10, 9:4, 10:12

Rule 35 (S plus Consonant)
    1:1, 2:19, 3:14, 4:11, 5:40, 6:35, 7:24, 8:7, 9:16,
    10:2, 11:37, 12:31, 13:21, 14:27, 15:26, 16:8, 17:35,
    18:3, 19:5, 20:29

Rule 36 (-T-)
    1:4, 2:24, 3:13, 4:28, 5:22, 6:31, 7:16, 8:34, 9:40,
    10:20, 11:2, 12:38, 13:10, 14:8, 15:36, 16:1, 17:33,
    18:26, 19:27, 20:18

Rule 38 (-TĀTE)
    1:5, 2:9, 3:8, 4:3, 5:2

Rule 39 (-TR-)
    1:10, 2:20, 3:14, 4:7, 5:18, 6:5, 7:16, 8:17, 9:12,
    10:13

Rule 40 (TY)
    1:13, 2:20, 3:27, 4:33, 5:9, 6:23, 7:38, 8:35, 9:24,
    10:17, 11:12, 12:29, 13:15, 14:3, 15:4, 16:40, 17:1,
    18:21, 19:8, 20:36

Rule 41 (Ū)
    1:10, 2:4, 3:13, 4:12, 5:8, 6:16, 7:15, 8:6, 9:2,
    10:13

Rule 42 (W-)
1:9, 2:3, 3:7, 4:1, 5:5

Rule 43 (X)
1:6, 2:5, 3:10, 4:13, 5:20, 6:8, 7:16, 8:2, 9:18,

10:11

GLOSSARY OF LINGUISTIC TERMINOLOGY

accent: (1) the distinctive character of a vowel or syllable determined by its degree or pattern of stress or musical pitch. (2) a mark indicating stress, musical tone, or vowel quality. The three commonest are the acute (´), the grave (`), and the circumflex (^).

affix: any meaningful element (prefix, infix, or suffix) added to a stem or base, as -ed added to *want* to form *wanted*.

affricate: a speech sound beginning with a stop and ending in a fricative, such as the ch in *church*, which begins like t and ends like sh.

alveolar: said of sounds produced with the tongue touching or almost touching the alveolar (or gum) ridge.

analogy: the tendency of inflections and word formations to follow an existing pattern, e.g. substandard English *heighth* 'height' patterned after *length, breadth, width,* and *depth.*

analytic: said of a language that tends to express syntactical relationships by the use of separate words ('free forms'), rather than by the use of prefixes, suffixes, and inflectional endings ('bound forms'). Chinese and English are often described as analytic (cp. synthetic).

antepenult: the last syllable but two in a word, as *bi-* in *ability* or RĪ in TERRĪBILIS.

apheresis: the omission of an unstressed syllable or sound at the beginning of a word.

apocope: the cutting off of the last sound of a word.

argot: the peculiar language or jargon of any class or group; originally that of thieves and vagabonds, devised for purposes of disguise and concealment.

articulate: to make the movements and adjustments of the speech organs necessary to utter (a speech sound). The 'point of articulation' is that part of the mouth where contact or constriction between the vocal organs is necessary to produce a given speech sound.

aspirate: (1) a puff of unvoiced air before or after another sound, represented in many languages by h, and in Greek by the 'sign of rough breathing' (‘). (As a verb) to release a stop consonant in such a way that the breath escapes with audible friction as in English *pit* . (2) to begin a word or syllable with an h sound, as in *when* (pron. *hwen*), *howl*, as opposed to *wen, owl.*

assimilation: the tendency to articulate a sound more like another (generally contiguous) sound in the same utterance, e.g. SEPTE *sette* (complete assimilation), COM'TE *conte* (partial assimilation).

atonic: unstressed (cp. tonic).

back formation: a word formed from one that looks like its derivative, as *pea* from *pease* (orig. singular, but later mistaken for a plural) or *typewrite* from *typewriter, donate* from *donation.*

bilabial: pronounced with the two lips brought close together or touching, e.g. p, b, m, w.

bilingualism: a condition generally due to conquests or migrations, wherein two spoken languages compete for supremacy in a given region.

checked vowel: a vowel situated in a closed syllable (q.v.). (Cp. free vowel).

close: said of vowels pronounced with a relatively small aperture above the tongue, for example, i, u. (Cp. open vowel).

closed syllable: a syllable ending in a consonant. (Cp. open syllable).

cognate: related in origin; said of languages, words, etc.

consonant: a sound subordinated in a syllable to another sound that has greater sonority (q.v.).

continuant: a consonant, such as f or m, which may be prolonged without change of quality.

dactylic: characterized by a sequence of one long syllable followed by two short ones (e.g. Latin MĀSCŬLŬ), or of one stressed syllable followed by two unstressed ones, as in Eng: dénsity, It: pópolo.

derivative: a form derived from another: *atomic* is a derivative of *atom.*

diachronic: covering a span of time.   (Cp. synchronic).

diacritical mark, point, or sign: a mark, point, or sign added or attached to a letter or character to distinguish it from another of similar form, to give it a particular phonetic value, to indicate stress, etc.

dialect: the language of a particular district or class, especially as distinguished from the standard language, as a provincial or rural substandard form of a language.

dieresis: a sign (¨) placed over one of two adjacent vowels to indicate separate pronunciation, as in Eng: coöperate, Sp: agüero.

digraph: a group of two letters representing a single speech sound, as *ea* in *meat*, or *th* in *path*.

diphthong: two contiguous vowels pronounced as one syllable with the less sonorous vowel subordinated to the other.   Diphthongs whose second element has greater sonority than the first (e.g. *ya, ye, yo, wa, we, wo*) are called 'rising diphthongs'; those whose second element has lesser sonority (e.g. *ay, oy, ey, aw, ew, ow*) are called 'falling diphthongs'.

dissimilation: the process whereby a speech sound is changed in an effort to differentiate it more clearly from another sound in the same word, e.g. ROTUNDU Sp: redondo, PEREGRINU Fr: pélérin Eng: pilgrim.

elision: the omission of a vowel in pronunciation, as Sp: l'otro for el otro.

enclitic: said of a short word which having no stress of its own is pronounced (and sometimes spelled) as part of the preceding word, e.g. the pronoun -me in Sp: dígame (Cp. proclitic).

epenthesis: the insertion of one or more sounds in the middle of a word, as the schwa in the substandard pronunciation of *elm* as [élam] or the e in dialectal Sp: tíguere for *tigre* 'tiger'.   In Old French an epenthetic i sound was often generated by a palatal consonant, as in RACEMU > *raisiéin, Fr, Eng: raisin.

esophagus: the tube connecting the mouth and pharynx with the stomach.

etymology: (1) the study of historical linguistic change, especially as applied to individual words; (2) an account of the history of a particular word; (3) the derivation of a word.

free vowel: a vowel situated in an open syllable, i.e. when absolutely final (as the o of AMO), in hiatus with a following vowel (as the Ĭ of VĬA), before a single medial consonant (as the Ĭ of VĬDĒT), or before a group consisting of a stop consonant + l or r (as the Ŭ of DŬPLU, the Ĕ of PĔTRA).

fricative: (1) (of consonants) characterized by a noise produced by air being forced through an opening, as in f̲, v̲, s̲,
etc.; (2) a fricative consonant.

haplology: error of speech which consists of omitting one of
two identical and consecutive syllables, as in *philogy* for
philology.

hiatus: a break or slight pause due to the coming together
without contraction of two vowels in successive words or
syllables.

homonym: a word like another in sound and perhaps in
spelling, but different in meaning, as Eng: *knows* and *nose*,
Fr: *louer* 'to praise' and *louer* 'to rent', Sp: *nada* 'swims'
and *nada* 'nothing'.

hypercorrection or ultracorrection: the act or result of a
speaker's fancifully attempting to 'restore' a sound or sounds
to a word which never had them. For example, in an effort
to correct the dropping of their h̲'s ('*is* '*at* '*his* hat'),
Cockneys may mistakenly aspirate words like *hour* and *honest*.

idiomatic: peculiar to or characteristic of a particular
language.

inflection: (1) a change in the form of a word, generally
by affixation by means of which a change of meaning or relationship to some other word or group of words is indicated; (2) the
affix added to the stem to produce this change. For example:
the -s in *dogs* and -ed in *played* are inflections.

interdental: pronounced with the tip of the tongue between
the upper and lower front teeth, as the *th* in *thick*.

intertonic: (of a syllable) situated between two stressed
syllables, as the e̲ in *ìntertónic*, or the second I of Latin
CĪVĪTĀTE.

intonation: the pattern or melody of pitch changes revealed
in connected speech; especially the pitch pattern of a sentence,
which distinguishes kinds of sentences and speakers of different nationalities.

isogloss: an imaginary line separating two localities which
differ in some feature of their speech.

labial: involving lip articulation, as p̲, v̲, m̲, w̲, or a
rounded vowel.

labiodental: with the lower lip close to the upper front
teeth, as in f̲, or v̲.

labiovelar: with simultaneous bilabial and velar articulations,
such as w̲.

larynx: the cavity at the upper end of the human trachea or windpipe, containing the vocal cords and acting as the organ of voice.

lateral: a speech sound, such as l̲, Sp: *ll*, in which the breath escapes on one or both sides of the tongue.

lax vowel: a vowel, such as the i̲ of *bit* and the u̲ of *pull*, pronounced with relatively relaxed muscles. (Cp. tense vowel.)

learned: said of words or expressions from the classical mother tongue introduced in the phonetic form of the traditional reading-pronunciation, into the formal speech and then into ordinary levels of a language. After they came into use, they were subject to the normal changes which thereafter occurred in the language, sometimes however, reshaped in the direction of the learned form.

liaison: in French sentence phonetics, the pronunciation of a usually mute final consonant as though it were the initial consonant of the following word, as in *un‿autre de tes‿amis est‿ici.*

linguistics: the science of language, including among its fields phonetics, phonemics, morphology, and syntax, and having as principal divisions descriptive linguistics, which treats the classification and arrangement of the features of language, and comparative (or historical) linguistics, which treats linguistic change, especially by the study of data taken from various languages.

liquid: *see* palatal.

loan translation: a word of one language adopted into another in translated form; for example, in Mexican Spanish baseball terminology, Sp: jonrón 'home run' is a 'loan word', while Sp: carrera 'run' is a 'loan translation'.

loan word: a word of one language adopted into another at any period in history. Examples: *wine* (into Old English from Latin), *blitz* (into Modern English from German).

medial: situated within a word or syllable, that is to say, neither initial nor final, as the t̲ of Eng: dated, or the group b̲l̲ of Sp: pueblo.

metaphony: especially applying to Portuguese; the closing of a vowel caused by the influence of a following closed vowel (as the unlauted vowels in German).

metathesis: the transposition of letters, syllables, or sounds within a word, as in Sp: quebrar for older Sp: crebar (simple metathesis) or Sp: milagro from older Sp: miraglo 'miracle' (reciprocal metathesis).

monophthong: a single, simple vowel sound.

morpheme: any of the minimum meaningful elements in a language, not further divisible into smaller meaningful elements, usually recurring in various contexts with relatively constant meaning: either a word, as *girl, world,* or part of a word, as *-ish* or *-ly* in *girlish* and *worldly.*

morphology: (1) the patterns of word formation in a particular language, including inflection, derivation, and composition; (2) the study and description thereof.

mouillé: *see* **palatal.**

nasal: (1) with the voice issuing through the nose, either partly (as in French nasal vowels) or entirely (as in m̲, n̲, or the n̲g̲ of *song*); (2) a nasal speech sound.

nasalize: to pronounce as a nasal sound by allowing some of the outgoing voice to issue through the nose.

oblique case: any case of noun inflection except nominative and vocative, or except these two and accusative: Latin genitive, dative, and ablative cases are said to be oblique cases.

occlusive: characterized by a momentary occlusion or stoppage of air at the point of articulation: p̲, t̲, k̲, b̲, d̲, g̲ are occlusive consonants.

onomatopoeia: the formation of a name or word by imitating sound associated with the thing designated, e.g. *cuckoo, bow-wow, click.*

open syllable: syllable ending in a vowel.

open vowel: pronounced with a relatively large opening above the tongue; for example, *sod* has a more open vowel than *sowed.*

oxytone: a word stressed on the last syllable. (Cp. paroxytone, proparoxytone.)

palatal: with the tongue held close to the hard palate: the y̲ of *yield* is a palatal consonant.

paradigm: the set of all forms containing a particular element, especially the set of all inflected forms of a single root, stem, or theme. For example: *boy, boy's, boys, boys'* constitutes the paradigm of the noun *boy.*

paragoge: (in linguistic change) the addition of a syllable, phoneme, or other element not originally present, at the end of a word, as the substandard pronunciation of *height* as *heighth,* the standard showing no change.

paroxytone: word stressed on the penult or next to last syllable.

parasynthesis: the formation of a word by the addition of an affix to a phrase or compound, as *great hearted*, which is *great heart* plus *-ed* (not *great* + *hearted*). A Spanish example is *ensimismado* (*en si mismo* + *-ado*).

patois: any peasant or provincial form of speech.

patronymic: (1) (of names) derived from the name of a father or ancestor, especially by the addition of a suffix or prefix indicating descent; (2) (of a suffix or prefix) indicating such descent; (3) a patronymic name, such as Williamson (son of William) or Macdonald (son of Donald); (4) a family name; surname.

pejorative: (1) having a disparaging force, as certain derivative word forms; (2) a pejorative form or word, as *poetaster*.

penult: the next to last syllable of a word.

periphrastic: (1) circumlocutory, roundabout; (2) denoting a construction of two or more words with a class meaning which in other languages or in other forms of the same language is expressed by inflectional modification of a single word. For example: *the son of Mr. Smith* is periphrastic; *Mr. Smith's son* is inflectional.

pharyngeal: articulated in the region of the pharynx (q.v.).

pharynx: the cavity to the rear of the tongue which connects the oral and nasal cavities with the esophagus and larynx.

phone: an individual speech sound.

phoneme: the smallest distinctive group or class of phones in a language. The phonemes of a language contrast with one another, e.g. in English, *pip* differs from *nip, pin, tip, pit, bib*, etc., and *rumple* from *rumble*, by contrast of a phoneme /p/ with other phonemes. In writing, the same symbol can be used for all the phones belonging to one phoneme without causing confusion between words: the /r/ consonant phoneme includes the voiceless fricative r̠ phone of *tree*, the voiced r̠ phone of *red*, etc.

phonemic: (1) of or pertaining to phonemes: a phonemic system; (2) of or pertaining to phonemics; concerning or involving the discrimination of distinctive speech sounds: a phonemic contrast.

phomemics: the science of phonemic systems and contrasts.

phonetic: (1) of or pertaining to speech sounds and their production; (2) agreeing with or corresponding to pronunciation: phonetic transcription.

phonetics: (1) the science of speech sounds and their production; (2) the phonetic system, or the body of phonetic facts, of a particular language.

phonology: in Romance linguistics, the historical study of sound changes, especially of the sounds of a given language.

popular: development of words from the mother tongue through the different stages of vulgar use, subject to the phonological and morphological changes peculiar to the language.

popular etymology: the deformation of a word due to its fancied relationship to some other word, e.g. colloquial Eng. sparrow-grass 'asparagus'; Eng: so long! (< Malay:salang < Ar: salam 'peace'). Eng: chaise lounge (< Fr: chaise longue).

post tonic: coming after the stressed syllable.

postverbal noun: verb form (other than a participle or gerund) used as a noun, as Eng: pay, take, go, exit.

prefix: an affix which is put before a word, stem, or word element to add to or qualify its meaning (as un- in unkind).

pretonic: coming before the stressed syllable.

primary stress: the principal or strongest stress of a word.

proclitic: said of a short word which having no stress of its own is pronounced and sometimes spelled as part of the following word, as the (i)t of 'twas.

pronominal: pertaining to or having the nature of a pronoun.

pronoun: a word used as a substitute for a noun, as Eng: I, you, she, it, this, who, what, which.

proparoxytone: stressed on the antepenult or last syllable but two, e.g. dángerous, télephone.

protected: said of a consonant which is treated as initial because the preceding syllable ends in a consonant. Cp. the -T- of AMATU Sp: amado with the T of AMANTE, which remains Sp: amante.

prothesis: the addition of a phoneme or syllable at the beginning of a word, as in Sp: escala 'ladder' from Latin SCALA. From this derives the adj. prothetic.

quality: the timbre or tonal color which distinguishes one speech sound from another and remains essentially constant for each sound, even in different voices.

quantity: the duration in time of an uttered sound.

resonance: the amplification of vocal tone by the bones of the head and upper chest and by the air cavities of the pharynx, mouth, and nasal passages.

Romance group: a late consonant cluster formed in any of the Romance languages through the dropping of a vowel still preserved in Vulgar Latin, e.g. VĪNDĬCĀRE > *vendegár > *vend'gar > Sp: vengar 'to avenge'.

root: a morpheme which underlies an inflectional paradigm or is used itself as a word or element of a compound. Thus *dance* is the root of *dancer, dancing*; Gm: seh is the root of Gm: gesehen.

rounded: (especially of vowels) pronounced with rounded lips, as the w̲ of *wet*, the o̲o̲ of *moon*, the u̲ of Fr: *une*, etc.

sandhi form: the phonetic or phonemic form of a word or phrase occurring in a context of other (preceding and following) forms, when different from the absolute form, e.g. in *Jack's at home* the 's̲ is a sandhi form, corresponding to the absolute form *is*.

schwa: (1) the indeterminate vowel sound, or sounds, of most unstressed syllables of English, however represented; e.g. the sound, or sounds, of a̲ in *alone* and *sofa*, e in *system*, i̲ in *easily*, o̲ in *gallon*, u̲ in *circus*. (2) the phonetic symbol [ə].

secondary stress: a stress accent weaker than primary accent but stronger than lack of stress, e.g. that of *in* in *introduce*.

semi-learned word: a word whose popular development has been checked or restrained by scholarly, legal, or ecclesiastical influence, as Sp: *siglo* SAECŬLU. The learned form would have been *século*, the popular form *sejo*.

semivowel: (1) a speech sound of vowel quality used as a consonant, such as w̲, y̲ in *wet, yet*; (2) the second element of a falling diphthong, as the w̲, y̲ of *now, nay*, in opposition to the first (and more consonantal) element of a rising diphthong, as the w̲, y̲ of *wet, yet*, which is termed a semiconsonant.

sibilant: (1) characterized by a hissing sound, denoting sounds like those spelled with s̲ in *this, rose, pressure, pleasure*; (2) a sibilant sound.

slang: (1) language of a markedly colloquial character, regarded as below the standard of cultivated speech; (2) the jargon of a particular class, profession, etc.; (3) the special vocabulary of thieves, vagabonds, etc.; argot.

sonant: (1) a speech sound which by itself makes a syllable or subordinates to itself the other sounds in the syllable; a syllabic sound (opposed to consonant); (2) a voiced sound.

sonorant: a voiced sound less sonorous than a vowel but more sonorous than a stop or fricative, as l, r, m, n, y, w; such a sound may be now a sonant, now a consonant; the n of *didn't* is a sonant or syllabic, while that of *dint* is a consonant.

sonority: *See* **resonance.**

sound: a segment of speech corresponding to a single articulation or to a combination of articulations constantly associated in the language; a phone.

sound shift: a change, or system of parallel changes, which seriously affects the phonetic or phonemic structure of the language, as the change in English vowels from Middle English to Modern. Such changes are generally operative only in a given speech area for a limited period of time, after which new words entering the language remain unaffected by them.

stem: the element common to all the forms of an inflectional paradigm, or common to some subset thereof, usually more than a root. Thus *ten-* or *tan-* would be the root of Latin *tendere* and *tend-* would be its stem.

strong position: the position (within a word) in which a sound tends to resist changes, the initial position generally being the strongest. For example, in TŌTU Sp: todo the initial T- has resisted change while the intervocalic -T- has voiced to -d-.

stress: relative loudness resulting from special effort of emphasis in utterance.

substratum: the traces of former linguistic habits (principally lexical, sometimes phonetic, rarely morphological or syntactical) which after a period of bilingualism the former speakers of an abandoned language carry over into the structure of their new language.

suffix: an affix which follows the element to which it is added, as *-ly* in *kindly*.

superstratum: the influence (fatal in some cases, negligible in others) that the language of a conquering people exerts upon the language of the vanquished.

surd: (1) unvoiced; (2) an unvoiced sound.

synaloepha: the blending of two successive vowels into one.

syncope: the contraction of a word by omitting one or more sounds from the middle, as in the reduction of *never* to *ne'er*.

syneresis: the contraction of two syllables or two vowels into one; especially the contraction of two vowels so as to form a diphthong.

synonym: a word having the same, or nearly the same, meaning as another in the language, e.g. *joyful, elated, glad.*

syntax: (1) the patterns of formation of sentences and phrases from words in a particular language; (2) the study and description thereof.

sentence phonetics: the way words are pronounced in connected speech as distinct from the way they are pronounced in isolation; also 'syntactical phonetics'.

tilde: a diacritical mark (~) placed over a letter, as over the letter n in Spanish to indicate a palatal nasal sound (Anglicized as *ny*), as in Sp: cañón.

tonic: stressed, especially with primary stress.

toponymics (or toponymy): the study of the place names of a region.

trachea: the windpipe.

trill: (1) to pronounce with vibrating articulation: Spanish rr is trilled with the tip of the tongue; (2) a trilled articulation.

triphthong: a union of three vowel sounds pronounced in one syllable, as in Sp: buey or Eng: quite.

trochaic: characterized by a sequence of one long syllable followed by one short one (e.g. Latin VĪTA, ĪP-SE) or of one stressed syllable followed by one unstressed syllable, as in Eng: máster, Sp: puéblo.

unvoiced = **voiceless:** pronounced without vibration of the vocal cords.

uvula: the small fleshy hanging lobe visible at the back of the throat.

uvular: pronounced with the back of the tongue held close to or touching the uvula; Parisian French uses uvular r.

velar: with the back of the tongue held close to or touching the soft palate (velum), as k, g, the ng of *sing*, the j of Sp: jota.

vernacular: (1) native or originating in the place of its occurrence or use, as language or words (often as opposed to literary or learned language); (2) the native speech or language of a place.

vibrant: (1) trilled; (2) a trilled consonant, as the rr of Sp: perro.

vocal cords: folds of mucous membrane projecting into the cavity of the larynx, the edges of which can be drawn tense and made to vibrate by the passage of air from the lungs, thus producing vocal sound.

vocalize: (1) to use as a vowel, as the l̲ of bottle; (2) to change into a vowel; (3) to voice.

voiceless: *see* **unvoiced.**

vowel: a speech sound, usually voiced but sometimes whispered, that is characterized not by audible friction of air in the oral passage but by a coupled-cavity resonance that varies with the shape and dimensions of the two cavities separated by the hump of the tongue.

vulgar: spoken by, or being in the language spoken by, the people generally; vernacular.

Vulgar Latin: popular Latin, as opposed to literary or standard Latin; especially those forms of popular Latin speech from which sprang the Romance languages of later times.

wau: a name sometimes given to the sound of semiconsonantal u̯ [w], as in Latin SAPU̯I, VĪDU̯A.

weak position: position in which a sound is readily dominated by sounds in its vicinity, and is liable to combinative changes of various types. Final, intervocalic consonants, as well as the first consonant of an intervocalic or final group, and the middle consonant of a group of three, are all in a weak position.

whisper: to speak without vibration of the vocal cords.

yod: name given to the semivowel i̯ [j].

SELECTED BIBLIOGRAPHY

1. General Bibliography

Grossman, M., and B. Mazzoni. 1974. Bibliographie de
phonologie romane. The Hague: Mouton.
Littlefield, M. 1974. A bibliographic index to *Romance
Philology Vols. 1-25.* Berkeley: University of California
Press.
Palfrey, T., J. Fucilla, and W. Holbrook. 1946. A biblio-
graphical guide to the Romance languages and literature.
3rd edition. Evanston, Ill.

2. Romance Linguistics

Bourciez, Edouard. 1967. Eléments de linguistique romane.
5 ème. ed. Paris: Klincksieck.
Elcock, W. D. 1975. The Romance languages. London: Faber.
Ferguson, T. 1976. A history of the Romance vowel systems
through paradigmatic reconstruction. The Hague: Mouton.
Iordan, Iorgu, and J. Orr. 1970. An introduction to Romance
linguistics: Its schools and scholars. Revised, and with a
supplement by R. Posner. 2nd ed. Cambridge: B. Blackwell.
Meyer-Lübke, Wilhelm. 1890-1902. Grammatik der romanischen
Sprachen. 4 v. Leipzig.
Meyer-Lübke, Wilhelm. Einführung in das Studium der
romanischen Sprachwissenschaft. 1920. 3. neubearb. Aufl.
Heidelberg. Introducción al estudio de la lingüística romance.
1914. Trad., rev ... de la 2a ed. alemana, por Américo
Castro. Madrid.
Meyer-Lübke, Wilhelm. 1972. Romanisches etymologisches
Wörterbuch. 5th ed. Heidelberg: C. Winter.
Pulgram, E. 1975. Latin-Romance phonology, prosodics and
metrics. Munich: Fink.

3. Classical and Vulgar Latin

Allen, W. S. 1978. Vox Latina: The pronunciation of classical Latin. Cambridge: University Press.

de Climent, M. Bassols. 1976. Fonetica Latina (Publ. del CSIC).
Ernout, A., and A. Meillet. 1967. Dictionnaire étymologique de la langue latine: histoire des mots. Nouv. éd. rev. Paris: Klincksieck.
Grandgent, Charles H. 1907. An introduction to Vulgar Latin. Boston.
Hammond, M. 1976. Latin: A historical and linguistic handbook. Cambridge: Harvard University Press.
Kent, R. G. 1932. The sounds of Latin: A descriptive, historical phonology. Baltimore.
Lewis and Short. 1945. A Latin dictionary. Oxford. (Reimpression of the 1st ed. of 1879.)
Marriet, A. 1975. La phonetique historique du latin dans le cadre des langues indo-européenes. Paris: Klincksieck.
Meillet, A. 1977. Esquisse d'une histoire de la langue latine. Paris: Klincksieck.
Niederman, M. 1953. Historische Lautlehre des Lateinischen 3rd ed. Heidelberg: C. Winter.
Palmer, L. R. 1954. The Latin language. London: Faber.

4. Italian

Grandgent, Charles H. From Latin to Italian: An historical outline of the phonology and morphology of the Italian language. Cambridge, Mass. 1927.
Hall, Robert. 1941. Bibliography of Italian linguistics. Baltimore.
Migliorini, B. 1978. Storia della lingua italiana. 5th ed. Sansoni.
Migliorini, B., and T. G. Griffith. 1966. The Italian language. London: Faber.
Pei, Mario A. 1940. The Italian language. New York.
Rohlfs, G. Grammatica storica della lingua italiana e dei suoi dialetti. I: Fonetica, II: Morfologia, III: Sintassi e formazione delle parole. Einaudi.

5. Spanish

Corominas, J. 1954. Diccionario crítico etimológico de la lengua castellana. 4 vols. Bern: Francke.
Entwistle, William. 1938. The Spanish language, together with Portuguese, Catalan and Basque. London: Faber.
Hanssen, F. 1913. Gramática histórica de la lengua castellana. Halle: Max Niemeyer.
Lapesa, R. 1962. Historia de la lengua española. 5a ed. Madrid.
Menéndez-Pidal, R. 1944. Manual de gramática histórica española. 7a ed. Madrid.
Spaulding, R. 1943. How Spanish grew. Berkeley, Calif.

Tovar, A. 1978. Einführung in die Sprachgeschichte der iberischen Halbinsel: Das heutige Spansch und seine historischen Grundlager.

6. Portuguese

Câmara, J. Mattoso. 1972. The Portuguese language. Chicago: University of Chicago Press.
Huber, J. 1933. Altportugiesische Elementarbuch. Heidelberg: C. Winter.
Williams, Edwin B. 1962. From Latin to Portuguese. Historical philology and morphology of the Portuguese language. 2nd ed. Philadelphia: University of Pennsylvania Press.

7. French

Anglade, J. 1965. Grammaire élémentaire de l'ancien français. Paris: Colin.
Bloch, O., and W. von Wartburg. 1968. Dictionnaire étymologique de la langue française. Paris: Presses Universitaires de France.
Bourciez, E. 1974. Phonétique française: étude historique. Paris: Klincksieck.
Brunot, F. 1905. Histoire de la langue française des origines à 1900. Paris.
Dauzat, Albert. 1938. Dictionnaire étymologique de la langue française. Paris.
Einhorn, E. 1975. Old French: A concise handbook. Cambridge: Cambridge University Press.
Ewert, A. 1969. The French language. London: Faber.
Fouché, P. 1966. Phonétique historique du français. 3 vols. Vol. 1: Introduction, Vol. 2: Voyelles, Vol. 3: Consonnes. 2ème ed. Paris: Klincksieck.
Foulet, L. 1928, 1967. Petite syntaxe de l'ancien français. Paris: Champion.
Fox, J., and R. Wood. 1968. A concise history of the French language. Oxford: Basil Blackwell.
Gamillscheg, E. 1957. Historische fransösische syntax. Tübingen: Niemeyer.
Godefroy. 1881-1902. Dictionnaire de l'ancienne langue française et de tous les dialectes du XIe au XVe siècle. 10 v. Paris.
Littré, Emile. 1885-1889. Dictionnaire de la langue française (5 vols.). Paris: Hachette.
Pope, Mildred K. 1934. From Latin to modern French, with especial consideration of Anglo-Norman; phonology and morphology. Manchester: Manchester University Press.
Sainte-Palaye. 1875-1882. Dictionnaire historique de l'ancien français, ou glossaire de la langue française depuis son origine jus qu'au siècle de Louis XIV. (10 vols.). Paris.
von Wartburg, W. 1971. Evolution et structure de la langue française. Bern: Francke.

8. English

Baugh, Albert C. 1935. History of the English language.
New York. 3rd revised. 1978. London: Routledge.
Jespersen, Otto. 1905. Growth and structure of the English
language. 4th ed. 1923. New York.
Matthews, Mitford. 1951. Dictionary of Americanisms on his-
torical principles. (2 vols.). Chicago: University of
Chicago Press.
Mencken, H. L. 1923. The American language. 3rd ed.
New York.
New English dictionary on historical principles (OED). 1884-
1928. (10 vols.). Oxford: Oxford University Press.
Pyles, T. 1971. The origin and development of the English
language. New York: Harcourt Brace.